Journeys of Love

Chicago Studies in Ethnomusicology

A series edited by Philip V. Bohlman and Timothy Rommen

∴

Journeys of Love

∵

KASHMIRIS, MUSIC, AND
THE POETICS OF MIGRATION

Thomas Hodgson

THE UNIVERSITY OF CHICAGO PRESS
CHICAGO AND LONDON

The University of Chicago Press, Chicago 60637
The University of Chicago Press, Ltd., London
© 2025 by Thomas Hodgson
All rights reserved. No part of this book may be used or reproduced in any
manner whatsoever without written permission, except in the case of brief
quotations in critical articles and reviews. For more information, contact the
University of Chicago Press, 1427 E. 60th St., Chicago, IL 60637.
Published 2025
Printed and bound by CPI Group (UK) Ltd, Croydon, CR0 4YY

34 33 32 31 30 29 28 27 26 25   1 2 3 4 5

ISBN-13: 978-0-226-84140-3 (cloth)
ISBN-13: 978-0-226-84142-7 (paper)
ISBN-13: 978-0-226-84141-0 (e-book)
DOI: https://doi.org/10.7208/chicago/9780226841410.001.0001

Library of Congress Cataloging-in-Publication Data

Names: Hodgson, Thomas E. (Thomas Edward), 1983–, author.
Title: Journeys of love : Kashmiris, music, and the poetics of migration / Thomas Hodgson.
Other titles: Kashmiris, music, and the poetics of migration | Chicago studies in
    ethnomusicology.
Description: Chicago ; London : The University of Chicago Press, 2025. |
    Series: Chicago studies in ethnomusicology | Includes bibliographical references
    and index.
Identifiers: LCCN 2024049319 | ISBN 9780226841403 (cloth) | ISBN 9780226841427
    (paperback) | ISBN 9780226841410 (ebook)
Subjects: LCSH: Pakistanis—Pakistan—Mirpur (Azad Kashmir)—Music—History and
    criticism. | Pakistanis—England—Music—History and criticism. | Immigrants—
    Pakistan—Mirpur (Azad Kashmir)—Social life and customs. | Immigrants—England—
    Social life and customs. | Pakistanis—England—Ethnic identity. | Music—Social
    aspects—England. | Music—Social aspects—Pakistan. | Cultural pluralism—England. |
    Pakistan—Emigration and immigration. | England—Emigration and immigration.
Classification: LCC ML3758.P327 M575 2025 | DDC 780.95491/38—dc23/eng/20241101
LC record available at https://lccn.loc.gov/2024049319

⊚ This paper meets the requirements of ANSI/NISO Z39.48-1992
(Permanence of Paper).

"Hill Speak" from *Us* by Zaffar Kunial and "England" from *England's Green*
by Zaffar Kunial, reprinted courtesy of the author and Faber and Faber Ltd.

For Mr. Khokhar, of Oak Lane, Bradford
and
Ustad Zulfikar Ali Khan, of Khari Sharif, Azad Kashmir

What we call the beginning is often the end
And to make an end is to make a beginning.
The end is where we start from.

T. S. ELIOT, "Little Gidding," from *Four Quartets*

Contents

On Language, Orthography, and Notational Conventions

The conversations featured in this book were primarily conducted in Urdu, Pothwari, or English, depending on where they took place. In Azad Kashmir (and across the border in Punjab), all my interactions were in Urdu, with moments of switching between Pothwari and Urdu. I have translated these conversations into English in the text. The same is true for the passages based in Doha, Qatar. The exceptions to this were when I encountered British Mirpuris in Azad Kashmir, who preferred to talk with me in English. For the chapters and sections based in the United Kingdom, most discussions took place in English, with some clarifications—especially regarding poetry—taking place in Urdu and Pothwari.

Where I have quoted passages of poetry, I have tried to include the original source script in *nasta'līq*, a transliteration, and an English translation. For the transliterations, I have mostly followed the American Library Association–Library of Congress romanization tables. That said, I have consciously written the book with a scholarly and nonspecialist audience in mind, and especially for those featured in its pages. In the main body of the text, I have therefore minimized the use of diacritics (which, to me, can often feel like their own language). Any inconsistencies are either deliberate, copied from the original, or else my own fault.

I have adopted a similar approach to musical examples, which are transcribed into an enhanced staff notation, again with a range of audiences in mind. To this end, where possible, I have mapped the North Indian *sargam* notational system above the staff. The intention of these transcriptions is to be descriptive rather than prescriptive: to give readers an idea of the sounds being described rather than a definitive fixing, on paper, of forms of music that are otherwise much more fluidly realized. "Music is of the heart," as my *ustad* would say, "not the notepad."

Illustrations

Introduction

سُن مُرلی دی لکڑ کولوں درد. وچھوڑا رُکھ دا

سبھناں دا ایہہ حال محمد، کہو کی حال اُنکھ دا

میاں محمد بخش، سیف الملوک

Sun murlī dī lakaṛ kōloṅ dard, vichhoṛā rukẖ dā
sabhnaṅ dā ih hāl Muḥammad, kahō kī hāl unkẖ dā.

Hear in the flute's wood the pain of its separation from the tree,
O Muhammad! We must all face the same fate.

MIAN MUHAMMAD BAKHSH, *Saif-ul-Malook*

I woke up under a heavy Kashmiri sky at the home of my *shehnai* teacher, Ustad Zulfikar Ali Khan.[1] Zulfikar's house was set against the side of a hill in the low Himalayan foothills, offering a good vantage point over the rest of the village. People began appearing on rooftops to hang out their washing, brightly colored *cheelas* (shawls) crisp against a monochrome sky. We had a busy day ahead: a three-hour drive around the vast Mangla Dam, up into the mountains to perform at a wedding. I was in the village of Khari Sharif in Azad Kashmir, Pakistan, resting place of the local Sufi saint Mian Muhammad Bakhsh and home to my *ustad*. Zulfikar, a local musician and renowned player of the *shehnai*, was teaching me his instrument and how to understand the Sufi poetic traditions of Kashmir.

Zulfikar's house was in many respects typical of those found in this area of Azad Kashmir: arranged on one floor with two or three rooms around a small courtyard. Inside, rooms were furnished with several *khat* (woven beds), used for a mixture of sitting, dining, and sleeping—occasionally all at the same time. On the lilac- and purple-colored walls, rows of shelves displayed the family's best crockery, sometimes plastic, sometimes china, decorated with colorful floral patterns. Stacks of blankets, quilts, and shawls, preserved in clear plastic bags lay in wait for winter. Over the coming months and years we would spend much of our time in these rooms, and in the small courtyard outside, with family and friends drifting in and out throughout the day to drink tea and shoot the breeze (*gapshap*).

Outside, Zulfikar's wife, Maqsood Begum, was preparing a breakfast of *paya* over an open fire: a watery stew of goat trotters cooked overnight with spices, onion, and garlic. We ate it with a pile of freshly baked tandoori *roti* lathered with melted *kyo* (ghee). I tore off a piece of the soft bread, still warm, and dipped it in the broth.

"Today we're playing at the function of a UK family," Zulfikar explained. "This is *shādi* [wedding] season, the best season. All UK families come here to get married, and every day we are busy." At this point, Zulfikar retrieved one of the bones from the broth and, looking at me with a raised eyebrow, sucked out the marrow. "But first I want to show you something."

We set off north into the mountains on his 125cc Honda motorcycle, hugging the side of the great Mangla Dam to our left. The monsoon rains hadn't yet fully arrived, and the water was low, the dam's beds temporarily reclaimed and turned into lush pastures of wheat. Reaching the north side, we began to wind our way up higher and deeper into Kashmir. The air cooled as we ascended and the land grew greener, thickening with vegetation. After a couple of hours, we reached the summit of the mountain and dismounted. The view was spectacular and vast. Our mountain dropped away sharply to an expansive green valley floor, peppered here and there with houses. We could hear the chatter and clanging of people on the valley floor, half a mile below, like one massive amphitheater. On the other side of the valley, the mountains rose again dramatically, reaching a distant crescendo with the snowcapped peaks of the Himalayas.

Zulfikar looked east, toward the mountains. "That's Indian Kashmir," he said, gesturing over the first set of hills. "Before Pakistan was born, my family would perform all over Kashmir. Now, just this side." Many local people had relatives, he told me, just a few miles away across the border. They hadn't physically seen each other since Partition in 1947. From where we stood, however, such a divide was hard to discern; the land appeared to continue uninterrupted, borderless except for where it met the sky.

Zulfikar reached into his pocket and, unexpectedly, withdrew a silver coin. He looked at it briefly before handing it over. It was a silver one-rupee coin minted in 1862 at the height of British colonial rule. I turned it over in my hand, rubbing my thumb across the contours of Queen Victoria's head. I had an unexpected urge to smell it, to bite it in the way prospectors do.

"It's for you," Zulfikar said.

I looked down at the coin and nodded, unsure what to say. What could I say? The coin was surely worth a lot of money, but I understood it also carried a heavier weight: a shared past hovering in the present—Britain and Pakistan—imprinted on two sides of an unearthed coin.

"Thank you," I said, turning my head to him.

"*Koi bāt nahīn*," he replied, waving me away: don't mention it. His dog—in a moment rich with symbolism—had dug up a small hoard of coins in a nearby graveyard. Once Zulfikar had learned of my visit, he decided to give one to me.

"But why?" I asked.

He turned to face me and, with a smile, replied, "Because this is part of your history. You're British, and you can take it home with you."

We fell into silence, looking out. There was a freshness on top of the mountain, the air thin and clear. The breeze bristled the grass, carrying with it the fading echoes of the plains below. Somewhere a cockerel crowed. I looked down at the coin and wondered at these same paths and plains the British had trodden at the time the coin was minted. Many details of this past were opaquely familiar to me, hinted at through the histories I had been taught and read about at school in Britain, and in the places in which I had worked and lived—spaces entangled with the legacies of empire, colonialism, and migration. The frequencies of here and there, now and then, were resonating in that moment, and yet their meanings came to me only distantly, like the breeze through the grass at my feet.

At some point, the coin with Queen Victoria's head on it had been buried along with the British Empire. In its place stood the newly independent countries of India and Pakistan, countries violently marked by the movement of people during Partition in 1947. The coin serves as a reminder of a past that shaped this land politically and economically. Its history as an object, and as a gift to me, also tells something of the relationship between migration and music in this part of the world. The coin had been minted during a time when this area of Kashmir was fertile ground for Sufi poetic traditions. Mian Muhammad Bakhsh, the poet with whom I began this book and whom we will revisit throughout, was born around 1830 in my ustad's village of Khari Sharif, twenty kilometers south of Old Mirpur, a region to which many British Pakistanis can trace their heritage and where they continue to maintain strong cultural and familial ties today.[2] It was in this part of Kashmir in 1870, just a few years after the coin was minted, that Mian Muhammad Bakhsh wrote his acclaimed book of poetry *Safar ul-Ishq*, translated and pluralized here as *Journeys of Love*.[3]

In what follows, I explore the poetics of these journeys through the music-making of Kashmiris in Pakistan and as they migrate around the world, from performances of nineteenth-century Sufi poetry in Kashmir to rapping on street corners in Bradford, England. I consider how the poetics of everyday performances relate to Kashmiris' experiences and memories of migration—past and present—and how they are collectively passed down to generations born in the diaspora through poetry and music (Halbwachs 1992).[4] There are parallels here with how Michael Herzfeld has described "social poetics": intricate everyday moments in which "people try to turn transient advantage into a permanent condition" (2005, 26). I am especially interested in how this "transient advantage" might be taken further: to understand and conceptualize the continuous movement—imagined to real, past to present—among multiple localities or, to turn it around, a state of transient permanence between Kashmir and Britain. To consider how this exists across generations, I draw on the work of early sociologists of memory Barry Schwartz (1996) and Eviatar Zerubavel (1996), who argued that performative acts, such those discussed in this book, constitute affective "memory repositories" in which understandings of the past are socially constructed and passed down to generations born far away from the ancestral homeland.

Yet a defining feature of the poetry discussed in this book is its ambiguity and what many Kashmiris have referred to as its mystical unknowability, not only by virtue of poetic metaphor but through its linguistic impenetrability to cultural outsiders. I suggest that this unknowability is crucial to an understanding of migratory experience. For migrant communities, the unknowability of their lives to outsiders allows for both a claiming of that experience in the face of often overwhelming pressures to assimilate and a space of maneuverability to adapt to different systems of government, ethics, and beliefs—skills vital to migratory survival. As such, unknowability is not to be deconstructed here but afforded space to articulate its ambiguous—and often self-consciously hidden—meanings. I show how, through this ambiguity, performances of music and poetry communicate the firsthand lived memory of migration to future generations, many of whom were born in Britain and yet are still often confusingly, and problematically, perceived and portrayed as migrants in scholarly, political, and media discourse.[5]

Despite the historical significance of music and poetry to Mirpuris, both have often been overlooked in the wider canonical literature in Pakistan and the Pakistani diaspora.[6] Studies of music in this region have tended to focus on prominent forms such as *qawwali*, which, after Partition, flourished in the established cultural and religious centers of Lahore and Delhi (Qureshi 1986), or else on major religious festivals and rites such as *muharram* drumming in Karachi (Wolf 2000; Hegland 1998). The highly localized sung poetic traditions practiced by Mirpuris in Azad Kashmir and Punjab—and indeed the diaspora—have long been neglected.[7] This is surprising given how in the nineteenth century, Sufi poets, such as Mian Muhammad Bakhsh, were known to be well plugged into the cultural elite and deeply influenced by contemporaries in the royal court of Rajit Singh.[8] Recent scholarship has revealed how colonial practice was to instead fetishize a reductive idea of "the folk" as a way to keep people in their place and legitimize imperial power dynamics, especially across Punjab (Kapuria 2023).[9] Foregrounding the sensory aspects of sung poetry, the performance contexts described in what follows—known as Pothwari *sher* and *mehfils*—provide an alternative window onto some of these legacies of empire, with important implications for how diversity and migration are culturally understood and politically regulated today.[10]

The geographic and scholarly marginality of Kashmiri music-making relates to what Alex Chávez (2017) has described elsewhere as "impoverished poetry": traditions that exist on the edges of the canon and of respectability. Lila Abu-Lughod's (1986) work on honor and poetry in Bedouin society is particularly relevant to what follows, as are Victoria Rowe Holbrook's (1994) studies of Ottoman oral poetry and Turkish modernity, and Zuzanna Olszewska's (2015) more recent work on poetry and personhood among young Afghan refugees in Iran. Situated as they are on the margins of permissibility, the ambiguity and "indeterminacy" (Holbrook 1994) of these traditions allow them to draw a veil over feelings and sentiments that might otherwise attract attention or even censorship (Abu-Lughod 1986). As we shall see, for Kashmiris, this unknowability is central to how they position themselves vis-à-vis a sharpening Islamic Pakistani nationalism on the one hand and a somewhat muddled secular multicultural Britain on the other. Poetry and music cipher memories of migration that, as we shall see, are for good reason often deliberately and self-consciously hidden from public view.[11] Across generations, memories of migration therefore become shrouded in poetic metaphor and ambiguity. It is this ambiguity that I bring to the foreground in this book.

Memories of Migration in Music

Kashmir and Britain are areas of the world shaped by the politics and poetics of migration, past and present. The end of the Second World War and the collapse of the British Empire brought about two periods of sustained migration, first within the Indian subcontinent and then between Kashmir and Britain. In 1947, when the British left and India was partitioned, an estimated fourteen million people were displaced, largely along religious lines. As many Muslims migrated northwest into the newly created country of Pakistan, and Hindus and Sikhs east into India, estimates of lives lost to sectarian violence range between several hundred thousand and two million. The 1951 census of Pakistan records some 7.2 million displaced persons.[12]

Within a decade, a second period of displacement came to the town of Old Mirpur with the construction of the Mangla Dam, built to regulate irrigation in the Indus basin and to create a new source of hydroelectric power for the wider region.[13] Completed in 1967, the dam is located on the border of Azad Kashmir and Punjab, where the western Himalayan foothills begin to rise out of the plain. Behind the first of these foothills, the dam occupies and claims an irregularly shaped geological basin. When the dam was completed in 1967, the water of the Jhelum River began to flow into the valley. Before the dam was built, the valley floor was home to hundreds of towns and villages, including the town of Old Mirpur: a wide and, historically, religiously diverse area that is the ancestral home to many of the Mirpuris who feature in this book.

In these old villages and towns, many inhabitants, refusing to believe the town would be lost, waited until the last moment before abandoning their homes, giving up only as the water lapped at their thresholds before rowing away in small boats.[14] A whole network of lives and relationships swept out to the peripheries by the rising tide. Some 260 towns and villages were submerged to create a ninety-seven square mile artificial lake. An estimated 100,000 people were displaced.[15] Azad Kashmiris in Britain have strong memories of this period and the migration it produced.

"It was *Eid-ul-udha* [religious festival] two days before. We couldn't eat for days, there was a lot of crying. There was a valley far below the old town so we'd seen that filling up with water for a while. After that, the water kept rising and our houses disappeared. . . . Ourselves, we only left when we saw the water around our ankles. It was so upsetting."[16]

Some of those who were displaced used compensation money they received from the Pakistani government to buy land in the development of New Mirpur, built on the edge of the dam, and the surrounding hamlets. Many others migrated, either to areas across Pakistan, such as Multan, Sargodha, or Gujrat, or else took up an invitation from the British government to emigrate and join relatives in northern mill towns like Bradford: at the time of Partition, in 1947, wages for low-skilled jobs in the UK were over 30 times that of equivalent jobs in the newly created Pakistan.[17]

FIGURE 1. Families in Old Mirpur row away as their homes are flooded
due to the creation of the Mangla Dam.

Can you imagine what it feels like when you see the graves of your fore-
fathers being covered by water, the graves you've been visiting year after
year? Can you imagine what it's like if that grave you're leaving behind
belongs to your sister, your mother, or your child? Only for the sake of the
nation! But I remember some people insisting they would rather drown
than leave.[18]

These memories of migration run deep among Kashmiris, both at home
and abroad. Over the decades that followed, music and poetry became
central to how such memories were produced and sustained across generations: they are rich in narratives of home and belonging, are historically
rooted in their relationship with nineteenth-century empire and nation-
state building, are patronized today through the circulation of people and
money between the diaspora and home, have a history of interacting with
state-led multicultural policies, and are inflected with cross-cultural influences stretching back centuries.[19]

Understanding migration through these "collective memories"
(Schwartz 1996), I want to suggest, cuts across some of the more established writing on migration that has tended to treat ethnicity and religion
as a first port of call, at the expense of more marginal, or even hidden,
musical and poetic traditions.[20] There are strong resonances here with
other studies of migration from the Indian subcontinent, which were

similarly propelled by the violence of Partition. In her ethnography of East Bengali migrant musicians in the Andaman Islands, for example, Carola E. Lorea has described how a sense of homeland would be realized via "a constant process of reconstruction through performances that provide a shared sense of history and territorial origins, a feeling of community and solidarity" (2018, 53). For the Bengali migrant musicians of her study, "performing the homeland" is a crucial means by which past and present, here and there, are mediated and reconciled. Elsewhere, Helene Basu has described how, for Gujarati migrants to Zanzibar, performances of *ngoma* are understood and experienced as a kind of "archive for remembering the past" (2008, 168). Experiences such as these point to the often ambiguous roles of music and poetry in nourishing familial and cultural memories along migratory routes (see also Niranjana 2006). Building on these studies, I explore how, during musical and poetic performances in Britain and Pakistan, Kashmiris' collective memory of migration is enacted in narrative form, encapsulating key values of family, kinship, and honor within the wider spiritual "grand narratives" of Sufism.[21]

The Poetics of Migration

How might we come to understand a poetics of migration? Or, rather, how might migration be understood as *being* poetic? Conceptually, I build here on Alessandra Ciucci's (2022) study of poetry and personhood among Moroccan migrants in Umbria, Italy.[22] Like the Moroccan men of her ethnography, the recitation of poetry by Kashmiris in Britain invokes a sense of "the rural" in the face of often overwhelming pressures to integrate into urban multicultural environments that have long been hostile to their presence. The way in which memories of migration are communicated in these urban areas is often shrouded in poetic metaphor and ambiguity. In her study of Ottoman poetic traditions at the dawn of the modern Turkish state, Victoria Rowe Holbrook wrote that "perhaps in any age a poetics has more often been devised by an interpretive community reflecting upon what it claimed as its own literary tradition" (1994, 2). In a similarly transitory context of Afghan refugees in Iran, the anthropologist Zuzanna Olszewska also identifies the composition, performance, and circulation of poetry as a means to make "collective claims about identity and to pursue personal ends" (2015, 6). Running through these studies is a sense of poetry in motion. In Holbrook's case, this relates to a somewhat turbulent moment in Turkey's history after World

War I and the birth of the modern Turkish state. Holbrook is particularly interested in what happened to Ottoman poetry and its emotional resonances during this period, as it moved from the realm of Persian mysticism into a Turkish modernity. For the women Afghan refugees in Olszewska's study, poetry set individual and collective identity in motion across Iranian and Afghan modernities in ways that destabilized and reimagined traditional gender dynamics. In both cases, it was the poetic movement of verses as they were being recited that afforded new imaginative and affective possibilities.[23]

Elsewhere, in the context of Bedouin society, Michael Meeker and others (Meeker 1979; Caton 1990) witnessed how important poetry was as an intellectual means to deal with the social and philosophical dilemmas of everyday life. If Meeker's study considered marginal poetic traditions in relation to what might broadly be described as "the political," Lila Abu-Lughod, in her classic study, *Veiled Sentiments*, sought to ground these interpretations more firmly in the quotidian. In doing so, Abu-Lughod vividly illustrates how daily experiences of frustration and anger in the face of racism or persecution find a kind of "veiled" expression through the "constellation of sentiments" made possible by poetry. Unknowable to those on the outside, there is a certain cultural safety in this veiled ambiguity. "Sentiments by individuals contribute to representations of the self, representations that are tied to morality, which in turn is tied to politics in its broadest sense" (Abu-Lughod 1986, 34).

For Holbrook, then, the sense of "indeterminacy" in Ottoman poetry serves to mediate between this world and that, between the temporal and the eternally divine. In Kashmiri migratory contexts, however, what they describe as unknowability can be taken further, since it mediates not only between the borders of the worldly and the divine but between the borders of here and there, home and abroad.[24] For Azad Kashmiris, their musical and poetic practices exist on the margins of not only South Asian scholarship but South Asia itself, across the borders of Kashmir and Punjab, Pakistan and India, and so its "claiming," in Holbrook's term, by Mirpuris at home and abroad does not constitute part of the wider literary and musical canons of Pakistani national mythology, of which there is a great deal written,[25] but rather becomes imbued with markers of a locally concentrated identity.[26] I suggest that with migration, such poetics become translocal rather than transnational, destabilizing ideas of citizenship in the process because, like poetry, ambiguity is at the heart of migratory experience.[27]

Poetic metaphor, such as our opening quote from *Safar ul-Ishq*, makes sense to many Kashmiris as it becomes relatable to their own lives in migratory contexts—"hear in the wood's flute the pain of its separation from the tree"—rather than how it sits vis-à-vis an established literary canon or national mythology. This theme of separation is not unique to Kashmiris and, perhaps unsurprisingly, is also present in neighboring Punjab—regions that were both arbitrarily and violently cleaved in two by Partition. In both places, the shared pain of separation is articulated and understood by those displaced through not only poetic metaphor but the physical materiality of things like musical instruments. Gibb Schreffler, for example, has shown how the *dhol* drum became a "sign of separation" for the way it "represents not only the emotional gap between loved ones, but also the spatial and cultural gap between Punjabis generally and the land of Punjab" (2010, 982).[28] In a similar vein, Stefan Fiol has described how, in the wider Himalayan region, Garhwali *gīt* (song) "offer[s] listeners multiple experiences of place, and how places (and mobility between places) prefigure certain kinds of listening" (2018, 114; see also 2017). We see, in other words, how migrant communities continuously weave a fine thread between the ambiguity of poetic metaphor and the reality that many things—songs, musical instruments—can also carry definitive meanings.

For Holbrook, these marginal yet "lived" literary traditions often become "rationalized [by scholars] for underdevelopment rather than poetics" (1994, 4). Holbrook was talking about semiotic literary theory, but arguably the same can be said for perceptions of the interpretive communities that surround poetic traditions. Kashmiris, particularly those from the Mirpur district, have been frequently dismissed by other Pakistanis as backward (McLoughlin 2006), of a low social status (Ballard 1994), and as adhering to orthodox forms of Islam that proscribe music (Baily 1995). That Kashmiri poetry remains a largely oral tradition propels this perception of marginality, further masking its poetics in a shroud of unknowability. While for outsiders, such unknowability serves to keep this tradition on the margins—and far away from literary analysis—for Kashmiris it paradoxically provides a shield against larger hegemonic forces, be it an ever-evolving Islamic Pakistani nationalism or a British multiculturalism preoccupied with questions of integration. Indeed, its positioning as what Chávez describes as "impoverished poetry" (2017) is in many respects what keeps it self-consciously unknowable to those on the outside, even while its mystical unknowability kindles shared intimacy for Kashmiris on the inside.

A poetics of migration reveals this mystical unknowability as a process that intertwines the spiritual with the quotidian: with micro-performances of unrequited longing for the beloved, it is a poetics full of ambiguities in which both the journey and the beloved can stand in for the worldly and the divine.[29] In this sense, the beloved can be God or the Prophet Muhammad, but recited in migratory contexts, it can also mean home, wherever that may be. Such ambiguity resonates so strongly with Kashmiris because their sense of home hovers across both Pakistan and Britain—Mirpur and Bradford—having been established over the longue durée, from the midnineteenth century, as we saw with the one-rupee coin, through to a history of postwar migration to places like Bradford in England that continues to this day. The musical performance and reception of *Saif-ul-Malook* discussed in this book provides a window onto how Mirpuris understand their

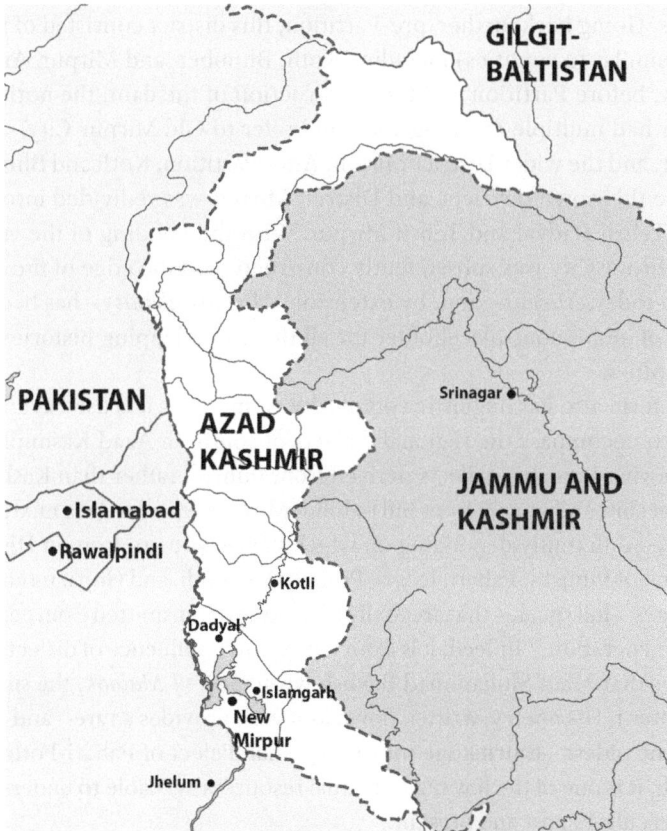

FIGURE 2. Mirpur today is located close to the southern border of Azad Kashmir, on the shore of the Mangla Dam.

migratory experience in ways that tie together these threads of politics, history and geography.

Locating Mirpur

Scholars and even those from this area of Azad Kashmir have often struggled to articulate exactly what or where Mirpur is.[30] The term itself is ambiguous, referring to a large area: one that covers parts of the Pothohar plateau of Punjab, and the hills surrounding Mangla in Azad Kashmir.[31] Before the construction of the Mangla Dam, *Mirpur* referred to the Old City, home to the shrine of Miran Mir, from whom the area takes its name. With the shrine being a site of pilgrimage, the surrounding area also came to be known as District Mirpur, encompassing dozens of distinct towns and villages. Going back further, pre-Partition, this district consisted of three *tehsil* (similar to counties) including Kotli, Bhimber, and Mirpur. And so already, before Partition and the construction of the dam, the notion of Mirpur had multiple meanings: it could refer to Old Mirpur City, *Tehsil* Mirpur, and the wider District Mirpur. After Partition, Kotli and Bhimber became their own districts, and District Mirpur was redivided into two *tehsil*: Tehsil Dadyal and Tehsil Mirpur. With the flooding of the valley, New Mirpur City was subsequently constructed on the edge of the dam. And so today, *Mirpur*—and, by extension, *Mirpuri identity*—has become a kind of ambiguous placeholder for all these overlapping histories and geographies.

The term also has linguistic complexity. Sometimes it is used as an umbrella to encompass the regional dialects of southern Azad Kashmir and neighboring Punjab—dialects derived from Punjabi rather than Kashmiri and that shift and morph from hill to hill.[32] Mirpuri is said to be a mixture— weighted differently depending on which village you are from in District Mirpur—of Punjabi, Pahari, Dogri, Pothwari, Lahndi, and Gojri: mountain languages—hill speak—that are orally learned and transmitted from generation to generation.[33] Indeed, it is from within this confluence of dialects and cultures that Mian Muhammad Bakhsh wrote *Saif-ul-Malook*, the subject of chapter 1. His poetry, written down as it was, provides a rare—and most likely the oldest—touchstone for the regional dialect of Pahari-Pothwari. As such, it is one of the few major textual resources available to understand Mirpuri culture past and present.

Partly because of this linguistic, geographic, and cultural ambiguity, Mirpuris often diverge quite drastically in how they describe themselves. Several people I met in Walsall, Birmingham, for example, pointedly told me that it was a made-up term, that "there is no such thing as 'Mirpuri.'" Instead, they advocated for *Kashmiri*, which I mainly follow here, taking their lead; indeed, in the Black Country, there is a political movement aimed at claiming closer identification with the historic state of Kashmir for important symbolic and linguistic purposes: the *Azad* in Azad Kashmir translates as "free" or "independent."[34] More northern Kashmiris in Pakistan, and indeed many metropolitan Pakistanis, however, would dismiss this terminology out of hand: "They're not Kashmiris!" I was told matter-of-factly by a music producer in Karachi. In Islamabad, I was also once confusingly told, "They're not real Pakistanis. We call Mirpur 'Little Britain.'"[35]

The term *Mirpuri*, in other words, is full of ambiguities that allow it to be many things to many people. As we shall see, it connotes a place, a people, a language, a culture, and a way of being. But it also connotes a place that doesn't fit and therefore suggests somewhere apart from the more obvious analytical and political poles of Pakistan and Britain. Indeed, those outside the community often use the term pejoratively, associating it with a supposedly backward, rural, peasant folk who do not belong in grander narratives about what it means to *be* Pakistani or *be* British.[36]

Yet within the community, the term carries strong, positive resonances that are felt more keenly along local rather than national lines. As one respondent put it,

> I could view myself as a member of the following communities, depending on the context and in no particular order: Black, Asian, Azad Kashmiri, Mirpuri, Jat, Marilail, Kungriwalay, Pakistani, English, British, Yorkshireman, Bradfordian, from Bradford Moor. . . . I could use the term "community" in any of these contexts and it would have meaning. Any attempt to define me only as one of these would be meaningless.[37]

Instead, markers of identity are more often expressed and *felt* in relation to localities of belonging and longing.[38] "Where are you from?" I would often be asked as I moved around Azad Kashmir. My response—"England"—would be met with blank stares. I would narrow down the scope to Bradford. "Ah, yes! Bradford! Where in Bradford? I have family there, in BD8 [postcode]." From there would follow a conversation about which postcode district I came from. My response of "BD9" would come with knowing approval due to its numerical and indeed geographic proximity to BD7 and BD8: locally specific places in Bradford where the families of people I met along the road in Kashmir had migrated to.

The original routes of migration, from villages in District Mirpur to Bradford postcodes, are still the primary points of reference for Azad Kashmiris across the diaspora. It also explains why the area surrounding Old Mirpur, submerged today under the water of the Mangla Dam, still retains a strong tidal pull for many Azad Kashmiris, drawing them back from both the edge of the dam and across the diaspora. Mirpuris are people who have been displaced by political decisions near and far, and yet Old Mirpur, still visible for a few weeks during the dry season, remains an anchor point. Generations born and raised abroad return here to visit relatives, to get married, to pay respects at the graves of their ancestors. Submerged today in the deep blue of the lake, it is the *memory* of Mirpur that provides historical and cultural depth for the people the water displaced, not just to the dam's periphery but to the margins of Europe and, more recently, to the Persian Gulf.

Methods and Memories

My first serious inquiries into Kashmiri music-making were met with a mixture of incredulity and thinly veiled contempt. One music producer in Bradford, England, whose parents were from Karachi, openly laughed at me: "They're not interested in music. We call them 'MPs' [short for Mirpuri]. They've got this village mentality, you see. When you said you were doing research on MPs I thought you were joking! I've seen everything now."

This dismissal did not mesh with my own experiences of Kashmiris and music in Bradford. The city's curry houses had the constant hum of Bollywood music in the background; a mixture of Dutch Pakistani singer Imran Khan and the late Nusrat Fateh Ali Khan would, more often than not, accompany a late-night taxi ride; and in its heyday, the Bradford Mela, one of Europe's biggest multicultural music and arts festivals, would draw over 150,000 visitors to the city every year. And yet, the dismissal also did something else. It highlighted a tension that had preoccupied me during the early stages of my research: I was back in Bradford—the place I was born—to learn more about Mirpuri poetry and practices of music, but three months down the line my inquiries had been met with incredulity among members of the wider South Asian community and blank looks in the local council. In terms of population size, Mirpuris account proportionally for the largest South Asian group living not only in Bradford but in the United Kingdom as a whole (McLoughlin 2006; Lewis 2007). How could it be that such a large number of people were supposedly without music?

I grew up in Manningham, a predominantly Pakistani area of Bradford in the north of England. Bradford's fortunes have risen and fallen like a breaking wave. In its nineteenth-century industrial prime, Bradford was one of the most prosperous cities in Europe. Today, the tide has gone out on much of that wealth. Decades of industrial and economic decline, neglect, and dubious urban planning have rendered a city center strewn with empty buildings, many of its once grand Victorian mills in decay. There is also a history of ethnic and religious tension in a city famed for the burning of Salman Rushdie's novel *The Satanic Verses*, for the Honeyford affair, for the Bradford riots, and for so-called segregated communities.

The vast majority of students at my local first school, Margaret McMillan on Scotchman Road, were also born in Bradford but, unlike me, were of Mirpuri heritage. We shared the same education, walked the same streets, played in the same park. In the final days of Ramadan each year, we would make decorations while singing Eid Mubarak songs. On the day of Eid itself, while most of the school's pupils celebrated at home with their families, the remaining half dozen or so of us non-Muslim pupils would have the run of the school, the undoubted highlight being unlimited access to crates and crates of half-pint bottles of free school milk. Margaret MacMillan wasn't a particularly academic school, it seems to me now, but then not all education is about what you learn from the teacher.

This was in the late 1980s, when competing views about multiculturalism in Britain were coming to the forefront of public debates.[39] Ray Honeyford, head teacher of nearby Drummond Middle School, had recently published an article in the conservative periodical the *Salisbury Review* that became a lightning rod for anxieties about immigration and multiculturalism. In the article, Honeyford criticized what he perceived as a misplaced use of multicultural policy in schools like ours, which, he argued, contributed to a lack of integration and a bias against what he saw as the native white population.[40] Of particular concern was what he perceived as an increasingly privileged status of ethnic minorities in schools—which, in his case, meant Mirpuri Muslims—citing the provision of halal meat, language, and dress code as examples. The response to Honeyford's article, from both the left and the right, was fervent: supporters saw him as raising valid concerns about educational standards and integration while his opponents saw instead a racist agenda that was discriminatory and damaging to community cohesion.[41]

What felt remarkable as I grew older, however, was the absence of Kashmiri voices in these debates. While these discussions swirled around us, my friends and I were experiencing multicultural education policy firsthand, and yet as children we were somewhat unaware of the stakes being set out.

The Rushdie affair and the Bradford riots of 1995 and 2001 that followed happened within a few hundred meters of where I grew up and went to school, but it strikes me now that the epistemologies surrounding Mirpuris that crystallized in their wake were peculiarly partial and damaging.

I have strong memories of these events, particularly the latter ones, but then I also have enduring memories of events in the area that were covered much less by politicians and the media at the time. For many years the Bradford Mela, one of Europe's largest multicultural music and arts festivals, occurred in Lister Park, across the road from my house. Every year, my friends and I would jump over the park wall, buy a bag of *pakoras*, and watch trapeze artists Skinning the Cat before heading to one of the many music stages to watch a *qawwali* ensemble perform a program of *ghazals* in front of thousands. From the age of twelve until I was sixteen, I worked as a paperboy and then shop assistant at the local corner shop run by Mr. Sheikh and his family. This was my first encounter with working life—come rain or shine—and through it I built up relationships with the family and, over the course of several years, attended many of their extravagant wedding celebrations. While enjoyable in their different ways, none of these experiences were extraordinary. They were all intimately tied up with my local neighborhood and my friends who lived there.

The music of the *mela* in Lister Park felt like a tonic to the kind of anti-multiculturalism sentiment swirling in the press and academia. Here was this multicultural festival, full of Bradford's different communities, new and old, experiencing and sharing each other's food, art, and music. The *mela*, in its size and scope, was unique to Bradford, a product of its history of immigration. Eating freshly fried *pakora* while listening to *qawwali* exposed me to a richness of music and cuisine often lost in debates about multiculturalism and Mirpuris in Britain that had frequently come to be understood through one lens: Islam. The majority of Pakistanis living in Bradford are indeed Muslim, and yet are there not other ways of understanding people's lives? Are there not many ways to *be* Muslim? Are there not other ways of understanding migration?

While my attempt to address these questions began in earnest during my first period of fieldwork in 2009, I don't think it is a huge stretch to say that, in an oblique sense, my interests began way back in these formative years.[42] Musically, I had grown up in an altogether different tradition, playing the cornet in the world of brass bands and wind orchestras. Later, when studying music at university, I was very much taken by the likes of Trevor Herbert (2002) and Suzel Reily (2013), scholars who took these working-class traditions—so important to postindustrial towns like Bradford—seriously and in doing so brought to the surface the value (and love) of the social relations hidden therein. But I also knew, looking around me, that even this was still a partial history. In the back of my mind was Manningham and the friends I went to school with. After all, the mills we played in the shadows of were the same mills that had sponsored brass bands back in the day; they were also the same mills that had brought the first Mirpuris to Bradford. Yet despite growing up among the Mirpuri community, for much of my child-hood their music and poetry had remained hidden from my experience of Bradford's cultural life, despite a proliferation of multicultural arts initia-tives in the city. It was only when I arrived in Kashmir in 2009 that I began to learn of a rich, proud musical culture deeply intertwined with the poetry of Mian Muhammad Bakhsh. Why had this poetry been so culturally hidden from view in Britain?

Such a complex question has necessarily involved a reckoning with my own positionality, first as a white Bradfordian and second as an ethnogra-pher: how should I situate myself in relation to a place that is intimately tied up with my own past while simultaneously remaining ethnically and religiously outside the community at the center of this book? There is no easy answer to this question. When writing about Bradford, I have always felt a kind of latent authority that, by dint of growing up there, my think-ing and writing in many respects precedes my positionality as an ethnog-rapher. On the other hand, when writing about Mirpuris, there is clearly an awkward inversion of that dynamic: I have no cultural authority, and I also don't necessarily believe that repositioning myself as an ethnographer can ever fully make up for that lack. It is also the case that my positionality affected the spaces and people I was able to work with. Throughout all my fieldwork in Pakistan, the world of female poetry and music was closed off from me (even as female domestic life was more open), and so what follows should be read primarily as an account of the world of *male* Mirpuri poetry and music-making. The challenge in writing this book, then, has been to navigate the ambiguity of my position as a Bradfordian (and musician) who, throughout his life and research, has come face to face with other Bradford-ians (and musicians) who also, in very different ways, grew up in a changing city shaped by migration (see also Niranjana 2006, 3).

Advice about how to navigate this ambiguity came from an unexpected source: my late grandfather, Ron, who, many moons ago, instructed me to always "listen twice, speak once." Ron was transposing one of the main rules of carpentry: measure twice, cut once; wood is valuable, and you must respect it. But it seems to me now that he was also saying something deeper about relationships and, unwittingly, about ethnographic methods (and participant observation in particular). Keep your ears open and lis-ten, pay attention to what people are saying (and not saying): words and gestures are fleeting and must be cherished. Coincidentally, it turned out to be similar to advice I received in Kashmir from my *ustad*, Zulfikar Ali Khan, who, during our first *shehnai* lesson, chastised me for wanting to write things down. "Music is not here," he rebuked, tapping on my notepad. "It is here and here," he said, pointing to my hand (for counting the beat) and heart (for feeling its meaning).[43] For this reason, I was always reluctant to sit down and conduct formal interviews where the flashing red light of a voice recorder or the scribbling in a pad could get in the way of meaningful, free-flowing conversations, the sheer presence of the technology affecting what might be said, its suggested permanence tempting inhibition.[44] When sitting down to write all this, then, it was the combination of the materials I gathered and deep reminiscence that rekindled all the intimately felt sounds and feelings that provide the background contexts to what I describe.

∴

What became clear throughout all my time in Bradford and Mirpur is that the multiculturalism debate in Britain largely came to be shaped by responses to Kashmiris, with little input from Kashmiris themselves. Yet as the multiculturalism debate stalled in the early 2010s, anxieties surrounding immigration have only grown, finding new expression through various populist movements across Europe and the Brexit referendum in Britain.[45] To see migration only through the lens of religion or ethnicity risks not only gliding over other ways of understanding the world but generating a narrow view of life that is reductive at best and deterministic at worst.[46] Much less heard in conversations about immigration in Britain are the voices and memories of Mirpuris themselves. And virtually silent are the rich music and poetry that have rendered migration between Pakistan and Britain meaningful and navigable for those people. It is this musical life as it is enacted across borders today that I call the poetics of migration.

The Path Ahead

There are two central arguments that I develop in this book. The first is a critique of pervasive assumptions about the politics of migration and multiculturalism. While I originally set out in this project to find the Mirpuri music-making that was so absent from scholarly texts (and my own experience), over time I came to realize that its hiddenness was itself a political act, one profoundly more meaningful to Kashmiris than the politics of race and identity. For a community so often accused of self-segregation and living parallel lives, I learned that Kashmiris have had good reason to keep their music and poetry hidden from public view. Moreover, researching an already marginalized community in the aftermath of the 2008 financial crash revealed the merits of economic insulation from the vagaries of government subsidies and funding initiatives. I thus interrogate scholarship on multiculturalism that has historically foregrounded race and ethnicity while situating socioeconomic integration as its ultimate aim (Charsley et al. 2020). Resisting and countering this, we see a community thriving through and by its cultural and economic self-reliance.

Second, I argue for a better understanding of the role of poetic metaphor not only in how migration is experienced firsthand but in how memories of those experiences are passed down to generations born in diaspora. I discuss how the affective turn of cultural theory over the past two decades (Stokes 2017) has seen a drift toward sensory aspects of migratory experience, in particular the role of memory and metaphor in cultural production. Building on Alex Chávez's recent work among Mexican migrants, I propose an idea of poetic metaphor as a constituent force in creating and sustaining the migratory experience (2017; see also Wolf 2021). Rather than seeing the hiddenness of Kashmiri sung poetry as a marker of marginalization, I emphasize instead the central role it plays for a community at the center of debates about migration in Britain.

I begin, in chapter 1, with a trip to a rural village on the outskirts of Mirpur, to visit a maker of musical instruments. I describe the process and materials involved in the construction of a *shehnai* (a kind of double-reed shawm common to this area of Kashmir) and its presentation to me as a gift. Through this, I introduce the local nineteenth-century Sufi mystic Mian Muhammad Bakhsh, who, like Rumi, used the wood of the flute as a metaphor for the pain of separation from the beloved. Through an analysis of contemporary performances at Mian Muhammad Bakhsh's shrine in Khari Sharif, I analyze this metaphor in relation to Kashmiris' own sensory experience of migration. I show how the *shehnai*—its materiality and poetics—represents a powerful home away from home through its usage in Kashmir and the diaspora to mark significant life-cycle events: births, marriages, and deaths. The poetics of the *shehnai*, I argue, run through these life stages, connecting the worldly with the divine, this world and that, Bradford and Kashmir. In the remaining chapters, I follow these routes of Kashmiri migration as they radiate outward from Mian Muhammad Bakhsh's shrine.

Chapter 2 charts the history of migration from Kashmir to Britain. Drawing on archival oral histories and ethnographic data, I show how the circulation of photographs and poetry between Bradford and Mirpur since World War II not only came to influence patterns of migration but began to shape the contours of what came to be known as the multiculturalism debate. While this debate situated Mirpuris as cultural outsiders, refusing to integrate into British society, an examination of Kashmiri iconography and music instead reveals hidden intimacies that point to deeply rooted senses of belonging in both Britain and Mirpur. Borrowing from Ruth Finnegan's classic study of "hidden musicians," I suggest that keeping their poetics largely hidden from public view does not necessarily mean they are living "parallel lives" but rather signals a means of fostering cultural intimacy in the face of repeated public criticism. The chapter thereby provides a counterpoint to a multiculturalism debate more often framed along racial and religious lines.

In chapter 3, I move beyond the multiculturalism debate by developing a theory of public poetics and consider more fully intergenerational dynamics. I examine the shifting relationship between Kashmiri rap in Bradford and state-led integration initiatives—in the form of rap workshops—aimed at "civilizing" Kashmiri youth. At stake here is the way in which the local council's integrationist agenda comes up, rather blindly, against the hidden intimacies described in the previous chapter. We see instead how emerging generations navigate their life at home, steeped in Kashmiri heritage, vis-à-vis their experiences growing up in the multicultural areas of Bradford and Birmingham—some of the most economically deprived boroughs in the country. I argue that top-down multicultural initiatives were often misplaced, underestimating the extent to which memories of migration shaped emerging generations' attitudes toward integration, which remain ambivalent at best. The public poetics of rap instead reveals a complex orientation toward life in both Bradford and Mirpur, full of humor and struggle, connecting the present to the past, and young Mirpuris to a much longer lineage of Kashmiri poets.

Chapter 4 further develops the theory of public poetics via the migration of South Asian festivals—*mela*—between Pakistan and Britain. These gatherings, which have traditionally been held across South Asia, are still practiced at the shrine of Mian Muhammad Bakhsh during his ʻurs celebrations, events that mark the anniversary of the saint's death. Since the late 1980s, *mela*s have also become common in the UK, initially as community-led festivals, but have since taken the form of state-sponsored celebrations of multicultural harmony. The chapter looks at this particular form of cultural migration and, through a comparison of the *mela* at Khari Sharif in Pakistan with the Bradford Mela in northern England, I examine the ways in which migrant musical practices change and become co-opted by the state for various ends. The history of *melas* in Britain, I suggest, shows that the relationship between Kashmiris and the state is fraught with contradictory narratives. When considered alongside the previous chapters, I show that integrationist approaches to nationalism and multiculturalism often ignore the complex ways in which migrants orient themselves across borders. Moreover, in the case of the Bradford Mela, integrationist initiatives by the local council—propelled by the multiculturalism debate—eventually came to exclude Mirpuris from its vision of multicultural Bradford.

Chapter 5 continues this exploration of the politics of belonging through emerging poetic traditions in Britain. The chapter examines the poetry of Zaffar Kunial, a British-born poet whose father was born in a village near Mirpur but whose mother is ethnically white British, and Mr. Khokhar, a first-generation migrant, barber, and poet in Bradford. Zaffar's contemporary poetry, recently published by Faber & Faber, explores the experience of growing up between the cultural and institutional traditions of his parents. The poetry speaks of coming to terms with a history of a land elsewhere, inculcated at a young age by his father, but that nevertheless remains distant and unfamiliar. I compare this to Mr. Khokhar's handwritten poetry, which reflects on his own spiritual and worldly journey from Mirpur to Bradford, to consider how poetic meaning becomes indexed against memories of migration—and home—in contrasting ways.

The concluding chapter returns to the imagery of the silver one-rupee coin with which I began this introduction, except this time we are in Qatar, almost ten years later. I examine the reception of *Saif-ul-Malook* among taxi drivers and migrant laborers working in Doha today. For these recent economic migrants, whose families remain in Pakistan, the narrative lessons of *Saif-ul-Malook* provide what they describe as a path home, even when a return may be many years away. As with the early circulation of photographs featured in chapter 2, new digital technologies have made this journey away from home more bearable, as the drivers interact with family members across the diaspora continually throughout their working day via messaging services such as WhatsApp, through which they share YouTube clips of sung poetry. As they drive through the city's streets, often working twelve to fifteen hours per day, the poetry reminds them that while they may be meandering down foreign roads, in a place where workers' rights are severely restricted, their spiritual path remains true.

∵

Taken together, then, the chapters in this book point to new directions for understanding the value of migration in a world increasingly marked by hardening national borders on the one hand and globalizing technologies that cut across these borders on the other. Bringing the insights generated throughout the book to bear on Azad Kashmiris' long and continued tradition of migration, the chapters look at how discursive and highly performative aspects of music and poetry serve to both establish and collapse time and space. In a world in which the value of migration is increasingly measured in economic terms, the book suggests the opposite: that music, like people, has always migrated and that its value is realized in culturally rich and socially profound ways. The book shows that the aesthetics of Mirpuri music-making, and its emotional resonances, continue to inspire new social formations that prove more porous and enduring than nationalist discourses might suggest.

CHAPTER ONE

The Wood of the Flute

اِکو فرش زِویں دا سارا اِکو یِنہ تراوت

بُوٹے رُکھ زِویں تے جِتنے سبھاں وچ تقاوت

میاں محمد بخش، سیف الملوک

Ikkō farsh ziweṅ dā sārā ikkō mēṅh tarāwat,
būṭe rukẖ ziweṅ te jitne sabhnāṅ vich tafāwat.

The land may be the same, and so too the rain,
But diverse are the plants which there reign.

MIAN MUHAMMAD BAKHSH, *Saif-ul-Malook*

We left the courtyard of my *ustad*'s house as day broke and followed a dirt track toward the river. We were in the shadow of the Mangla Dam, and the water below us flowed from its great hydroelectric turbines. The bulging Jhelum River carried with it the unpredictable force of ninety-seven square miles of pent-up water. Its surface appeared pillowed, lightly patterned by the powerful currents pushing underneath.

"Grown men drown in this river," Zulfikar warned.

We eased ourselves in, careful to hold on to the bank. The icy water tugged at my feet, beckoning me to follow it on the journey downstream. We closed our eyes and ducked our heads under. Water swirled around us, filling our ears, drowning our senses.

This water had begun its journey on the Indian side of the Himalayas and would not stop until it reached the Arabian Sea and, from there, the world. Climbing out, Zulfikar recited the verse with which I began this chapter.

"Water," he went on to explain, "is life, here and there, everywhere." The dam holds it up for only so long.

Submerged as we were, there was something about being suspended in its flow, enveloped by another element. We were in Pakistan, yet through his allusion to the poetry of Mian Muhammad Bakhsh, Zulfikar hinted at how the water that filled our ears and held our bodies also connected us physically and symbolically with lands elsewhere: the banks and soil of Kashmir, yes, but also places far away across the seas. For Zulfikar, the water connected us to the past and the future, to India, Pakistan, and Britain. Such philosophical ruminations were typical of my time with Zulfikar, especially during our *shehnai* lessons. (Zulfikar himself belonged to a long patrilineage of local *shehnai* players and described, proudly, that he had ninety-four students [*shagirds*] across Azad Kashmir and Punjab who would visit him fortnightly for lessons at his home.)

We climbed out, pulled on our *shalwar kameez*, and returned to Zulfikar's village just as the summer sun started to make itself felt. After a light breakfast of *paratha* and tea, we set out for the day to meet a local *shehnai* maker, a ten-minute walk up a steep-sided creek from my *ustad*'s house. His home was smaller than Zulfikar's, more isolated, perched as it was above the creek, looking down its arid course. In the small open courtyard, three puppies came running up to us. Their white coats had been patterned with black dye, giving the impression of young dalmatians. Chickens and a cockerel ambled about, pecking at the dusty ground.

Mr. Zuman embraced us, shaking our hands. His palms were rough from a lifetime of working wood. Beckoning us in, he brought out a selection of the instruments he was working on. As he ran his hands over the wood, his skin made the coarse sound of sandpaper. Zulfikar withdrew from his pocket his own *shehnai* just as Mr. Zuman pulled a toolbox from underneath his bed. The instrument maker took the *shehnai*, pincered it between his legs, and immediately, roughly, started gouging it with a chisel. There was a hairline crack in the wood, and Mr. Zuman intended to get to the bottom of it. Blowing the thin curls of wood away, he began to vigorously sand the area down. He then filled the crack with wood filler, pushing it in with his thumb before sanding smooth again. He blew the dust away and handed the instrument back to Zulfikar, who immediately angled the instrument to the horizon and looked down its barrel as if it were the bore of a rifle. His mustache twitched as he looked up to the ceiling, rummaging in his *kurta* pocket for the reed (*patha*). Inserting it into the *shehnai*, Zulfikar took the instrument through its paces up and down *Rāg Pahari*, testing its sound and intonation.

"*Theek*," he said, nodding toward Mr. Zuman, who looked on attentively: good. The whole episode took perhaps five minutes. Quick enough, anyway, that I was still drinking my *chah* by the time they finished.

Zulfikar smiled at me and started to more fully explore *Rāg Pahari*—mountain *rāg*—the melodic tones of which I would hear again later that day, at the wedding of a British Mirpuri, set to the poetry of Mian Muhammad Bakhsh.

∴

For many Mirpuris in Britain and Kashmir, the *shehnai* is a powerful symbol of a home away from home. It is often used and heard in musical performances that mark life-cycle events—births, marriages, deaths—within the family and the wider kinship network (*biraderi*), and at the *'urs* of local Sufi saints.[1] The patronage of the *shehnai* in these settings affords deep memories of home, especially during performances, a process intensely shaped by the instrument's materiality and, by extension, its aurality. Indeed, the specific type of *shehnai* made by Mr. Zuman is quite literally rooted in this part of Azad Kashmir: the timbre of the sound it produces flows from the grain and texture of its wood and its double-reed mouthpiece—materials that grow in the soil near where it is made and also where Mian Muhammad Bakhsh wrote his verses. Its use in Kashmiri life-cycle events is therefore valued not only because it accompanies sung poetry but because its materiality conveys something of the physical geography and soil from which it originates, with important affective ramifications for Mirpuri identities and feelings of longing and belonging.[2] By following the relationships that develop around this instrument's production and use, we will see how the circulation of money within musical performances intersects with local memories and industry, connecting Mr. Zuman, through Zulfikar, to the Kashmiri diaspora: production, performance, and migration.[3] It is this combination of sonic ephemerality and instrumental physicality that makes the *shehnai* such a powerful and instrumental symbol of a home away from home, especially as its sounds become intertwined with the poetics of Mian Muhammad Bakhsh.[4]

The *Shehnai* Maker

The *shehnai* can be found across the Indian subcontinent in various forms, having migrated, mutatis mutandis, into the subcontinent from central and western Asia during the middle of the fourteenth century. The name itself is often said to derive from *shah* (king, great) plus *nay* or *na'i* (reed, pipe, flute).[5] The particular type of *shehnai* I held in my hands, made by Mr. Zuman, is common across this area of Kashmir and Punjab. It is thirteen inches in length, with eight finger holes—seven along the top and one on the underside for the thumb (see fig. 3). The shaft of the instrument is one inch in diameter all the way down until the bell, which opens up to three inches. The *shehnai* is primarily an outdoor instrument, an attribute that can immediately be understood when one hears it for the first time. It is loud. To make a sound, the pinched *patha* is placed just inside the mouth, perpendicular to the lips, which form a seal as air is pushed through the instrument, causing the reed to vibrate. Variations in pitch are then controlled with the fingers, which sit on top of the shaft, with the thumb below. Moving up an octave requires close control of the air speed as it moves through the instrument.[6] The instrument itself is made of a single piece of hard, dark wood taken, Mr. Zuman informed me, from the *thali* tree, which grew down the creek from his workshop.

"*Jeyra raaso, uwa kapso.*" Mr. Zuman smiled: you reap what you sow.[7]

Mr. Zuman went on to describe how the materials he used were all gathered from the natural habitat surrounding his workshop. The lead pipe (*neer*), he explained, pointing to the top of the instrument, connected the mouthpiece (*patha*) to the main body of the *shehnai*. He pointed out the open door: "This *patha* is from the *ker* plant, over there by the creek." The *patha* was bound to the mouthpiece by string wound tightly around it, and the reed was pinched at the end, creating a tight aperture, and shielded

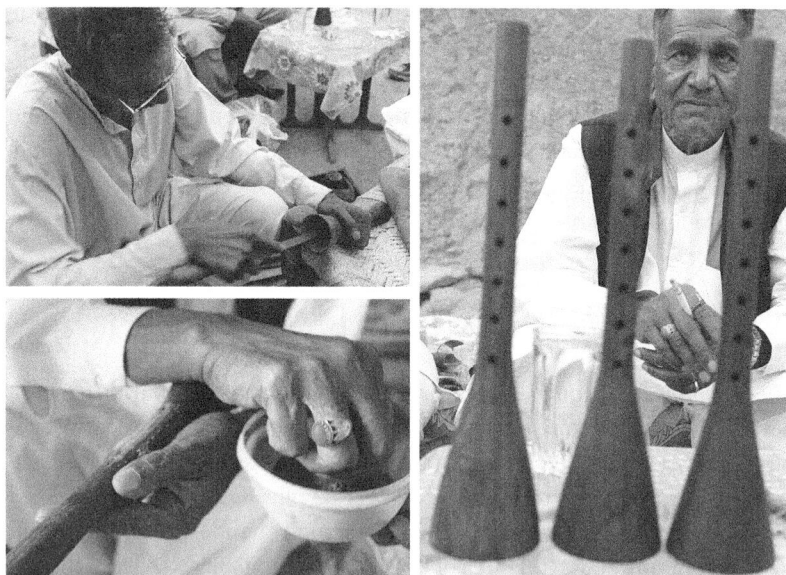

FIGURE 3. *Top left*, Mr. Zuman working on a new *shehnai* at his workshop. *Right*, completed *shehnai*, with *shehnai* player Ustad Yunis Khan in the background. *Bottom left*, Mr. Zuman repairs a crack in Zulfikar's *shehnai*.

from the *neer* by a circular plastic disk called a *pacheer*. "The *patha*, you see, is the mouth [*mū*] of the land."

I could see a small pile of wood outside, rough approximations of what would eventually become the instrument Mr. Zuman was holding. The unworked wood and the pile of reeds held latent possibilities: fire, fettling, music. Through the aperture of the doorframe, I could see three stages of production, from the trees in the distance to the woodpile in the courtyard to the instrument in my hand—separation, pain, and movement of the kind evoked in Mian Muhammad Bakhsh's poetry. Mr. Zuman and Zulfikar picked up this theme and began to discuss the materials of the *shehnai* and how they "gave voice" to the poetry of Mian Muhammad Bakhsh. Here, Zulfikar said, were the literal roots (*jat*) of Mian Muhammad Bakhsh's metaphors of the separation from the beloved, only a few hundred meters from where he had composed his verses in nearby Khari Sharif. Mr. Zuman smiled and gestured outside as he recited an early verse from *Saif-ul-Malook*:

جہلم گھاٹوں پر بت پاسے میرپورے تھیں دُکھن

کھڑی ملک وچ لوڑن جہڑے طلب بندے دی رکھن

Jehlam ghāṭoṅ parbat pāse Mīrpure thīṅ dakhkhan,
Kharī mulk vic loṛan jeṛe ṭalab bande dī rakhan.

Those who look will find me at Khari [Sharif]
Follow the bank of the Jhelum [River], toward the hill, to the south of Mirpur.

The poetic means by which Mian Muhammad Bakhsh described his whereabouts neatly mapped onto the landscape outside Mr. Zuman's workshop, finding meaning today—social and economic—in the lives of instrument makers and Kashmiris both near and far. These lines could even be read today as approximate directions to Mr. Zuman's workshop: descriptions of a topology that resonates with followers of Mian Muhammad Bakhsh across the wider Kashmir and Punjab region and beyond.[8] We begin to see, in other words, why an instrument such as the *shehnai* becomes meaningful not just for the sounds and music it produces but because it comes to be poetically intertwined with a particular landscape and the myriad shared experiences connected to that land.

The poetics of the *shehnai*, in other words, actuate the rhetoric of Mian Muhammad Bakhsh's verses as they are performed into being. The word for "flute" that Mian Muhammad Bakhsh uses in his poetry, for example, is *murali* ("*sun murali di lakar kolon dard*"—hear the pain of the flute's wood), which adds a layer of ambiguity to its translation. A *murali* can refer to a range of aerophones across the Indian subcontinent, including the *bansuri* and the *shehnai*. In Hinduism, the *bansuri* is closely identified with Krishna, in particular the love story between the god and Radha. It is a divine instrument, revered by Krishna and used during the god's *rasa lila* dance ceremonies. In many of these stories, *murali* is used as an alternative word for the *bansuri*. Unlike *shehnai*, however, the *bansuri* is played parallel to the mouth and is commonly made from bamboo. Yet, as Bruno Nettl recognized, since at least the fifteenth century, sculptures and paintings in India have also shown the *bansuri* being played perpendicular to the mouth, as the *shehnai* is today. For Nettl (1998), this change in playing style is likely to have been caused by migration from Persia into North India and the influence of Islamic musical culture that ensued. Writing in the middle of the nineteenth century, Mian Muhammad Bakhsh described a *murali* that likely was closely related to the *shehnai* heard today in Khari Sharif, fashioned in the workshop of Mr. Zuman.

The ambiguity attached to the word *murali* means that it also points in different historical and religious directions. Indeed, such ambiguity lends an adaptability to a verse that in many respects is a product of the culturally diverse and religiously heterodox time in which Muhammad Bakhsh wrote his poetry. The wood of the flute may be separated from the tree from which it once grew, as Mian Mohammad Bakhsh tells us, but through the vibration of the *patha* and its amplification via the instrument's wooden body today, an imagined connection remains—one that, in the minds of many Mirpuris in Britain, remains deeply rooted in the soil of Kashmir, as we shall now see.

∴

The memory of this time at Mr. Zuman's workshop came back to me several months and several thousand miles later, in the barbershop of Mr. Khokhar on Oak Lane in Bradford, England. As we sat in his shop after the last customers had left, Mr. Khokhar would often reminisce about the master musicians he knew back in Kashmir. I asked him why he never mentioned musicians who were based in the UK.

"These are not really musicians," he replied, and he let out a wistful sigh. "Only in Pakistan are there real musicians. They are the best. You see," he said, settling into his theme, "over there, they learn from their dads. All their life. Just playing, playing, playing [music]. Here, it's not like that. Children go to school and get jobs; they don't play music anymore. So when we want to put on concerts [in the United Kingdom], we bring musicians over. The best musicians in all Pakistan."

He talked on, telling me again how beautiful Kashmir is, how green, how free. "Like paradise." He smiled. Outside the window it was a gray, wet day in Yorkshire. He glanced at the street, then back inside, as though he'd seen all he needed to see. He had been working for seven days straight; the only time he would take off work was to travel to Mirpur once a year. In the meantime, he would listen to recordings on his phone of Zulfikar playing his *shehnai*, write and recite his own poetry from a small handwritten notebook, and invoke Mian Muhammad Bakhsh.

Music, musicians, and instruments became deeply intertwined in these moments of reminiscence.[9] When Mr. Khokhar talked wistfully about music and musicians in Pakistan, as he so often did in his Bradford barbershop, he was not talking just about music per se but about the feelings and memories of a place that the sound of the *shehnai* afforded: home, Kashmir. When he held the *shehnai* made for me in Mr. Zuman's workshop, he smiled, and there was a solidity to these memories and emotions. For Mr. Khokhar, music, poetry, and the materiality of the *shehnai* would combine and afford memories of Kashmir and feelings of homeliness. Depending on where he was at any given moment—outside an instrument workshop in Kashmir or in a barbershop in Yorkshire—these poems and objects activated meaning that was rooted in his memories of the past and became animated through performances: the *shehnai* is played, the poem is sung, memories of home are kindled.

In migratory contexts such as Bradford, we see how the complex feelings and emotions evoked through the performance of poetry are amplified by geographic distance from Kashmir and the passage of time experienced by early generations of migrants such as Mr. Khokhar. Central to these emotions are the poetic ambiguities of Mian Muhammad Bakhsh's verses. Mian Muhammad Bakhsh implores the listener, for example, not just to imagine but to *hear* [*sun*] the pain of the *shehnai*'s wood as it becomes separated from the *thali* tree and to *feel* the flow of water over time and space. Emotion and space. "O Muhammad!" he writes, "We must all face the same destiny." Like so much Sufi poetry, couplets such as these sustain meaning on multiple levels.[10] As Mr. Khokhar explained, for him and his friends, who were also sitting in the barbershop, the pain of the wood's separation from the tree spoke to the trauma of being separated from loved ones in Mirpur (indeed, the word for "pain" here—*dard*—can also signify "grief"). But there is also a sense of collectivity, established in the verse through the pronoun "we": this is not just your pain, Mian Muhammad Bakhsh suggests, but part of our shared fate and condition. The couplet also held a double meaning for Mr. Khokhar and those of his wider kinship group (*biraderi*), who remain and live in Mirpur while their relatives live and work abroad: the feeling not just of being separated (*vhichhoraa*) from loved ones but of being left behind (*vhichhoraa* translates more literally as "left out"). It is this ambiguous pain and longing that Mian Muhammad Bakhsh invites us to hear in the *shehnai*.[11]

The Journey of Love

Mian Muhammad Bakhsh was born around 1830 in the village of Khari Sharif, twenty kilometers south of Old Mirpur, a region to which, as we have seen, many British Pakistanis trace their heritage and where they continue to maintain strong cultural and familial ties today. It was in this area of Kashmir that Mian Muhammad Bakhsh wrote his acclaimed book of poetry, *Safar ul-Ishq* (*The Journey of Love*), more commonly known as *Saif-ul-Malook*.

Widely regarded by Kashmiris across the subcontinent as the Rumi of Kashmir, Mian Muhammad Bakhsh was thirty-three years old when *Safar ul-Ishq* was published (coinciding almost precisely with the year when the one-rupee coin that was gifted to me by Zulfikar had been minted). Mian Muhammad Bakhsh was well versed in Persianate poetic traditions and Rumi in particular: the imagery of the wooden flute's "separation from the tree," for example, references the opening of Rumi's famous *Masnawī*.[12] Belonging to the *Qadiri tariqa* (the latter meaning "way" or "order"), Mian Muhammad Bakhsh was part of a long line of local Sufi leaders (*sheikh*) stretching back to Pir Shah Ghazi Qalandar Damri Wali Sarkar (d. 1739).[13] He was a prolific writer, producing ten large volumes and numerous shorter poems (Shackle 2007). Like much Sufi poetry of the region, Mian Muhammad Bakhsh's work drew upon Persian storytelling and narrative themes, reimagining them in the local Punjabi vernacular. Among his major works, as noted by Christopher Shackle (2007), are the romance *Sohnī Mahīnwāl* (1857), the *Qissa Sheikh Sun'ān* (1857–58), an adaptation of the well-known Persian Sufi poem *Mantiq al-Tayr* (*Conference of the Birds*) by Farid al-Din Attar, a translation of Ghanimat Kunjahi's romance *Nayrang-I 'Isq* (1859–60), and a version of the Persian classic *Shīrīn Farhād* (1860) that, Shackle suggests, was itself a corrective to previous treatments of the poetry by Nizami and Amir Khusrau (2007, 127).

It was, however, Mian Muhammad Bakhsh's rendering of the Persian epic *Saif-ul-Malook*, taken from *One Thousand and One Nights*, that widely came to be regarded as his masterpiece.[14] His collection of poetry, *Safar ul-Ishq*, includes some 9,249 rhyming couplets and is written in Punjabi but includes a wide range of local dialects, including Pahari and Pothwari, and a rich vocabulary of Persian and Arabic—a mixture of languages that itself alludes to migrations past. There exists only one original manuscript, printed by Mian Muhammad Bakhsh during his lifetime; what circulates today has been passed down orally through performances, published as excerpts, or as Urdu translations at later dates, or handwritten in notebooks.[15] While the story of *Safar ul-Ishq* follows the same narrative arc as the Persian *Saif-ul-Malook*, Mian Muhammad Bakhsh's long elaborations and reflections on human actions, such as "hunting, fighting, feasting [and] music" (Shackle 2007, 128), serve to anchor the poetry to this particular part of Azad Kashmir and, in doing so, carry strong resonances for Kashmiris living in diaspora. It is worth briefly outlining the story of the *Safar ul-Ishq* to see why.

The epic poem tells the story of a handsome Egyptian prince, Saif ul-Malook, who was born into riches and wants for nothing. The prince grows increasingly restless, and one day his father presents him with two concealed pictures. Upon revealing the pictures, Saif ul-Malook encounters two likenesses: one of himself and the other of a woman of unimaginable beauty, the likes of which had never been seen before. Saif falls in love with the image of the woman, who subsequently visits him in his dreams. She introduces herself in this dream state as Badi-ul-Jamala, daughter of Shahpal, king of the fairies in the garden of Irum in golden Shahristan. Upon awakening, Saif becomes desperately lovesick and tells his father that he must leave home at once in a bid to find the woman. The epic then tells of his journey away from home in a desperate search for the object of his longing and desire, despite his father's discouragement. As the story unfolds, the narrator, Mian Muhammad Bakhsh, becomes the protagonist's interlocutor and spiritual guide (*murshid*), warning Saif of the perils ahead and questioning the wisdom of leaving one's home. As Saif embarks upon his journey of love, the obstacles that he encounters become morality tales through which Mian Muhammad Bakhsh interpolates both the protagonist and the listener.

Stories such as these are popular parables of spiritual and worldly movement. With its themes of remaining true to one's home and one's family, of the oppressed being saved from the oppressor, and of the need to be patient, to keep hope and faith in God, the story of *Saif-ul-Malook* is highly valued by Kashmiris in Pakistan and in Britain. Its verses are performed and sung regularly throughout the year by hereditary musicians at weddings and festivals, and recited by amateur musicians everywhere from taxis and barbershops to people's homes.[16] It is, in many respects, *the* story of movement and displacement, but it is also one of coming together, not only in terms of its narrative arc but through the way it has accompanied Kashmiris on their own migratory journeys, as we shall see. Importantly, it is in this respect, too, that Mian Muhammad Bakhsh's *Saif-ul-Malook* departs from the Persian original: Saif and his beloved are ultimately united. It is a story with a happy ending—reassuring, should you ever find yourself far from home.

Marriage and Money

After our visit to Mr. Zuman's house-cum-workshop, Zulfikar and I set off again to perform at a wedding directly across the Mangla Dam, the vast reservoir that played a pivotal role in the migration of Mirpuris to Britain. To get there, we climbed the high banks of the dam on Zulfikar's motorbike, rising up slowly before zigzagging back down. Crops swayed in the fields as we passed. Zulfikar switched off the engine midmotion, allowing us to freewheel down the slope. Braking, leaning into each hairpin, releasing the brake, and picking up speed again, we gradually wound our way toward the reservoir's basin. After an hour we turned a corner, and the vastness of the dam opened up beneath us. We pulled over to take in the view. I could see the city of New Mirpur shimmering in the distance, on the other side of the dam—a mere eight kilometers as the crow flies, yet to journey across the dam would take another hour or so.

With our instruments in our pockets, we were on our way to perform at the wedding of a British Pakistani family. On the way, we met up with some of the other musicians in Zulfikar's ensemble at a gas station: another *shehnai* player, three *dhol* players,[17] a *chimta* player, and two singers. Several instruments were lying around, including four *dhol*, standing several feet off the floor, each the size of a large barrel. The musicians chatted about the day's work. We would be traveling down the receded shore of the lake and taking a small ferry to the sunken city of Old Mirpur, where we would meet the family at a *darbar* (shrine) that had recently reemerged due to the dam's low water level. Afterward, we would go to the family's home in Islamgarh for the evening's celebrations. As we drank sugary tea and ate freshly made *dahi* (homemade yogurt), I counted the instruments and musicians in our party. Four *dhol*, two *shehnai*, one *chimta*, nine musicians in total. I counted the number of 125cc motorbikes: three.

"OK," Zulfikar said, "*challo*." Let's go.

I climbed onto the pillion of one of the bikes. With no small trace of a smirk, Habib, one of the other musicians, lifted one of the large *dhol* up onto my right knee.

"Hold," he said.

Grappling the drum with my right arm, I watched as Habib moved back to the group, picked up another *dhol*, walked around the bike, and deposited the barrel onto my other knee. "*Challo*," he bellowed, slapping my back twice sharply with his hand.

With a nod, Zulfikar kick-started the bike. Not wanting to move lest I spill the cargo, I clung to two drums for dear life. And so we gingerly set off, three by three, the weighed-down bikes ballasted on each side by the drums, like laden galleons out to sea, listing this way and that as we navigated the potholes of a dirt road leading down to the water's edge.

The ferry was a small wooden boat with one outboard motor. The bikes were hoisted perpendicular onto the side of the craft, the front wheels sticking out over the water (fig. 4). The men and cargo sat on the other side, providing a counterweight. As we puttered low in the water across the small lake, Habib struck up a rhythm on his *dhol*, mingling the lapping of the water and the putter of the engine with the beat of the drum.

I sat facing the stern, watching as New Mirpur receded, and thought about the distance between here and Bradford. Far away and yet also proximate; I had grown up around Mirpuri culture in Bradford for much of my life, and here I was, sailing toward its center. There was a familiarity to the things we were doing that surprised me. As much as I felt the weight of a colonial past with the one-rupee coin described just a few pages ago, here I could feel a tie to the present, a deeply rooted connection between Bradford and Mirpur, yet one hidden from view until it was performed into being through the *dhol* and the *shehnai*. Twisting around, I looked out across the bow; the water prickled with light. The Old Mirpur Road appeared amphibious, unexpectedly climbing out of the water on the far

FIGURE 4. *Left*, musicians load their motorcycles and instruments onto the ferry.
Top right, the destination, a green *darbar*, can be seen in the distance.
Bottom right, Yunis Khan and Hussain on the old Mirpur road.

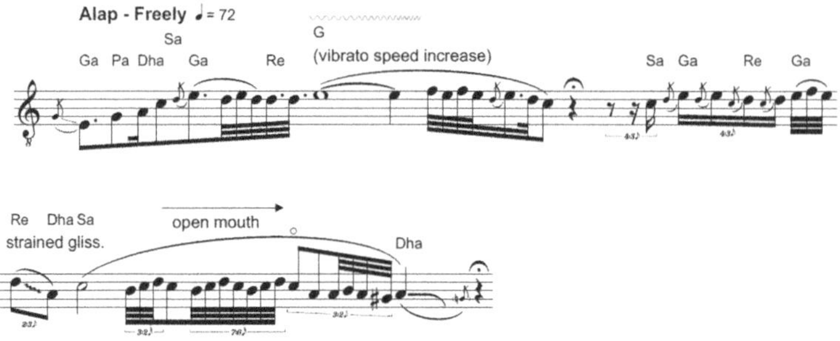

FIGURE 5. Mr. Javid begins *Saif-ul-Malook* in *Rāg Pahari*, unaccompanied in a *darbar*. Transcribed into fluid nonequal temperament (ca. A = 450 Hz); *sargam* above staff; accidentals do not carry; all fermatas = variable-length breath.

bank (fig. 4), flanked on either side by luscious grass and framed by the rubbled outlines of lost buildings. To the left, I could see the tower (*shikhara*) of an old Hindu temple, the Shivala *mandir*, precipitously leaning to one side, its foundations compromised by forty years of water. Land was lost to the rising tide of the dam and, along with it, the archaeology of religious and ethnic plurality. This was a diverse area, first divided by Partition and finally displaced by flood; much of the area's cultural and religious plurality has itself migrated elsewhere, creating new diversity in places like Bradford. Some distance to the right stood our destination, the *darbar* of Miran Mir, from which the district of Mirpur is said to take its name. In contrast to the *mandir*, the *darbar* is meticulously and lovingly restored each year as the waters recede. Silt and sediment are washed away, and its walls are repaired and painted brilliant white and green. The *darbar* stands there among the ruins of Old Mirpur as new, a symbol of both what's lost and what remains (see fig. 7 below).

We had time to spare and entered the *darbar* to cool off from the midday sun. As we sat down around the central tombstone, one of the vocalists in Zulfikar's troupe, Mr. Javid, began to sing a short *alap* (fig. 5).

As he paused, his voice echoed against the walls of the shrine, fading into the wind and birdsong outside. Zulfikar nodded his head knowingly. The two musicians briefly looked each other in the eye before Mr. Javid looked upward, inhaled deeply, closed his eyes toward the heavens, and sang (fig. 6).

Verse (parentheses indicate repeat):

(اوّل حمد ثناء اِلٰہی)، جو مالک ہر ہر دا

اُس دا نام چتارن والا، ارے میدان نہ ہر دا

Awwal ḥamd sanā ilāhī, jo mālik har har dā,
us dā nām citāran wālā, are maidān nah hardā.

First, praise and glorify Allah, who is the Master of all
Whoever remembers His name does not falter in the field.

كام تمام ميسر هوندے)، نام اوهدا چت دهرياں
رحموں سكے ساوے كردا قهرون سارے هرياں

Kām tamām muyassar honday, nām ohdā cit dhariyāṅ,
raḥmoṅ sake sāve karda qahroṅ sāṛe hariyāṅ.

All tasks are rendered simple when His name is remembered,
He showers mercy and averts misfortune.

Chorus:

قُدرت تھیں، جس باغ بناۓ، جگ سنسار تمامی
رنگ برنگی بُوٹے لاۓ، كجھ خاصے كجھ عامی

Qudrat thīṅ, jis bāgh banā'e, jag sansār tamāmī,
rang-birangī būṭe lā'e, kujh khāse kujh ʿāmī.

By His power, He created this garden, the entire world
He brought forth colorful plants, some special, some widespread.

The words Mr. Javid sang, which are transcribed here, flowed from *Saif-ul-Malook*. He sang them unaccompanied, the rest of us gathered around him drinking sugary pink Kashmiri tea. The melody bounced off the stone walls of the shrine, holding us within while the words he sang transported us without. The opening lines introduced a section of *Saif-ul-Malook* about love and loss, hope and despair, humility and redemption through God's grace—a motif that forms the basis of so much of Mian Muhammad Bakhsh's poetry. In its sung form, the poetry, as in Mr. Zuman's workshop, also alluded to the topography around us: the land, the wildlife, the water. The melody Mr. Javid sang followed *Rāg Pahari*, a North Indian musical mode often associated with light classical music. The name of the *rāg* was seemingly no coincidence: *pahar* means "mountain." This was music for a grand scale. Sitting as we were, with the mountains of Kashmir as our backdrop, the mountain *rāga* resonated

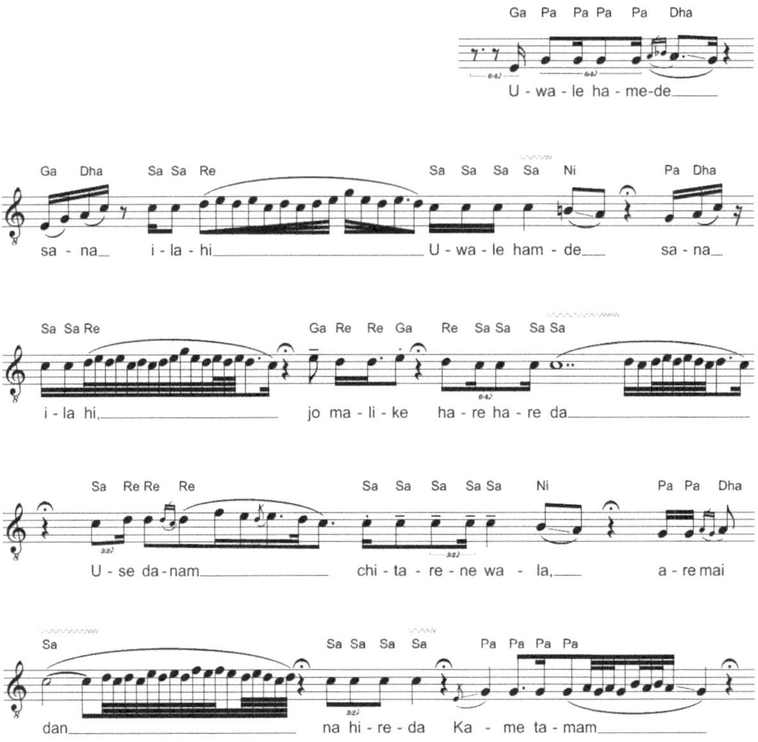

FIGURE 6. After the *alap*, Mr. Javid continues to sing *Saif-ul-Malook*.

with our surroundings, with those sitting among us, and, as I would later learn, with Kashmiris far away in Bradford.[18]

Why might this be the case? Scholars of Hindustani music understand *rāga*s as complex intermedial entities that take both a sonic form, as a kind of musical mode, and an iconic form—namely, as a painting or image or else visualized through dance.[19] The sonic form of the *rāga* is meant to evoke its iconic form and the emotional associations this generates in the listener. In other words, what you hear is also supposed to relate to what you see, in terms of both the external world and one's internal and spiritual experience of it. And so, given what we know about how a *rāga*'s sonic *and* iconic forms are intertwined, we can begin to understand how the melody we were listening to that day, as it traveled up (*aroh*) and down (*avroh*) the scale (*thāt*), provided a kind of contour to Mian Muhammad Bakhsh's couplets, a contour that in that moment seemed to echo the surrounding mountain peaks. It also gives a hint as to why this sung poetry is important in migratory contexts. Kashmiris at home and abroad don't just hear this poetry; they also see *and feel* this landscape.

Dha Dha Sa   Sa   Sa   Sa   Ga   strained   Sa   Sa   Sa   Sa

ma - y - sa - re ho - ne - de,_____ Ka - me ta - mam_____

Pa   Pa   Dha Sa Sa   Ga   strained   Ga   Ga Re Ga

ma - ye - sa - re hon - de_____ na - me o - da___

Sa   Sa   Sa   Sa   (Pa)_   strained   Ga Ga   Sa   Sa Re Sa Ni   Pa

chi - te dha - ri - yam_____   Rah - mon sa - ke__   sa - ve ka - re - da,___   qah -

Dha Sa Sa   Re   Sa   Sa   Sa   Ga Ga Ga Pa Pa Pa Pa Pa   Dha

-ro - ne sa -   -   -   - re_____ ha - ri - yam Qu - de - ra - te thin, ji - se ba - ge

Pa Pa   Ga Ga Ga Re   Re Re Pa

ba - nae,   ja - ge sa - nesan - sa - re_____

Re Sa   Sa   Sa   Re Re Re Re   Sa   Sa   Sa   Ni

ta - ma - mi____   Ran - ge bi - ran - gi___   bu - te - la - e___

Pa   Pa Dha Sa   Sa   Sa   Sa

ku - jhe kha_ se_____ kujh   a - mi

FIGURE 6A. After the *alap*, Mr. Javid continues to sing *Saif-ul-Malook*.

With the dam's water having drained away at the end of the dry season, there was a glimpse of this landscape from a time gone by—a time when Mian Muhammad Bakhsh wrote his poetry. What would soon be filled once again with water had once been filled with people, histories, memories. As the water recedes, swaths of fertile pastures are offered up, and the ruins of District Mirpur are revealed. Old Muslim *darbar*s, graveyards (*qabristan*s), Hindu temples (*mandir*), and a Sikh *gurudwara*s emerge from the depths, exclaiming the area's multireligious, multiethnic heritage pre-Partition (the Mangla Dam itself takes its name from the older Mangla hamlet, which in turn took its name from Mangla Devi, the Hindu goddess). Over the years, as the waters receded during these months, I would join Mirpuris from near and far as they tentatively moved down, back into the valley. Ancient family graves would be tended to and the *darbar* restored to its former glory, while the *mandir* further crumbled. Wedding parties, preceded by rhythmic *dhol* and melodious *shehnai*, would descend from the wedding halls that lined the shores to receive blessings at the restored shrine of Miran Mir.[20] Memories of Old Mirpur became rekindled.

Mr. Javid finished singing, and we left the shrine to descend farther into the dam's emptying basin on the motorbikes. Looking over Zulfikar's shoulder, I could clearly make out the shape of the old town below. The footprint of the town was obvious, although the walls had gone, leaving only their lower stones visible among the green pasture. Houses, courtyards, and the remnants of streets appeared like imprints of the past, excavated by the receding waters. The graveyards and *darbar*s, conversely, appeared new, having been tenderly restored—resurrected—by local and British Mirpuris each year (fig. 7). Mirpuris in Bradford had described to me, in vivid detail, where their old plots of land were located, and they would always return here during these months while the tide was out. Perfectly circular pools of water occasionally punctuated these plots—old water wells (*khoo*) plunging deeper into the dam's bed. The whole neat layout of the town could be easily imagined, although decades of submersion had blurred the lines. The

FIGURE 7. *Left*, a crumbling Hindu *mandir* in Old Mirpur. *Right*, the newly painted *darbar* of Miran Mir, restored each year when the water recedes.

subsiding Hindu temple was a reminder of how quickly histories can crumble when not attended to and when people are partitioned along religious lines.

We were running late for the wedding. I asked Zulfikar where the function would take place. He pointed to our feet and smiled.

"Purana Mirpur," he said: Old Mirpur. We set off back in the direction of the *darbar* in which Mr. Javid had sung.

As we approached, the wedding party began to arrive in 4×4 Toyota Land Cruisers from the opposite direction. The groom remained in a car while the other men and the musicians gathered along the path leading to the *darbar*'s entrance. Our *dhol* players struck up a rhythm (*taal*) while the two *shehnai* heralded the groom out of the car, loud and high pitches producing an immersive soundscape of tangled reeds with thundering *dhol* underneath. As the groom emerged, dressed in brilliant white *shalwar kameez*, a garland with banknotes and flowers stapled to it was placed over his head. A videographer appeared, carefully capturing the garland and its presenter. The groom slowly began to make his way along the path, flanked on either side by dozens of family members. Younger members of the family started to dance to the music, surrounding the young groom. As they did so, whole bags of rupee notes were thrown up in the air, raining down over the groom and dancers. Amid the dancing, the music would periodically stop as one-thousand-rupee notes were individually placed above the groom and his family's heads, an act carefully performed in front of the videographer, who was capturing each gesture and offering. During these moments, the *chimta* player would also act as the ceremony's *nāzim* (master of ceremonies/emcee) and take the notes from above the groom's head. The drums would pause, and the name of the gift giver would be sung out for all to hear, the *nāzim*'s virtuosity increasing as the stakes were raised. This money, along with the cash that had been thrown up in the air, was all carefully collected by the *chimta* player, who would later turn it over to Zulfikar. This was the money with which the musicians would be remunerated after the day's performances finished.

After receiving blessings in the *darbar*, we left Old Mirpur and traveled to the wedding hall; we would eventually end the day at the groom's large family house in New Islamgarh—another town rebuilt after the old settlement flooded—for more celebrations. The wedding party was yet to arrive, and so we sat on the floor by the side of the road, across from the hall. The motorbikes shielded us from the road while on our other side a tributary river to the dam flowed silently by. We didn't speak. The bodies of the old motorbikes ticked from heat as they cooled off, and the air smelled of warm oil. Other sounds and smells came to me: the mango seller across the road, car horns, the rush of engines and tires as they drove by, their sound de-tuning in pitch as they drove away. A few yards down the road from us, also on the bank between the road and the river, a horse and cart stood immobile. The horse gazed forlornly down the road; bony shoulder blades stretched its haunch. The cart's wheels had been reclaimed from a van or small truck—old and new. I continued my panorama to the river, settling my gaze on the slow-moving water.

"The river flows to the sea," Zulfikar explained, following my gaze, "and returns to the mountain as rain." Across the road, the wedding party had begun to arrive. I could hear familiar accents, Yorkshire mixed with Pothwari. "They," he continued, pointing at the wedding party, "have also returned here through clouds." Zulfikar smiled and fixed me with his eyes. A goat nibbled the grass near my feet.

I realized somewhat belatedly that Zulfikar was alluding to the couplet from *Saif-ul-Malook* he had invoked earlier in the day, with which I opened this chapter:

> The land may be the same, and so too the rain,
> But diverse are the plants which do reign.

People may be born in the same area or even in the same house, yet migration creates change. This is true even, or perhaps especially, when that movement—of people, of culture, of matrimony—happens over great distances. Yet Zulfikar was also suggesting that return migration brings its own changes and opportunities. For him, the transnational weddings of Mirpuris meant remuneration and, by extension, business for Mr. Zuman. Mian Muhammad Bakhsh's couplet had interlaced our day, connecting the river to the Mangla Dam, to the migration and return of Mirpuris abroad. It had connected the past to the present, the near to the far. The poetics of migration runs deep in the musical lives of Mirpuris, its ambiguous meanings mediated through these musicians and the *shehnai*, connecting migrant experience to the great lines of Sufi mysticism.

∵

We crossed the road and preceded the wedding party down the street toward the wedding hall. Our *shehnai* and the *dhol* created a soundtrack for the walk, drawing all eyes to us. As we approached the hall, its outside walls looked tired, with mirrored windows designed to reflect the heat but adept at attracting dust from the road and traffic. Inside, the air was cool and dry. We walked over a marble floor of geometric opulence, past the tables and chairs where guests were starting to take their seats, pausing their conversations for a lunch of chicken drumsticks and onion *bhaji*.

I was ushered toward the back of the hall, to the stage where the bride, the groom, and their immediate family members sat slightly elevated from the other guests, conferring their status. The groom stood up and offered me his hand, small and soft, from beneath a lustrous *shalwar kameez* sparkling with light reflected from hundreds of beads. On his head was a turban of gold-colored cloth. It had a shimmering quality, catching the light and drawing eyes toward him. His face was slender and had been freshly shaven that morning. Everything would be done for him that day. He seemed amused by my presence. I began to speak to him in Urdu, and his amusement gave way to a laugh. "Where are you from, mate?" he asked in a thick Lancastrian accent. He introduced himself as Mo from Oldham, and we sat down.

"Almost done?" I asked, noticing the slightly jaded look on his face and the cluster of empty Red Bull cans by his side.

He gave me a wry smile and replied cheerily, "Cut the cake and that's it!" We settled into our seats, looking out over the feasting guests. "So what do you make of it over here then?" he asked.

"I like it. Everyone's friendly. The food's delicious. Good music."

I reflected the question back to him. "It's all right. It's family, innit, but I get bored out here, do you know what I mean? There's fuck all to do over here except chill. I have to drive up to Mirpur to get a KFC!" We laughed.

"So what happens next?" I asked.

"Back to our house for more of this [music and food], innit? Come on."

The drummers struck up a beat, and Zulfikar and his troupe began playing in front of us. Along with approximately a hundred men, we followed the musicians out of the wedding hall and across town to the groom's family house, an opulent three-story villa surrounded by an imposing wall. Therein began fireworks and *bhangra* dancing under the night sky (fig. 8). Mo's uncle appeared with an AK-47 and fired it, *rat-a-tat-tat*, into the air.

"*Now* it's a wedding celebration," said Mo, snapping his fingers as he joined the dancers.

The father of the groom, Shakoor, caught sight of me at the back of the crowd and beckoned me over to a line of chairs on the veranda of his house, where he and his close relatives sat. After introductions, Shakoor took me to the quieter inner sanctum of the villa for tea. He explained that he had traveled from their home in Oldham, Lancashire, to see his son marry Shakoor's sister's daughter, Mo's first cousin.[21] Much like Mr. Khokhar, Shakoor spoke nostalgically about when he had first gone to England in 1967 to work in the textile mills. In those days, he said, the English had been warm and

FIGURE 8. Dancing at a wedding outside Shakoor's family home in Islamgarh.

welcoming, and he'd gotten along well with them. He contrasted this sharply with new Eastern European migrants, whom he blamed for unsettling his community and taking jobs. He also drew parallels with his own community's migration, saying how the Polish were similarly setting up their own shops and restaurants in England. There was a reverse nostalgia, not for a lost Mirpur but for a changing Oldham.

Later in the evening, I spoke again with both Shakoor and the bride's father, Aftab, on the roof of the villa, taking in sweeping views of the Mangla Dam and the guests who filled the courtyard below. We spoke about Mian Muhammad Bakhsh and their own lives across Pakistan and England. Both families owned taxi companies back in England and spoke in thick Lancastrian accents. They were full of characteristically northern English humor—dry, irreverent, and just a bit sarcastic—that was often directed, in a low, bumbling drawl that only I (not the guests) could hear, at the local Mirpuris, whom they joked were backward and illiterate. Their humor was deployed in a semiserious, self-referential way yet seemed to also draw a distinction between those who, like Shakoor and Aftab, had migrated and therefore advanced economically and socially and those who had not.

"These are simple people," Shakoor told me, gesturing at the guests below. "They'll believe anything. At these weddings," he continued, half laughing, half mocking, "people from all over turn up like vultures just for the food."

There was no industry in the area, they explained, except for that paid for by their own British money.[22] All the newly built houses, the infrastructure, the weddings, the musicians: they all revolved around money from England. There was no government support for infrastructure, they said. The roads we could see from the top of his house had been paid for by taxi fares in Oldham.

This was an area, in other words, that continued to be shaped, socially and economically, by money, marriage, and migration, each serving to reinforce and propel the other.[23] The town we were in, Islamgarh, on the edge of the dam, was itself a replacement for the older city that had flooded. Before Partition in 1947, this old town had been known as Akalgarh and had been predominantly Hindu. Like Old Mirpur, Shakoor explained, looking out across the water, Akalgarh had contained many Hindu temples, all of which—buildings and congregations—had been lost, first to Partition, then to flooding and migration.

Shakoor turned away from the dam and said that his family were about to be displaced again. The capacity of the dam was to be increased, and the village was once again being threatened with flooding. He led me back downstairs and out of the house to show me the rising water up close. Houses near the waterline had already been looted and reduced to rubble. His house had narrowly escaped the same fate the previous year, being on slightly higher ground, but he expected it to flood later that year. There would be no compensation this time from the government. Shakoor was surprisingly philosophical, looking out over the water. "We've rebuilt before. We can do it again," he said with a confidence I was by then becoming familiar with among Mirpuris. He turned to me and, code-switching between Pothwari and English, said:

مالی دا کم پانی دینا، بَھر بَھر مشکاں پاوے

مالک دا کم پُھل پُھل لانا، لاوے یا نہ لاوے

Mālī dā kam pānī denā, bhar bhar mashkāṅ pāwe,
mālik dā kam phal phul lānā, lāwe yā nah lāwe.

The gardener's job is to water the plants.
It is up to God to allow the fruits and flowers to blossom.

"That's Mian Muhammad Bakhsh for you, mate!" he chirped with no small hint of irony, and then he led us back to the wedding party.[24]

∴

After the wedding, I met up again with Zulfikar and the other musicians, and we retired to Hussain the *dhol* player's sister's house, which was also precariously located in the area marked for submersion by the raising of the dam. Her house (fig. 9) had already been half destroyed the previous year by the rising water, but the family had returned and cleaned it up, determined to live there one more year while their new plot of land was developed—it was a halfway house in an especially sobering way. Unlike at Shakoor's, the mood among the musicians in this house was melancholic. Villages that had stood for hundreds of years were being destroyed, and what were once strong and close-knit communities were fanning out over large distances. The musicians didn't have the option of returning to Oldham. This was their home.

As we unwound after our performances, the musicians chatted and were affectionate to one another. *Shagird*s (students) held their *ustad*s' hands and respectfully touched their knees and feet. The usual ritual of chitchat (*gapshap*) began, and vividly colored fizzy drinks were distributed. Zulfikar started to divide up the money he had collected from all the performances throughout the day at the *darbar*, the wedding hall, and Shakoor's house. The day had yielded a total of Rs. 43,000 (Pakistan rupees)—around $190 in 2016. The highest-ranked performers—*ustad*s, like Zulfikar—each took Rs. 5000. The *nāzim* who had announced the names of all the patrons

FIGURE 9. Musicians regroup at Hussain's sister's house for *gapshap* and tea between performances.

received Rs. 3000. Two lower-ranked musicians, including the one who played the bagpipes, received Rs. 750 each, and another facilitator who had helped drive some of the performers around received Rs. 1500, which included money for his gas. I was given a share of Rs. 750.

Zulfikar distributed the money with an air of solemnity and gravity. The rupee notes were blessed by the receivers, who touched them to their foreheads. Any money that was left over was laid out on the *khat* (rope bed) for everyone to see before it was democratically offered first to the senior musicians as a show of respect. These musicians would show humility when offered this extra money, refusing it at first but then either accepting it or, often, redirecting it to others. With all the money distributed, Zulfikar was pleased. The day's labor, he explained on the ride home, had yielded ten times what he might normally expect outside of *shādi* (wedding) season. With tired smiles, *salāms* were given, the men embraced, and Zulfikar, Yunis, and I sped off on his motorbike through the clear night, the banks of the Mangla Dam to our right, the lights of New Mirpur flickering in the distance. Somewhere in the dark void of the dam lay the ruins of the old town. Shakoor's words replayed in my mind: "We've rebuilt before. We can do it again. . . . That's Mian Muhammad Bakhsh for you, mate."

∵

These conversations with Shakoor, and later with the musicians, surfaced the contrasting fortunes and perceptions of those who have migrated from Mirpur and those who have not. Migration holds a powerful attraction for Kashmiris because of its perceived promise of wealth and the prestige that this wealth can bring: the building of extravagant houses, the patronage of music, the status of being seen as looking after one's family. Yet it also produces an ambiguous sense of belonging. Zulfikar's neighbor Tariq, for example, had spoken to me of his experience of being "left behind" as each of his siblings had migrated to Britain. He was the last of the siblings still living in the village near Khari Sharif, looking after his elderly parents as his brothers and sisters migrated in search of work or having married a cousin abroad, as Shakoor's son had done. Tariq spoke solemnly of being left out even as he continued to resolutely study for his English language exams—twice as hard, he explained, as his peers at the local college. Yet Tariq was also philosophical: His wait in Mirpur was the result of forces beyond his control. It was God's will. It was also the product of being a less-favored son, born at the wrong time or in the wrong order. One of the children in his family was expected to stay in Pakistan to look after their parents. And so Tariq remained and watched as his siblings left for lands elsewhere. The first step, Tariq explained, was to reverse this situation and migrate to where the action was, or at least where he perceived it to be. He spoke of his anxiety over feeling like he was in the wrong place and missing out; he wanted to be elsewhere. Tariq's sense of being out of place in some respects stood in opposition to Shakoor's fortune, which had been brought about through migration. For some, time in Mirpur was a respite from the rigors of work in Oldham and Bradford. Life in Mirpur was easy for them. This was a home away from home.

∵

The *shehnai* that Mr. Zuman had made for me and that had been used at the wedding in Islamgarh had been produced just a few kilometers from where Mian Muhammad Bakhsh was laid to rest at his shrine in Khari Sharif. It is likely that the aurality Mian Muhammad Bakhsh described in his verses—the sound he turned into a metaphor for pain and separation: "hear the pain of the flute's wood"—came from instruments made of similar materials and in the same instrument-building tradition that Mr. Zuman uses today. The *shehnai*'s acoustic properties (the high, thin, reedy pitch) and its considerable dynamics (as mentioned, the *shehnai* is an outdoor instrument; it is built to be heard) stem from its materiality. In Mian Muhammad Bakhsh's time, in the midnineteenth century, the sound produced by the *shehnai* would have been familiar to all those who lived nearby, used as it was (and still is) during weddings and ʿ*urs* rituals and to mark moments of worldly death: moments of pain and separation. It is not hard to imagine the trees that Mian Muhammad Bakhsh alluded to in his poetry growing near Mr. Zuman's workshop; indeed, one can still find them today—they are the same trees used to make my own *shehnai*. Mian Muhammad Bakhsh played with this relationship between sonic and material worlds, between this world and that, and used it to produce new life: the separation of wood from the tree produces the *shehnai*, which in turn marks the time of life and death, the separation of home from home, and this world from the spiritual. And yet, the pain of separation can ultimately also be inverted: finding meaning in the *coming together* of love and loss. The pain of separation from the beloved, from home, is instead grounded and brought together in the materiality of these local memories and experiences.

Over the following months and years, as Zulfikar and I traveled on his Honda between the functions of British Mirpuris such as those described above, our instruments were tucked into the pockets of our *shalwar ka-meezes*, ready to be taken out at a moment's notice. This was often the case as we received a nod from the organizer of a function. The instruments were rough and ready yet carefully hewn from local materials. They were, above all else, functional instruments, not holding the kind of economic or symbolic value associated with forms of high-art music. Indeed, the reverse was true. Given the lower social status of many musicians in this part of Kashmir and South Asia more broadly, the symbolic value of the *shehnai* connotes the stratum of society its owner occupies.[25] And yet, within the world of musicianship across the Pothwar Plateau, the *shehnai* rides high in the hierarchy of musical instruments among musicians.[26]

For Zulfikar, the instrument was a means to an end: money to feed his family. The music itself was the real thing of value that existed in the mind and in the heart (*apki dil mein hai*). And yet, the *shehnai* also reveals something of the interconnected musical and poetic life of Kashmir, between the past and present, Mirpur and the diaspora. The instrument evokes an idea of Mirpur, coming as it does from the soil that surrounds Mr. Zuman's workshop, the trees that line the creek by his house, and the river that feeds the dam. Mr. Zuman, like Zulfikar, supported his life and family from the harvesting of this wood, hewing it into something that creates value of an altogether different sort. Zulfikar used the instrument for teaching and performing at functions across Kashmir and Punjab—functions patronized by British Mirpuris from places like Bradford and Oldham, who traveled back to Mirpur each year for weddings and family gatherings.

By tracing the life cycle of this instrument, we see how poetics come to be transmuted and enacted in multiple directions: for its maker, for Zulfikar, and for those, such as Shakoor and his son, who would come to hear the sounds it produced. Indeed, during performances we see how the music becomes deeply intertwined with social lives and values: the family unit, collective memories, beliefs and spirituality. Unpicking these overlapping values, especially as they become manifest through performances, provides a window onto how Mirpuris understand a sense of belonging across time and space.

The poetics of migration provides a way of picking apart the complex relationship between people, music, and movement while bringing into focus some of the contrasting narratives surrounding Mirpuri culture.[27] That the old villages of District Mirpuri are submerged for most of the year has the counterintuitive effect of providing a landing point for Mirpuri identity and culture. The dispersal of people to the peripheries—of the lake, of places like Bradford—leaves an imagined space in the center of the dam, a place that, as we have seen, has a long history of hosting a plurality of cultures and religions. When the dam was built and the water flowed in, flooding the valley and the old towns, the people of the diverse yet tightly knit communities who resided there were displaced, and the geographical and cultural ambiguity that resulted created room in which a broader sense of Mirpuriness could flourish. In the following chapter, we will follow some of this movement as it radiated outward from the dam, through the history of migration from Mirpur to Bradford. We will examine how the circulation of people, photographs, and poetry between Kashmir and Britain since World War II has come to shape the contours of the multiculturalism debate and how this contributes to what I describe as the hidden poetics of migration.

FIGURE 10. A photograph of three Mirpuri men, taken at the Belle Vue Studio in Bradford. Date unknown.

[CHAPTER TWO]

A Home Away from Home

Before I came to this country I would see the photographs of my relations which were sent to us in Pakistan. We would like to know the level of their prosperity and their well-being. We would look at their jackets, how expensive they were, or their shoes. And we would yearn for these things. People would say "I wish I were there and could buy such nice clothes." When I came to this country I realised that the photographs were . . . that there was some exaggeration.[1]

These words, spoken in 1994, are of a man from Mirpur who, along with many others from Azad Kashmir, had come to join relatives in Bradford and work in the city's textile mills during the 1960s and 1970s. He was reminiscing about photographs taken at the Belle Vue Studio in Bradford, located on the outskirts of the city center in Manningham—photographs that would be sent thousands of miles back to his home village in Kashmir and that had been carefully curated to project an image of wealth and success. The kind of photographs he described—of a romanticized, prosperous life abroad—were familiar to migrant communities across South Asia in the postwar period.[2] Indeed, images such as these developed into a significant cottage industry during cycles of postwar migration to Britain and played an important role in projecting an image of wealth that encouraged thousands more to emigrate from Azad Kashmir.

The circulation of photographs and poetry between Bradford and Mirpur worked in tandem to help establish patterns of migration while also kindling imagined futures and hidden intimacies between family members across the diaspora.[3] But the printed photographs also concealed a corresponding negative image. The images of wealth and prosperity projected in the photographs contrasted sharply with the realities of life as an immigrant in Bradford during a period in which the textile industry—the foundation of that promised wealth—was in sharp decline and racial hostility toward immigrants was widespread.[4] It was also a moment in which Mirpuris were increasingly finding themselves in the public spotlight and at the center of debates about immigration and multiculturalism in Britain. And yet, despite these challenging realities on the ground, the images taken at the Belle Vue Studio still secured their desired effect: encouraging relatives to join family members in Bradford and establishing a pattern of movement that came to be known as chain migration.[5]

As our opening quote suggests, upon arrival in Britain the picture looked somewhat different, and by the end of the twentieth century, the gap between what the images projected and the reality of life on the ground had only widened. The increasingly diverse society brought about by postwar migration was coming under fire in political circles and the media, and Mirpuris in particular were being criticized as an apparently self-segregating community. Academic accounts of this period described young Mirpuris as failing at school, embroiled in crime, and increasingly turning to more radical interpretations of Islam.[6] Reports commissioned by the UK government warned that Mirpuris refused to integrate and were not contributing to society.[7] Against this backdrop, the very idea of multiculturalism was seemingly crumbling.[8] Britain was becoming divided, with Mirpuris living parallel lives and interacting with other communities only "when forced to."[9] In practice, and as we have already seen, Kashmiris occupy rich and diverse cultural and musical worlds that are central to how they navigate and understand their own migratory journeys. As this chapter shows, after successive public debates about multiculturalism in which Muslims were repeatedly blamed for its failure, Mirpuris had good reason to instead look within their own community for support and cultural meaning.

For early migrants, as the realities of work and daily life set in, writing and performing poetry remained an activity, as in Azad Kashmir, in which an imagined future could be articulated and realized, one that was able to traverse the distance—geographic, cultural, spiritual—between Mirpur and Bradford. That these poetics remained largely hidden from public view during this period does not necessarily mean Mirpuris were living parallel lives but rather signaled a way of fostering hidden intimacies in the face of repeated public criticism. The photographs, music, and poetry of the Kashmiris described below reveal a counterpoint to a multiculturalism debate that came to dominate public life toward the end of the twentieth century. Kashmiri music and poetry are rich in narratives of home and belonging; they are historically rooted in the relationship between nineteenth-century empire and nation-state building; they are shared today through new media and the circulation of people and money between the diaspora and home; they have histories of interacting with state-led multicultural policies; and they are inflected with cross-cultural influences stretching back centuries. My focus on the hidden intimacies and poetics of migration in this chapter, I suggest, reveals a kind of connoisseurship from below that allows us to examine how this happens in ways that cut through established epistemologies surrounding Kashmiris and Islam in Britain.

The Belle Vue Studio, Bradford

> He, the young man carbuncular arrives,
> A small house agent's clerk, with one bold stare,
> One of the low on whom assurance sits
> As a silk hat on a Bradford millionaire.
>
> T. S. ELIOT, *The Waste Land*

I set out to find the Belle Vue Studio. Standing on the opposite side of the road from where the studio is supposed to be, I look down at an old black-and-white photograph of the building. I glance up and across the street for confirmation. Cars and buses blow me backward. In the photograph, the studio looks smart. In the top half of the window, stained glass paneling depicts a pastoral scene in the arts and crafts style. Low, rolling hills provide a cushion for a small church and what looks like a castle. On either side, thin tree trunks shoot up to the top of the window frame, supporting a billowy canopy. The hills and the canopy frame the shop's name: B. Sandford Taylor, Photographer & Photographic Dealer (fig. 11). In the lower half of the window are the shop's wares: cameras, films, plates, and papers. The building itself is made of Yorkshire stone, like so many in the surrounding area. Above the sign is a large Victorian bay window, and the yellow sandstone has been blackened by soot, the breath of the Industrial Revolution that brought so much prosperity and migration to Bradford.

I look up again. The terrace row of shops is still there, except the soot has been sandblasted away, the residue of the industry that once supported their trade wiped clean. The buildings today look both new and old. Of the four shops in front of me, there is now an Islamic bookstore, a chartered accountant, and a travel agent specializing in trips to Mecca and Medina for Hajj. One of the shops is empty, and I wonder if that's where Sandford's once was. The door numbers run from 126 to 120. I look down at the photograph. Above the door is number 118. It's been demolished.

In the nineteenth and early twentieth centuries, the Manningham area of Bradford was a wealthy district in one of the richest cities in England, supported by a buoyant textile industry famous for its high-quality worsted cloth, silk, and velvet. According to the Bradford Mechanics Institute

FIGURE 11. B. Sandford Taylor, known locally as the Belle Vue Studio,
on Manningham Lane in Bradford.

(est. 1832), Bradford was once home to more Rolls-Royce owners than any
other city in the country.[10] Manningham Lane was a hub of commerce, full
of shops and businesses including a grand Victorian-gothic shopping ar-
cade at its eastern end, which came to be occupied by the upmarket Busby's
department store. Yet the human and economic devastation wrought by

the Second World War accelerated the demise of an industry that was already declining. The loss of life during the war left large employment gaps in Britain's textile and manufacturing industries, a problem that particularly affected northern industrial towns like Bradford. This need for cheap labor saw a political approach to economics and migration in Britain that was in many ways the opposite of what we see today. Increased taxation and the nationalization of much of the country's industry was coupled with a policy of not just welcoming immigration but actively seeking it. The Labour government, led by Clement Attlee, introduced the British Nationality Act 1948, which granted rights to former subjects of the empire to live and work in the UK without the need for a visa, kick-starting a period of migration to Britain of workers from the Caribbean, India, and especially Mirpur in Azad Kashmir, Pakistan. At the time of Partition in 1947, wages for low-skilled jobs in Britain were over thirty times those of equivalent jobs in the newly created Pakistan.[11]

> At the time they [the British] were desperate for labour and they were pleased that we were coming. They had this man in a kiosk and he never even looked up, just had his head down and stamped away at the passports. Two men from labour firms approached me at the airport about giving me work because they needed workers so badly.[12]

The postwar economy had ebbed, and migration was encouraged to flow. But while Bradford's textile industry continued its decline, Britain's wider postwar economy began to recover, prompting amendments to the 1948 act with a view to once again restrict the flow of migration into Britain. This culminated in the Commonwealth Immigrants Act 1962, which permitted only those members of the Commonwealth with government-issued employment vouchers to settle in the UK.[13] These vouchers were extended in particular to Mirpuris who had been displaced by the construction of the new Mangla Dam.[14] With the recent upheaval brought about by Partition, and then with the construction of the dam, Mirpuris now had two incentives to migrate—motivations rendered all the more vivid through the circulation of photographs (fig. 12).[15]

The photographs featured in this chapter form part of a collection of seventeen thousand images that were rescued from the building in which the Belle Vue Studio had been based. The negatives were discovered in a refuse skip by its last proprietor, Tony Walker, before the business was sold. The pictures he saved form a rich archive of portraits of Mirpuris who had migrated to Bradford between the 1940s and the 1980s.[16] They display lives of prosperity and yet are also reminders that there is often

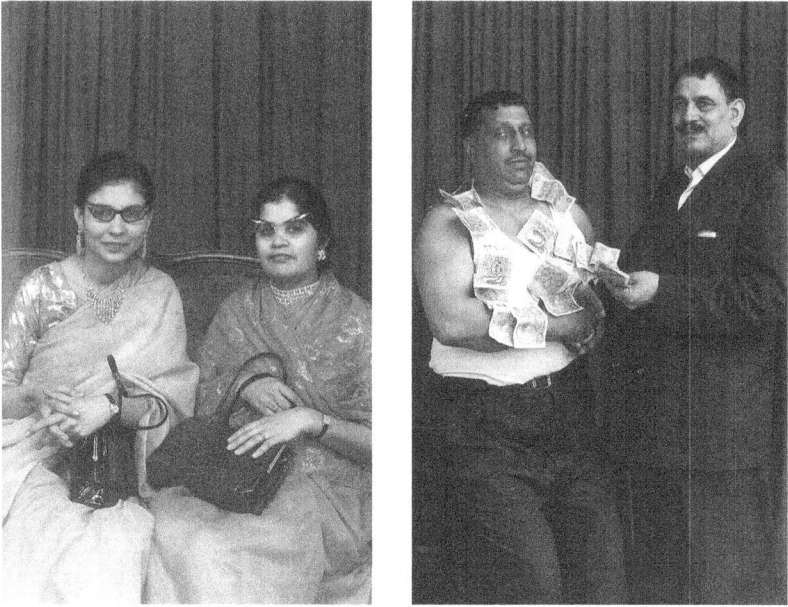

FIGURE 12. *Left*, two women in fine clothes and jewelry. *Right*,
a wrestler poses with his winnings.

more to an image than meets the eye. In figure 10, for example, we see
three young men, possibly brothers, posing in smart suits with shirts,
ties, dress shoes, fountain pens clipped neatly into top pockets, and silver
watches. They are well groomed, chests puffed out, chins raised. Their
crossed legs have been placed just so, projecting a relaxed yet business-
like demeanor.

In the hands of one of the men is a £5 note, resting perpendicular to his
knee, drawing the eyes down, calling attention. As with the one-rupee
coin in the introduction, we are once again faced with a British monarch
imprinted on money. This time, Queen Elizabeth II stares out of the image, and I am reminded of that moment on top of the Kashmiri mountain with Zulfikar. What message does the monarch send out this time,
in the aftermath of the Second World War? The empire is no more, India
has been partitioned, Pakistan has been created, and the British have left.
Some kind of relationship between Britain and the Indian subcontinent
remains, but the direction of the flow of people and money has reversed.
Queen Elizabeth stares out of the photograph solemnly, much like the
man holding the note. This—money and the prosperity it brings—was
primarily what motivated those early migrants to relocate from Mirpur
to Bradford. But sending these pieces of paper back to Mirpur was not

enough. The money itself conveys only so much. The photographs suggest something more.

> When someone left our village and sent his first letter from England or some money, that in itself was an advert for England. You'd receive a money order or a letter or a present, or when he returned, he'd bring his luggage from England that would create an idea of glamour among our people. They wanted to go as well.[17]

The images conveyed an ideal of orderliness and prosperity. They were sending a message of hope, of a life that might come to pass. It was a message internalized as much by the subjects of the photos as by those who received the images thousands of miles away in Mirpur. As Roland Barthes theorized in *Camera Lucida*, photographs have the capacity to "puncture" realities and connect people across time and space.[18] They are also able to powerfully connect people with ideas and with the suggestion of something or someplace else. The Belle Vue photographs' dreamlike vision of a future, of a life elsewhere, beckons the viewer: look at what you could have. Until an idea is rendered into form—audible, visible—it can remain indistinct in the mind. Like the film in a camera, ideas and hopes do not develop fully until they are exposed to light and air. Take a leap, the images say; trust that the net will appear. Look, we are here. Set out on your journey.

The first migrants from Mirpur to Bradford were almost exclusively men. Early pioneers often intended to stay in Britain only briefly, earning enough money before returning home to Mirpur—what came to be known as the "myth of return."[19] Yet the photographs of Belle Vue Studio seem to say the opposite. Look at these suits, these briefcases, the uniforms, the money— these trappings of work, consumerism, and comfort. These are not images of an imminent return home; they are a call to join. They are images of a home away from home.

However, the photographs are also partial, limited as they are by what they leave out of frame. Working in the textile mills was hard, and living conditions were cramped and often dangerous. Early migrants soon realized that the prosperity presented in the photographs—wherein the smart suits, watches, and shoes were rented in the studio rather than owned by the subjects—did not correspond with life on the ground (fig. 13).[20]

> We had this image, it was all beautiful modern life, all these luxuries. And when we got over to Britain we thought it was, in comparison to Mirpur, what we had over there, it was luxury. But looking back on it now after twenty years I'm convinced the house we were living in was

FIGURE 13. Bradford's skyline in 1975, with Drummond Mill in the center.
Photograph by Ian Beesley.

a dump. Living conditions were bad. No bath, no toilet, a back-to-back
house. Money was plentiful, jobs were plentiful. There was a stereotype
from people in England who were living better than they were before.
The stereotype was Britain is all rosy, but when we got here we suddenly
realized it wasn't. People had to work hard, twelve hour shifts, seven days
a week.[21]

And so while jobs were plentiful, much of the money that was made
was sent back to families in Pakistan. This circulation of money and photographs between Bradford and Mirpur changed the social and economic landscapes in both places. In Kashmir, the money early migrants sent
home transformed the material circumstances of family members, allowing them to build larger houses and increase the family's small holdings,
as we saw in the previous chapter. In Bradford, areas of inward migration
such as Manningham also underwent change as Mirpuris opened shops
and restaurants and established mosques. These demographic changes
soon made Bradford one of the most ethnically diverse cities in Britain.
During this period of highly localized social change and upheaval, in which
many white Bradfordians began to move farther out to the suburbs, areas
such as Manningham came to be more tightly associated with Mirpuri life
and culture.

These changes to the ethnic and religious makeup of the city played a central role in shaping the contours of the multiculturalism debate that followed, as politicians grappled with the challenges of supporting a culturally and linguistically diverse society with different educational and public health needs. Mirpur also experienced radical change brought about by emigration and the flow of remittances back home. The gap between families in Kashmir whose relatives had migrated to Bradford and those who had not migrated widened, producing, in effect, a two-tier economy in which grand mansions were constructed next to adobe houses and cars began sharing the road with donkey-drawn carts.[22]

Also left out of the frame at the Belle Vue Studio were those left behind in Pakistan. While their material circumstances improved through remittances sent from Britain, there was the pain and trauma of being separated from close family members, especially fathers from their wives and children who remained in Kashmir, as this child of an emigrating father recalls:

> He wrote and sent us money obviously, and he sent pictures of himself and he looked very healthy and he looked very smart. I remember that. And our material circumstances changed in Pakistan when he was here because we had a lot more money. You know he sent things, presents when someone went to Pakistan. We had clothes which were made in England of good quality so materially things changed, but got a bit harder, I think, not having him here as we missed him as children.[23]

Such prolonged separation meant that the need to tighten the family kinship network (*biraderi*) over great distances via the circulation of photographs and gifts became all the more important.[24] Rather than becoming diluted by migration, then, Mirpuri family units were instead strengthened by these hidden intimacies, performed through the circulation of highly curated photographs and, as we shall see, sung poetry.[25] As communities became more firmly established over the coming decades, frequent visits between Bradford and Mirpur further entrenched these intimacies. On each occasion, returning relatives were expected to bring material gifts for each member of their family. In the direction of Pakistan, these often included children's toys, garments, and jewelry from high-street stores in Bradford; on the return leg, suitcases were filled with designer clothes from Mirpur's shopping malls.[26] These Maussian circulations of gifts among family members in Bradford and Mirpur show that while economic remittances brought a range of benefits to those back home,[27] they also carried what

Steven Vertovec has described as "'social remittances' and other reverse-cultural flows—of ideas, values and tastes, practices and material cultures—back to migrants' societies of origin" (2009, 162).[28]

> When I first came, I didn't want to live here such a long time, I was just thinking that I'll live here for a couple of years and then I'll go back and live with my family. But it's just like a trap once you start living in a country, your children went to schools and then you didn't want to interrupt their education once they've started. And then when they finished their education, they get jobs in this country, and I've got a job myself. So I just keep going and visiting my family whenever I can. I feel this is my home, I've lived here more than I've lived in Pakistan but it's still different when somebody's born somewhere else. I still feel love and sympathy with Pakistan, it could be because I have such strong family links there.[29]

The sense of a home away from home was thereby continuously maintained through the circulation of hidden intimacies—photographs, gifts, poetry—between Bradford and Mirpur; intimacies that nevertheless produced a transformative effect on local economic and social hierarchies in both places. It also allowed Mirpuris to more fluidly feel at home in both Bradford and Mirpur.[30]

∴

The effect of this circulation of people and gifts between Britain and Kashmir can be felt across Mirpur and Bradford today. In late 2014, for example, I found myself driving with Mr. Khokhar from New Mirpur City to his family village, Takipur, just a few miles away. At a junction in the road, we pulled over by a small whitewashed building, two stories high. The store was adorned with a large red sign, written in both English and Urdu script: Mirpur General Store, British Produce. The air smelled heavy with spices. Children were playing with a tatty football outside the store, where two old men sat watching the world go by. The children shrieked, laughing wildly as the ball pinged around, seemingly at random. The men sat unmoving and unfazed by the risk of a ball in the face, protected perhaps by an assuredness that flowed from the children's respect of their elders, but quite possibly just out of sheer luck.

I was in Kashmir, but the whole scene—the signage, the produce, the smells, the men, and the children—were as familiar to me as the sights and sounds of Bradford, where I had lived for so much of my life and where so many Mirpuris had also chosen to call home, open shops, and have families. I had played with children like these myself as a child decades ago, on a different continent. Walking down those streets in Yorkshire, I had breathed in these smells, seen these men, heard this language. I closed my eyes and pictured Oak Lane in Bradford, a street lined with Kashmiri takeout restaurants, chicken shops, and greengrocers. Even down the side streets near my house, away from the main strip, a cloud of spices would hang in the air, drifting out of people's homes. The senses—sounds, smells, and sights—that reached me in Bradford were those of multiculturalism, composed by the politics and economics of postwar Britain. They were the sounds and aromas of my youth, present here, thousands of miles away in Kashmir. This sensory memory is one that rarely comes to mind when we think about migration. Phyletic memory, it's called. It is a reminder that places are connected by forces beyond geography, by these phyletic memories conjured through smells and through sounds. Can you be in two places at once? Surely. All you have to do is close your eyes, open your ears, and breathe in. A home away from home must be sensed to feel real.

Sung Poetry in Britain: Rochdale Town Hall

Since the 1960s and 1970s, the performance and reception of Kashmiri spoken and sung poetry (*mushai'ra*) has been widespread in Britain yet rarely advertised publicly. For reasons set out below, the self-conscious "veiling," in Lila Abu-Lughod's term (1986), of these poetic traditions is at least in part related to racism experienced by migrants in and since the 1970s and the multiculturalism debate that ensued. As a hidden tradition, performances of Pothwari *sher* (poetry written and sung in the Pothwari dialect) are important spaces in which memories of home, belonging, and status are continuously sustained and enacted away from the critical glare of a press and national politics that above all else privileged integration. As with the photographs of the previous section, an important component of this hidden tradition is the visual circulation of money during performances and the projection of wealth that this creates. Nowhere is this more vividly apparent than when audience members shower the musicians with bank notes for all to see.

∵

Mr. Khokhar's barbershop in Bradford lies just around the corner from where the Belle Vue Studio once stood. Rows of Victorian terrace shops line the junction of Oak Lane and Manningham Lane. Manningham Mills, the destination of so many migrant workers, looms large at the top of the hill, its chimney visible across much of Bradford. The terraced houses and shops are, from the first floor up, more or less identical, their yellow sandstone bricks still charred by century-old Victorian soot.[31] The variety occurs at street level. Each shop displays its wares: fruit, vegetables, spices, Kashmiri food, chicken. The first time I met Mr. Khokhar was on this street in 2009. It was dark outside, with drizzle coming down at an angle in sheets, illuminated by the yellow streetlights. The boutiques of Oak Lane had closed their shutters, and the road was quiet. Mr. Khokhar's shop radiated light, its front one big window. I could see movement inside, but the figures were indistinct, the condensation obscured the view. I hesitated before going in, unsure what I would say. Was this where I would find music? It seemed unlikely. I had lived in this area for much of my life, and yet Mirpuri music-making had remained opaquely hidden from public view; much like the inside of the barbershop that day.

It was summer in Bradford and my timing was impeccable: for the past few months Mr. Khokhar had been helping to arrange visa sponsorship for a Pothwari singer, Abid Qadri, to come to Britain and perform. Mr. Khokhar was excited: Abid Qadri was a widely known and highly regarded singer from Rawalpindi, Punjab, who had won numerous competitions across the region. His arrival in the UK would also mark a moment of particular prestige for Mr. Khokhar among the wider Kashmiri community. For Abid Qadri, too, a visit to the UK to perform at Mirpuri functions would be both socially prestigious and financially lucrative. His tour of England would visit the migratory destinations of Kashmiris: northern postindustrial cities such as Bradford, Keighley, Rochdale, and Birmingham.

A few months after my first visit to the barbershop, the singer arrived in the UK. Mr. Khokhar invited me along to a concert in Rochdale, a town with a large Kashmiri community, approximately forty miles west of Bradford, on the outskirts of Manchester. We agreed to meet at the barbershop later that day. The shop had closed to the evening's trade, but the door was open, and Mr. Khokhar sat inside with the last customers of the day. After saying our *salāms*, the customers got up to leave, and Mr. Khokhar offered me some food. Having just eaten, I politely refused and waited in the shop while he went downstairs. Three of his friends came in dressed in traditional *shalwar kameez*. We chatted briefly about my recent trip to Pakistan, the places I had visited, music I had performed and listened to, and the extreme flooding that had recently hit the Northwest region. There was a feeling of anticipation in the barbershop, and Mr. Khokhar's friends impressed on me that Abid Qadri was a supreme singer: "One of the best!"

The men probed me about my knowledge of Kashmiri music and poetry. A few weeks earlier, I had been to a music academy in the town of Dina, on the Grand Trunk Road, northern Punjab, where I had heard a short recital of the type of sung poetry we would soon be hearing in Rochdale: Pothwari *sher*. In Dina, there had been only a few people in the room and no electronic amplification. I expressed how impressed I was with how loud the *ghara* was and that my ears had been ringing for days afterward. Mr. Khokhar's friends were pleased that I had seen Pothwari *sher* in Pakistan and that I had some knowledge of the instruments involved but were also amused that this had been my only experience of the music thus far.

"Tonight's concert will be much, much bigger!" one of the men said, and they looked at each other knowingly, grinning.

Mr. Khokhar reappeared with a plate heaped with food. "There you go," he said, "you try this."

The earlier offer of food, it transpired, was less of a question and more a rite. Like in Kashmir, food, drink, and *gapshap* are an important precon-cert ritual in Mirpuri culture in Bradford. As I ate my second dinner of the day, verses from the *Saif-ul-Malook* were recited and discussed, each a mini performance, eliciting knowing nods and appreciative cries of "*Wah wah!*" and "*Sach hai!*" (It is true!). Such rituals are themselves intimate spaces in which male social bonds are reaffirmed and strengthened through micro recitations of poetry.[32] This was especially important at the end of long days of manual labor, providing spiritual and emotional anchorage in the face of external pressures. The verses also transported those in the barbershop elsewhere, producing images and memories of home, friendship, and love, dissolving distances across time and space, this world and that—temporal reminders of the path ahead. One of the men recited:

بے دردال دی یاری اوہی جیویں دکان لوہاراں

کپڑے پاویں کنج کنج بہیے پر چھندر پیں ہزاراں

Be dardāṅ dī yārī oheṅ jīeṅ jeoṅ dukān lohārāṅ,
kapaṛe pāweṅ kanj kanj baihīe par chhandar paeṅ hazārāṅ.

Friendship of those who feel no pain is like being in a blacksmith's shop:
Your clothes, even when sat very carefully, will be covered by sparks.

He paused, looking at each of the men, who were nodding their heads in ap-proval, deep in their own thoughts. He pointed upward, seemingly through the ceiling, to a higher being, before continuing:

درد منداں دی یاری اوہں جیویں دکان عطاراں

سودا پاویں لیے نہ لیے پر ہلے ملن ہزاراں

Dardmandāṅ dī yārī oheṅ jīeṅ jeoṅ dukāṅ,
'aṭṭārāṅ sawdā pāweṅ li'e nah li'e par hile milan hazārāṅ.

Friendship of those whose heart is filled with pain is like a
perfume shop:
Even without buying anything, your clothes are filled with a
thousand smells.[33]

The men went on to discuss the thematic word that runs through these
two couplets, *dard*, which can be roughly translated into English as "pain,"
and yet, from their discussion, it was clearly being utilized by Mian Muhammad Bakhsh to produce a number of further connotations. The second couplet, they explained, begins with the word *dardmandān* (درمنداں), which
translates as "those with pain," setting up the rest of the verse to imply a
person who, through their own suffering, has learned to be empathetic,
kind, and compassionate.

Even in this brief example, we begin to see the depth and complexity of
poetic meaning in Mirpuri everyday life. In this context, for example, the
root of this word, *dard*, connotes not only pain and agony but also a deeper
tenderness. With the Persian suffix -*mand*, the word is transformed into an
agent of another noun: for example, *danish* (wisdom) with -*mand* becomes
danishmand (the one with wisdom). With *dardandān* (the -*ān* pluralizes the
noun), then, we have an image of those who are both afflicted and compassionate.[34] Through this play on the word *pain*, recited by Mr. Khokhar and
his friends, Mian Muhammad Bakhsh teaches that if you surround yourself
with those who have experienced pain and suffering, you will absorb their
great wisdom and compassion almost imperceptibly, like a mist of perfume.

Yet these verses could also be understood against the backdrop of Mr.
Khokhar and his friends' experiences of migration and life in Bradford—the
pain of separation from family in Mirpur and the experience of living in a
culturally diverse city, of suffering racism and prejudice for the family cause.
When recited in small gatherings such as these, these past experiences of
migrant life are lifted out of and above the daily grind of work and recontex-
tualized on a spiritual level. Pain, then, is reimagined *as part of the journey*—
indeed, as part of the pathway toward *rahma* (divine mercy). Your suffering
is not in vain, Bakhsh promises; its forbearance is part of all of our collective
experience; it is what makes us who we are. In the context of Mr. Khokhar's
own experiences of suffering, of the hardships he faced working in the textile mills, of his work seven days a week in the barbershop, these hidden intimacies kindled between him and his friends through micro-performances
of poetry were plain to see. The metaphor also points to why the Mirpuri

community is so tightly knit: so that these experiences of migration, and the hardships endured, can be passed down to generations not as pain but reimagined as part of a higher purpose.

∴

With my stomach bursting from two full meals, we left the barbershop and set off in Mr. Khokhar's blue Ford Focus. I drove, and on the way to the concert we picked up two more of his friends from Great Horton Road before joining the M62 motorway to Rochdale. We arrived at Rochdale Town Hall at about 9:30 p.m., and there were only a few cars parked in the lot, suggesting that even at that hour we were a little early. Mr. Khokhar laughed and said that people would be amazed that there was a "white guy" there; he, at least, had never seen a *gora* at a Pothwari concert before.[35] We got out of the car and made our way into the hall, stopping to say hello to people as we did. The hall itself was large, rectangular, with a stage up front and seats for around 150 people. The high walls on either side of the stage were lined, floor to ceiling, with black cloth, punctuated with sparkling lights to create a starry night effect.

There were already a few dozen people milling about. At the back of the hall there was a sales desk, set up on an old folding trestle table, with DVDs of previous concerts. The desk had a small television and a DVD player showing Pothwari sung poetry. The television was surrounded by groups of men. We sat down for a few minutes and various people came over for a chat, including Mr. Khokhar's thirteen-year-old grandson. He sat down next to me, and I asked whether he liked Pothwari music. He shook his head coolly.

"So what music do you like? What are you into?" I asked.

He shrugged his shoulders.

"Imran Khan? What about Tupac?" I suggested.

"Yeah, yeah!" he replied, perking up. "We do music in school—rhymes, tunes and stuff, but it's boring." With it being the summer holiday, he lamented that he had spent most of his time "being dragged around" to these concerts. "It's not all bad, though. I get paid a tenner [£10] for picking up all the [bank] notes!"[36]

It did not look like the performance would start anytime soon, so we got back up from our seats and headed out of the hall via the fire escape and down to a taxi rank located directly underneath the hall. There were several men hanging around the rank—radio operators or drivers—and most knew Mr. Khokhar. The atmosphere was convivial, and they greeted us as we came in, offering us tea or coffee while we waited for the concert to begin.

We sat on some couches for coffee and *gapshap* while another TV played a DVD of a Pothwari concert in Pakistan. The DVD was a good taste of what was to come; indeed, I later recognized some members of the audience in the Pakistan video in the audience in Rochdale. As ten p.m. approached, the hall was getting busy. Around one hundred men had turned up, and as the night progressed a further fifty or so arrived. The reason for these late and staggered arrival times, Mr. Khokhar explained, was that most Kashmiris in the area worked as taxi drivers or in restaurants, and so they had to wait until their shifts finished. The concert's schedule was flexible and shaped around audience availability rather than the other way around.

We made our way to our seats as the evening's *nāzim* (master of ceremonies) took to the stage; he cleared his throat, and the audience began to settle. The evening began with prayers said by the local imam, who blessed the event.[37] Once prayers were completed, several people, including the imam and Mr. Khokhar, were invited onto the stage to recite their own Sufi poetry. During the journey over from Bradford, Mr. Khokhar had been fidgeting with bits of A4 paper filled with his own handwritten poetry. He had practiced reciting his couplets in the car, eliciting encouraging cries of "*Wah!*" from his friends in the back seat. Sitting in the hall, however, his anxiety level was palpable as he thumbed his notes, silently rereading them and looking skyward for inspiration. The two audience members who were the first to take to the stage and recite their verses received warm applause from the attentive audience. Next on stage was the imam, whose couplets received a chorus of "*Wah ji wah!*" from all corners of the hall. It was clear that as a natural orator, the imam would be a hard act to follow.

As the applause for the imam died down, Mr. Khokhar's name was read out, and he audibly swallowed. He walked up onto the stage, received the microphone, and took a moment to compose himself. He began his recitation smoothly but haltingly. Soon after starting, he forgot his lines. He made a few quips to the audience, who were encouraging him along. He visibly relaxed and, despite his lapse in memory, began:

ہتھ رہندے مصروف نے کار ولے
دل ہر دم اُس دی ثنا وچ ہے

Hath rahnde maṣrūf ne kār vale,
dil har dam us dī sanā vich haī.

My hands are busy with work,
but my heart is every moment busy in His praise.

As Mr. Khokhar finished this first couplet, the man next to me nodded in agreement, rocking forward and back, saying, apparently to himself, "*Wah ji wah*." He turned to me, raised his eyebrows, and said, "*Ye sach hai*"—it is the truth. Like many other men in the hall, he had just finished his long shift as a taxi driver and was now letting go of the day's grind. More than that, his daily grind at work was, through Mr. Khokhar's couplet, being elevated to a higher plane. Mr. Khokhar continued more confidently through his verses, pausing here and there at the end of a particular line, giving space for the audience to react. The cries of approval became more emphatic.

کسے یاد وچ کھوکھر نہیں لطف اتنا

لطف جتنا یادِ خدا وچ ہے

Kisē yād vich Khōkhar nahīṅ luṭf itnā,
luṭf jitnā yād-i khudā vich haī.

No thought holds such bliss, oh Khokhar!
As the joy in God's remembrance.[38]

The man next to me exclaimed his approval—"*Wah wah*"—yet again, but louder, and not directed to himself but outward, to the audience and to Mr. Khokhar on the stage. Mr. Khokhar was speaking from his own experience, his own heart, of the hardship of work, the long hours. Through his poetic metaphor, he was also saying something about why it all mattered. It had a higher purpose, for the remembrance of God and for the love of his family. Life was hard, yes, but his path—his own journey of love—remained true. He was, it became clear—looking around the hall, seeing the nodding heads, hearing the cries of approval—speaking for many of the men there that night.

At the conclusion of his poem, the audience applauded, and Mr. Khokhar left the stage to retake his seat, receiving pats on the back as he shimmied along the aisle. The man next to me leaned across me and shook Mr. Khokhar's hand. "*Shabash, shabash*," he said warmly. Well done, well done.

The poetry, written and performed in Pothwari, followed the same metrical and thematic structure used by the great Mian Muhammad Bakhsh. And as in the *Saif-ul-Malook*, Mr. Khokhar situated himself within his poetry as the audience's interlocutor and spiritual *murshid* (spiritual guide). Through these performances, not only do these local poetic traditions thereby become situated within a much longer lineage of Sufi wisdom, but the poets themselves are established by the wider community

as bearers of Kashmiri traditions and values in a land far away from Khari
Sharif and Mirpur. Indeed, despite the number of people in attendance at
the concert, it was a deeply intimate space, strikingly similar to performances I had attended in Kashmir. Those present were entirely men of
the Kashmiri community, and the language spoken throughout the evening was entirely Pothwari. Most of those in attendance wore traditional
shalwar kameez and greeted one another with a familiarity that spoke of
their shared experiences and culture. Outside the hall was Rochdale, but
for Mr. Khokhar, this was also a kind of refuge, a kind of Mirpur, poetically
performed and performatively enacted.

∴

Once the spoken poetry portion (*mushai'ra*) of the evening was over, the
stage began to be set up for the musicians, and the hall filled again with ambient chatter. By then the venue was full. When the stage was set, the *nāzim*
(emcee) began to introduce each musician individually to applause from
the audience.[39] There were eight musicians on stage: two *ghara* players,[40]
Usman Shah and Raja Tajammal, sat with their backs to the audience, as

FIGURE 14. Musicians sit onstage at the Pothwari concert in Rochdale,
Greater Manchester, with banner reading "Mehfil-e-Sher-Khwani"
(gathering for poetry recital/singing).

did the *dholak* player, Mohammad Yaseen.[41] Next to the *dholak* sat a harmonium player, Talat Hussain, who positioned himself at an angle facing toward the audience. He was flanked by the stars of the show, Abid Qadri and Ch Javed, the singers, who sat adjacent to the *sitar* player, Syed Irfan Shah Sahib (fig. 14).

In this arrangement, performances of Pothwari *sher* generally follow a similar pattern: the singer will recite the first two lines of *sher* solo, and the remaining instruments join in thereafter.[42] The singers are the focal point of a Pothwari ensemble as they compete against each other with verses of poetry. The instrumentalists are arranged either side of the singers, in a *U*-shaped formation with the singers at the apex or in a circular formation.[43]

With the musicians introduced, the harmonium played a flurry of notes (fig. 15). Abid Qadri stood up, pointing to the sky, and began to sing, joined by the sharp earthen percussion of the *ghara*:

گلیاں وچ چکر تے مینہ وسدا

اسدا ،، دور ہے در جس دے نال یاری

Galiyāṅ vich chakkaṛ te mehṅ vasdā.
Usdā, dūr hai dar jis de nāl yārī. . . .

The streets are muddy from all the rain,
And my beloved's door is far, far away. . . .

Abid Qadri's vocal style was high pitched but full and powerful (*bhari hui moti*). He directed his voice at the audience, gesturing, pleading with them, questioning them with refrains and themes of love and loss common to so much Sufi poetry. The audience, in turn, reacted and responded to his singing with cries of approval and recognition, hearing themselves and recognizing their individual experiences in the words he sang. In this way, Abid Qadri was appraised by the audience according to how well he vocalized the emotion of the poetry and connected it with the audience's worldly and spiritual journeys. The quality of his voice and its ability to convey sentiment would also play a large part in determining how well Abid Qadri would be remunerated during his performance, as we shall now see.[44]

THE CIRCULATION OF MONEY

The concert in Rochdale, as in Kashmir and indeed elsewhere on Abid Qadri's tour, offered free entry. Audience members were welcome to come and go as they pleased. But their financial appreciation and patronage were

FIGURE 15. Excerpt of Abid Qadri singing with a Pothwari ensemble in Rochdale.

dramatically expressed during the concert itself. While the singers were singing, members of the audience would go to the evening's *nāzim*, who stood at the side of the stage holding a bag full of low-denomination rupee notes, and buy wads of them for £5 or £10, then subsequently shower the musicians with them so the money rained down like confetti. This kind of performed patronage continued throughout the evening. The first time I saw this happening, I strained my eyes to see what denomination the money was, but Mr. Khokhar, with a laugh, informed me that they were rupees, not pounds. At the same time, audience members would hand the *nāzim* pieces of paper with the names of people in their party, who then passed the list to the singer. Before the beginning of each verse, the singer would stop the music (the harmonium would keep improvising with the *rāg*)

FIGURE 15A. Excerpt of Abid Qadri singing with a Pothwari ensemble in Rochdale.

and announce the names of the benefactors with honorifics and where they came from: "Raja Khokhar Sahab, Bradford," and so forth.

Throughout the evening, all the musicians remained in a seated position, usually cross-legged, with the exception of the singers, who stood when it was their turn to sing. When a performer was approached by a member of the audience and showered with money, the performer would not usually respond unless a rupee note fell somewhere that interrupted their technique. At the show in Rochdale, the only musician who responded to the offering of money was Abid Qadri. Similar to the context of *qawwali*, the musicians at a Pothwari *sher* gathering receive money only implicitly as remuneration. In this way, the social status of the performer is explicitly realized through their ability to convey the emotion and meaning (*matlab*) of the poetry (Qureshi 1986, 111).[45]

With hundreds of rupee notes surrounding the musicians, the youngest or most junior member of the ensemble would collect all the fallen banknotes and return them to the mediator; at that evening's concert, the honor fell to Mr. Khokhar's grandson. The circulation of money truly was cyclical, with the rupees constantly being recycled by the *nāzim* to be used again by the next patron. The monetary value of the rupees would not usually correspond to the equivalent value of the pounds sterling and so instead carried symbolic significance.[46] For Mirpuris, the circulation of Pakistani rupees during the concert in Rochdale carried important and symbolic connotations of home. And as the singer announced to the wider audience the names of those showering the musicians with rupees, it was not only money that was being exchanged during the performance; status, too, was part of the transaction.

The second means through which money was transferred from patron to performer bypassed the *nāzim* altogether. This type of exchange often occurred at a more progressed stage of the evening, in a manner that could be described as a kind of one-upmanship. Because the original value of the donation could become lost in translation as it was converted from pounds to rupees, a more ostentatious method of patronage could be employed. When this happened, five-, ten-, twenty-, and occasionally fifty-pound notes were handed by audience members directly to the singer, who acknowledged the donation with a nod before pocketing the note himself. If the same gesture was offered to an instrumentalist, they would proceed until the end of their solo and then also pocket the money. When this exchange took place, the patron made sure that the color of their money was clearly visible to the rest of the audience.

MALE RITUAL, CONNOISSEURSHIP, AND CLASSICIZATION

> Qawwali music conveys to its listeners affirmation of traditional structures, whether ideological or social. It does so by its very dependence on those structures of successful articulation. But there is no doubt that the same music also concurrently articulates, and even promotes, individual self-assertion.[47]

As the monetary exchanges described above suggest, there is more than money at stake during performances of Pothwari sung poetry. Concerts such as these are almost always exclusively attended by men with Punjabi or Kashmiri heritage.[48] While there is no formal seating plan or reservations for the majority of seats, most concerts I attended had one row of seats to the side of the musicians where higher-status individuals sat. These were often the owners of the venue, successful businessmen, or the principle patrons of the visiting musician (i.e., those who had helped finance and sponsor the trip from Pakistan to the UK).[49]

The public displays of emotion by audience members during performances conveys what Magnus Marsden (2007) has described in other contexts as a form of male cultural connoisseurship—a demonstration, for all to see, of a depth of knowledge of and fidelity to the historical traditions of Pothwari culture. This cultural connoisseurship is performed audibly (through cries) and visibly (through nods), demonstrating one's knowledge and appreciation of the *sher* and the quality of the artists at the correct moments of a performance. The giving of money produces similar displays of connoisseurship. In relation to performances of jùjù music among Yoruba elite, Christopher Waterman discusses the act of "spraying," whereby the patron will very publicly shower the musician with money. While spraying takes place within the confines of a particular performance context, Waterman shows that its desired effect is felt further afield: "Gossip circulates quickly, and ceremonies are nexus points for positive and negative re-evaluations of social status and personal power" (1990, 175). As we have seen, the showering of money during a Pothwari *sher* is highly ritualized and of great importance for both the performer and the individual patrons, the effects of which are felt far beyond the confines of the concert. For these musicians visiting from Pakistan, the degree to which they were looked after and patronized meant that they would return to Kashmir and the Punjab with stories of their host's generosity. These stories would circulate widely and thereby affect the host's standing in the community both in Bradford and in Mirpur.

The giving of money, and the very public way in which it is done during a Pothwari performance, is therefore a heavily loaded and public gesture. It is a way of saying, "I am staying true to my roots" while also implicitly asking everyone else, "Are you?" In this sense, ostentatious displays of patronage provide a way to *be* Mirpuri that continue beyond the realm of the *mehfil*. This *being Mirpuri* is enacted, and reaffirmed, through the appreciation of music, and conversely, the appreciation of music is an important part of *being Mirpuri*, especially thousands of miles away from Kashmir, in Rochdale, England.

Audience members effectively perform their status through their public patronage and appreciation of music. At the Rochdale show, for example, some men would make multiple trips to the stage throughout the evening while others moved to show their higher status by handing over £10 and £20 notes directly to a musician, circumventing the middleman and making sure the color of their money was clearly visible to all watching. Others would mark their performance of patronage by standing onstage with the performers, drizzling their wad of rupees over the head of a particular musician while nodding appreciatively. Others still would stand in front of the stage and dramatically throw their notes upward in one burst, creating a monsoon of rupees. Such performances of patronage are declarations of appreciation, knowledge, and wealth aimed not just at those within the *mehfil* but—via the returning musicians—to those back in the ancestral homeland, all of which can both confer *and* alter status within the community home and abroad.

As in a *qawwali* gathering, then, these offerings "constitute the social gesture *par excellence* for expressing high status and a position of patronage" (Qureshi 1986, 129). Waterman, too, recognized the importance of patronage in determining and maintaining status, showing that "anyone can achieve wealth and high status through the cultivation of patron-client networks" (Waterman 1990, 1). These ostentatious demonstrations of patronage are important not only for reenforcing levels of status but also as a means of income for the performers. The musicians' levels of remuneration depend entirely on the largesse of the audience rather than ticket sales.

For the audience, their financial support is also indicative of a deeper understanding of and connection to a longer history of Kashmiri musical heritage and culture.[50] Yet these were also spaces in which certain gender expectations were formed. Writing about *mehfil*s during the period of Aurangzeb in seventeenth-century Mughal India, Katherine Schofield (née Brown) has described how the "differentiated yet complementary roles of patron and musician were embedded in Indo-Persian discourses of gender and social strata, and the mirza's successful negotiation of his prescribed role in this relationship signified his mastery of elite male codes" (Brown 2006, 67).[51] By patronizing traditional Pothwari music and poetry, male Mirpuris display their love of and appreciation for a deeply rooted articulation of Kashmiri culture. The "performance of patronage" (through showering the musician with money) of Pothwari sung poetry, both by the musician's sponsor and by those attending the concerts, demonstrates, for all to see, a level of cultural connoisseurship that embodies and codifies a particular type of male Mirpuri subjectivity, one that is shrouded in hidden intimacies between audience members and also largely hidden from wider public view—subjectivities that are tightly indexed to memories of migration and of longing for/belonging to Kashmir, even while home is in Britain.[52]

∴

While researching the Khalifa community in Bradford, John Baily observed that "Mirpuris are regarded by other Asian communities in Bradford, and apparently elsewhere, as rather unsophisticated people. . . . There can be no doubt that there is strong pressure within the Mirpuri community to maintain a way of life which is in harmony with the values of Mirpur" (Baily 1990, 157). Yet within the performance contexts described here, this desire to live a life in harmony with the values of Mirpur is seen entirely positively within the community. For some Mirpuris, music is outwardly regarded with relatively little interest, as an activity to pass the time while at work or simply something that happens in the background. And yet, even in these cases, Kashmiri poetry is repeatedly held up as a highly valued aspect of culture that is central to Mirpuri heritage. For example, when meeting Mirpuris in other locations around the country—Oxford, Newcastle, Walsall—their interest was always piqued and their eyebrows raised when I mentioned Mian Muhammad Bakhsh. In these snatched conversations—in taxis, kebab and curry houses, shops, and so forth—it was always clear that poetry was deeply felt as an esteemed marker of Mirpuri identity and culture. Rather than simply being of a low stratum in society that is "backward" and not interested in music, then, the context of the Pothwari *mehfil* shows that Mirpuris occupy a social position that is culturally rich and deeply complex, in which music plays a critical role in kindling a sense of community interlaced with memories of home.

And so the sense of Mirpuriness that was cultivated in the male-only barbershop was further negotiated and asserted within the *mehfil* in Rochdale, where modes of masculine behavior were learned, performed, and thereby passed down to generations born in Britain. This was particularly the case for the younger British-born Mirpuris present, whose emotional connection with Mirpur was reinforced by poetry and established as a crux of their heritage. Relationships among and between men, based on a sense of Mirpuriness, would be forged and realized; their status as flag-bearers of Mirpur tradition was established, both within the community and without.

In places such as Bradford, Mirpuris have become increasingly prosperous and, subsequently, great patrons of music. The higher wages, compared with equivalent jobs in Pakistan (Shaw 2000), that drove migration to Bradford have since contributed to an elevated economic status of Mirpuris at home and abroad, with domino effects for individuals' social status within the community. The ways in which these changes have been revealed through and by music have a real and profound impact on current epistemologies of both Mirpuris and the patronage of music in modern Muslim societies. Here, individuals or groups who are very much of the working class rather than the ruling elite display their connoisseurship and social mobility through the patronization of music and sung poetry. For Mirpuris, subscribing to and attending Pothwari performances is an act of connoisseurship full of hidden intimacies (Herzfeld 2005, 3) whereby the music is used simultaneously as a mark of group belonging and as a mark of cultural pride in a wider environment that is often hostile to immigrants.

∵

A few days after the concert in Rochdale, I asked Mr. Khokhar whether he thought there were any notable Pothwari singers in the UK. He shook his head sadly and replied, "No, the only good performers are in Pakistan." It was an opinion that was by then becoming familiar to me. I'd elicited a similar response on the eve of the Bradford Mela, when I'd asked Mr. Khokhar if he would be going to see any of the *qawwali* groups performing that year. I had often heard *qawwali* being played in his barbershop, and based on his participation at Pothwari *sher* concerts, I assumed he would be attending the public two-day festival.

"These are not real performances," Mr. Khokhar had said dismissively. "Only people from London. Only in Pakistan are there real *qawwals*." For Mr. Khokhar, the Bradford Mela, which I explore in more detail in chapter 4, existed outside the sphere of his own life and experience, in the outward-facing public domain of "multicultural" Bradford. Only the Pothwari concerts organized by the community and for the community, such as the one in Rochdale featuring the Pakistani singer Abid Qadri, during the summer of 2010, were *real* and authentic.

CLASSICIZATION OF POTHWARI *SHER*

Attending and patronizing Pothwari gatherings in towns across the north of England trigger collective but dynamic cultural memories of migration and home. These memories are performed into being through displays of connoisseurship during performances and the recitation of poetry in everyday spaces such as the barbershop, that only those within the community would recognize. The audience in a contemporary Pothwari *mehfil* is *expected* to respond to the musicians and orators, in the right way and at the right time, with shouts of "*Wah wah!*" These important indications of connoisseurship demonstrate an ability to identify particularly moving passages of verse or a particularly skilled flourish on a solo instrument (see Silver 1984, 321). Doing so reveals, both to the musician and to other audience members, that the acknowledging audience member possesses a high degree of cultural knowledge and literacy. This has always been an important part of *adab* (etiquette) in South Asian *mehfil* culture, but arguably, it takes on additional significance in migratory contexts. Such public displays of connoisseurship are also part of a broader display of loyalty and belonging whereby cultural knowledge and literacy of music serve as markers of one's identity. The performance of patronage within a Pothwari *mehfil* and its relationship with status thus endows the gathering with the capacity to act as a medium (to paraphrase Qureshi 1986) for social change and mobility. While the gathering serves to articulate existing social hierarchies, then, the circulation of money also allows for new values and socialities to develop that can, in turn, transform traditional hierarchies within the community and of the music itself.

When describing Pothwari music as traditional, for example, Mr. Khokhar would often also emphasize its value and quality by calling it classical. This duality of how the music is imagined suggests an underlying process of "Ashrafisation," whereby the music is elevated from *desi* (local, or village style) to something closer to *mārga* (a more privileged, universal *tariqa* or way) (Schofield 2010, 491).[53] It is a process that situates Kashmiri music-making within a much longer social history of elite music-making on the Indian subcontinent. In Schofield's (2010) study of the classicization of Hindustani music by the Mughals, for example, several discursive markers are used to identify processes of classicization that occurred in precolonial times. For one of these markers, Schofield draws on the work of Harold Powers (1980), which states that "for music to be classical, it must be 'patronized by individuals or groups, belonging to the ruling elite, who profess *connoisseurship*'" of that music (11; emphasis in original).[54] With musical patronage, then, come alternative ways of asserting musical values that are indexed against social status in an inverse way to the Mughal elite. To paraphrase Appadurai (1986), gatherings of Pothwari sung poetry can be thought of as "tournaments of status" wherein members of a community historically seen as low status publicly assert their love of the music through patronage, to reaffirm or renegotiate their high status in society.

The relationship between patronage, connoisseurship, and classicization has important bearings for the way Pothwari concerts can be understood in the UK, particularly vis-à-vis their wider multicultural landscape. The performance of patronage reveals complex moments of exchange between and among Mirpuris. But what is at stake in these moments is complicated.

Money plays an important role but not simply as a means of remuneration for the musician. The performance of patronage is also a social performance, and its meanings are local and particular. The recitation of poetry, the showering of money, the reading out of patrons' names, and the emotional cries of approval are all part of asserting levels of connoisseurship about Mirpuri culture and history. This connoisseurship is under the constant scrutiny of those who are there, and so there is much to be lost and much to be gained. Pothwari *mehfil*s are thus active spaces of Mirpuri male subjectivity, the ramifications of which are felt across the city and beyond, in Mirpur.

In this sense, Pothwari *mehfil*s must also be understood in relation to, and connected with, wider political pressures.[55] While they are very much located within the industrial landscapes of Bradford and Rochdale, the sense of place and space that is represented therein is, in Giddens's terms, "thoroughly penetrated by and shaped in terms of social influences quite distant from them" (1990, 18). Vertovec (1997) identified such duality as being integral to a "diaspora consciousness" marked by social identifications that point in multiple cultural directions: hence an "awareness of decentered attachments, of being simultaneously 'home away from home,' 'here or there' or, for instance, 'British and something else'" (282). In the UK, pressures about what it means to live a good life take many forms: from internal familial pressures such as marriage, paying taxes, and maintaining *biraderi* ties to external social pressures such as the expectation in the media to integrate and broader political events involving Islam and Muslims.[56] In a society that is becoming increasingly diverse, to the extent that the term "super-diversity" (Vertovec 2007; Grillo 2010) has been coined to describe the demographics of UK cities, cultural practices such as Pothwari *sher* assume an increased significance for Kashmiris in places like Bradford. Rather than signifying segregation, Pothwari *mehfil*s are conversely understood by Mirpuris as arenas of hidden cultural intimacy wherein assertions of a home away from home are performatively brought into being.

CHAPTER THREE

Public Poetics

On the cusp of New Year's Day 2019, Zeshan Sajid, a young British Mirpuri actor from Birmingham, England, posted his latest skit on YouTube: "Saqib—shafaqat no taqat ft liaquat (official music video)."[1] The satirical video features his popular character, Saqib, a fictional eight-year-old boy (played by a bearded Sajid) who wryly observes the world of adults around him. In this video, he's recording a "diss" track in response to his *chacha* (uncle, also played by Sajid), who had, in a previous post, teased his nephew for thinking he was a "big man": "*Na na na yaara*," his uncle Shafaqat had rapped, "*Saqib thinks he's bou bara!*" (No no no, bro! Saqib thinks he's the big man!)

In the new video, we catch up with Saqib several months later. He's wearing a red hoodie and a backward green baseball cap. He is at home, sitting in front of a computer with Apple's Logic open, WAV files displayed across the screen, and studio monitors to his left and right. He has created his backing track, which we hear playing in the background—up-tempo EDM with a bass-line beat—but he is stuck staring tearfully at a separate computer screen, which is playing his uncle's mocking YouTube post. The young Saqib—replete with a luxuriant beard—is theatrically whining to his dad, like an upset toddler, about not knowing what to say in response to his uncle Shafaqat's diss. The camera cuts to his father—who, yes, is also played by Sajid—dressed in a traditional *shalwar kameez*. His father takes off his sunglasses and exclaims, "*Fikr na!* [Don't worry!] I will help you! *Chal!* [Come!] Let's make diss track!" The screen fades to black, and the track's title appears in white lettering: "Shafaqat No Taqat" (Shafaqat's Got No Power). We find ourselves in a vocal booth, with Saqib's dad in front of a condenser microphone against a soundproofed backdrop:

"Shafaqat no taqat [Uncle, you've got no power] / You look like a crisp packet!"

When I watched the video for the first time in 2023, I laughed so loudly that the other commuters on the bus turned around and stared. I was thousands of miles away from Birmingham, but the video, the accents, the dialect, the humor, put me right back in my childhood, thirty years ago in Bradford and its streets. Back then, as we will see in this chapter, young Mirpuris seemed to relentlessly find themselves on the receiving end of public criticism, portrayed, somewhat fatalistically, as uneducated and destined for a life of crime by the media, politicians, and other South Asian communities in both Britain and the subcontinent. Thirty years later, as I sat on that bus, Zeshan Sajid's satire appeared to turn all of that on its head, cutting through the tensions—and indeed epistemologies—that surrounded young Mirpuris back then, only to be solidified in the intervening decades.

Zeshan Sajid's comedy is dry, self-referential, playful. Its target audience, evidenced in the interactions below his videos across social media platforms, is not just his own Mirpuri community but, more narrowly, those with the experiences of Sajid's particular generation: teenagers and young adults who were born and grew up in places like Bradford and Birmingham, yet whose parents still largely orient themselves elsewhere, toward the ancestral homeland of District Mirpur. I pressed "play" again, and after the "crisp packet" (x4) diss intro, Saqib replaced his dad at the microphone (fig. 16):

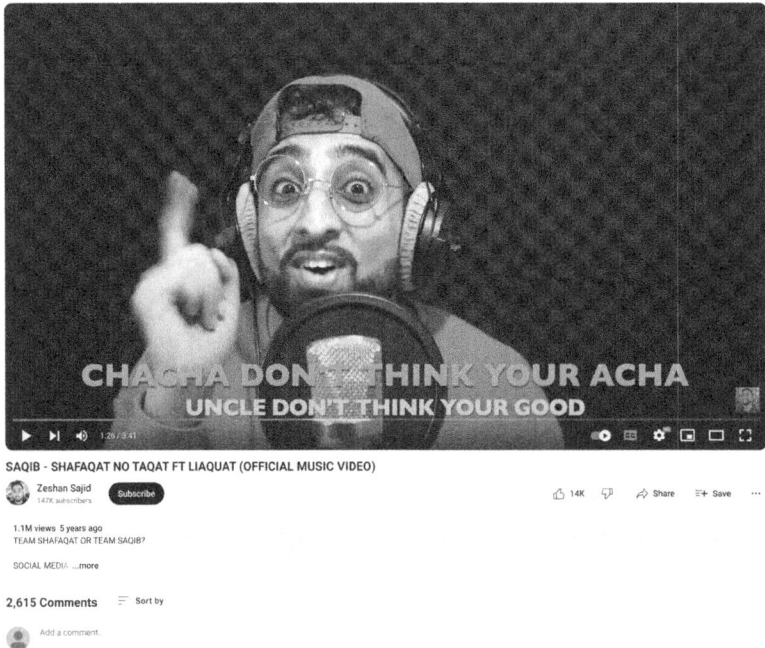

FIGURE 16. Still from the YouTube video "Saqib—shafaqat no taqat ft liaquat (official music video)."

> *Chacha* [uncle], don't think you're *acha* [good]!
> You don't even wear a *kacha* [underwear]
> Don't even use a *lota* [water pot]
> Your son is a *khota* [donkey]
> Have you heard about your *murra* [son]?
> Cousin Abid is very *burra* [bad]
> *Woh school koni jana* [He doesn't go to school]!
> *Woh bas jutiya khana* [All he eats are slippers]!
> *Marey naal koni laro* [Don't mess with me]
> *Ukal istamal kao* [Use your common sense]
> *Chacha*, you wear *shalwar kameez*
> But you don't have any *tameez* [manners]
> Yes you're my *abba's bhai* [dad's brother]
> But don't come round for *chai* [tea]
> Call yourself Shafaqat?
> But you don't have any *taqat* [power]!

Sajid's humor is not epiphenomenal to the efficacy of the video's appeal among its audience. Rhyming *lota* with *khota* is toilet humor in its finest figurative as well as literal sense: poking fun at his uncle for both his lofty "village mentality" and an apparently erstwhile lax veneration of the old ways of restroom sanitation. It is an in-joke deployed frequently in Sajid's videos to produce the kind of effect that Michael Herzfeld would no doubt recognize as a kind of "cultural intimacy:"[2] Sajid takes the worn stereotypes leveled against Mirpuris and skewers them, recasting them into self-knowing points of pride (for context, at the time of writing, his YouTube channel had 144,000 subscribers, 536 videos posted since 2016, and a combined stream count of over 87 million; "Shafaqat No Taqat" is his most popular video to date, with over 1 million streams).[3]

In the previous chapter, I described the dislocating sensation of being in two places at once. I had been in Pakistan back then, at a dusty junction in the road facing a grocery store with the signage "Mirpur General Store: British Produce." I described how the sounds and aromas I sensed back then had transported me back to Bradford. I'd closed my eyes, breathed in, and not just imagined but *felt* my childhood in Bradford coming back to me. Several years had since passed, and I had moved to another continent on the other side of the world. Sitting on the bus, watching Zeshan Sajid's videos in 2023, it was a different sense that yet again brought me back to those streets of Yorkshire. As I watched Sajid's videos in California, where I had moved for work, it was the sense of humor, detectable in the fine particularities of code-switching and references to local places and customs—at once quintessentially Mirpuri, British, and northern—that transported me again across space and back through time, to both Britain and Azad Kashmir. I was reminded of exactly this kind of irreverent humor from school: slapstick and throwaway; put-downs as sharp as a razor and as crunchy as a crisp packet.

It is probably not a stretch to say that few of my fellow commuters on the bus that day would have had the same response to Sajid's humor that I did. To get the joke, you would also need to get the cultural idiosyncrasies, the references to Mirpuri life in Britain and in Pakistan. As I paused the video and looked out the window, I thought about how closely aligned Sajid's humor was with Shakoor's when I'd been on his rooftop in Islamghar, described just a few pages ago. Of course, this was also perhaps the point: the sense of humor, through its rhetorical use of language—and in particular the rhymed code-switching between English and Pothwari—drew a line around a certain kind of collective experience, recognizable to those within the community, unknowable to all else. As Maurice Said (2016) once wrote, humor is a device, an observational way of teasing apart the push and pull of generational dynamics and expectations.[4] It is also a means to overcoming injustices on your own terms.

These videos are, relatively speaking, a new thing, brought about by the emergent technological possibilities of social media. Over the decades, avenues for creative expression, especially for young Mirpuris, have both contracted and expanded in Britain. Contracted because, as we will see throughout this chapter, state-led initiatives—even when deployed with the best intentions—have repeatedly failed to address Mirpuris' particular creative needs to the point of abandonment; yet also expanded because recent digital technologies have opened up spaces for a different kind of public poetics, away from schools and away from the more censorious gaze of parents: a space I describe in what follows as "the street-online nexus," wherein those institutions—both public and private—can be effectively lampooned.

In what follows, I examine three contrasting spaces of young Mirpuri music-making: schools, state-run rap workshops, and the street-online nexus, a space theorized here as existing across local geographies and spilling into online worlds. There is a chronology to how I approach these spaces, and deliberately so. In the case of the former—schools and music workshops—I focus primarily on Kashmiri youth culture in Britain from the late 1970s to the early 2010s. This period in many ways marked the apotheosis of state-led (i.e., publicly funded) music initiatives directed toward young Mirpuris, which often led to naught. In the years since, little has changed in terms of music education policy in Bradford, and if anything, expressive opportunities for young Mirpuris in these public places—schools, festivals—have only become further constricted: in 2023, music curricula in the few remaining schools to offer music as a subject remain unchanged, focusing exclusively on Western popular music (blues, rock, grunge, Brit-pop), a brief (and uncritical) nod toward world music, and a survey of repertoire from the Western canon (Beethoven, Bach, and the usual suspects). Instead, local publicly funded arts organizations stepped in, somewhat haphazardly. These organizations, dominated by music promoters of primarily Indian Hindu heritage from Punjab, were highly articulate in the bureaucratic language required to attract state funding and so came to symbolize the multicultural agenda of the municipal council, shaping it around their own tastes while dominating public arts programming in the city. As a result, opportunities for Mirpuri creative expression were, as we saw in the previous chapter, often pushed to the margins, to places like Mr. Khokhar's barbershop and Rochdale Town Hall.

In the subsequent section, I further develop the idea that young British Mirpuris had good reason to develop economic and cultural self-reliance—expressed on the street and on social media—especially in the face of various "civilizing" projects organized and funded by the local council. At school, we see an education system anxious to avoid provoking perceived sensitivities around the permissibility of music in Islam, especially within more orthodox mosques in Bradford, with the result that actual Mirpuri music-making was largely ignored. And so, with Mirpuri youth culture being systematically squeezed out of the very institutions ostensibly there to support them, it should perhaps come as no surprise that these young people instead look elsewhere—to their streets and to platforms such as YouTube and TikTok—for creative expression, spaces that are nominally public yet coded—hidden, even—through linguistic and cultural particularity.

A History of South Asian Music in Bradford

Broadly speaking, South Asian youth culture began to flourish in Bradford in the mid- to late 1970s, when a small group of students from Bradford College and Bradford University started putting on live Bollywood nights. The concerts proved extremely popular. Until then, despite growing numbers of South Asian migrant workers arriving in the city, there had been little in the way of public events that might appeal to them. Champak Kumar, a student at Bradford College at the time, noticed that Bollywood film screenings in local cinemas were booming in popularity among the city's Pakistani, Indian, and Bangladeshi communities. He saw a gap in the market and organized what he described to me as the first live, public South Asian concert in Bradford:

> About 300 to 340 people attended. All the artists that performed were local. A combination of students, you know, my group and the people from the community that did some dance. So there were girls, and we got some members of the communities involved to actually make some costumes, colorful costumes, get some imitation jewelry for the girls to wear. Audience makeup was, majority was Asian community: a makeup of Hindu, Pakistani, Gujarati Muslims, students. We had some English students as well, all of our friends. Basically, we said, "Look, guys, you have supported us up 'til now in the college atmosphere, but you now come out of the college atmosphere and you support us in this atmosphere." And they came and everybody enjoyed it. Everybody started saying, "When is your next concert?" and we said, "Give us some time! Because we don't have money, we don't have funding, we don't have anything." We approached [the council] and said, "Just look. . . ." We found out that they used to have some types of English concerts, you know, like classical and folk, so we approached the manager and we said, "Look, we want to actually do an Asian concert."[5]

Following the success of these early concerts, Champak formed a music promotion company, Oriental Arts—one of the UK's first South Asian arts organizations—with a view to establishing a program of South Asian music in the city. I spent a year volunteering for Oriental Arts, working with Champak to apply for funding from Arts Council England and from the local municipal council.[6] Our office was just about large enough to hold three people, located in a converted Victorian warehouse in the Little Germany area of Bradford: a district named after nineteenth-century German mercantile migration to the city, refashioned as a place of late twentieth-century South Asian cultural production.

In the early days of Oriental Arts, applications for funding submitted to the local council were met with flat refusals. Indeed, Champak explained how his first proposals for a concert in the city's municipal library elicited confused responses:

"Asian concert? What does it entail? What does it mean, 'Asian concert'?" the venue manager replied.

"Well, you know, music and dance," Champak ventured.

"Is there such a thing?!"

Champak believed this kind of response, common at the time, was a product of South Asian areas of the city becoming geographically and culturally isolated from the rest of Bradford, pushed out to the suburbs, resulting in fewer opportunities for cultural exposure and exchange. In many respects, these were early indications of the kind of racial and cultural segregation that fed into the multiculturalism backlash in the years that followed.[7] Champak saw Bollywood concerts, and live music in particular, as a way of countering this by increasing cultural exchange between new migrant populations and longer established Bradfordians. In lieu of financial support from the municipal council, Champak relied on contributions from local Pakistanis, Indians, and Bangladeshis to put on shows and promote them around Bradford. Donations were needed to buy microphones, stands, speakers, and instruments as well to pay for venues. A nominal amount of 20p was charged for entry into the concerts—something that was regulated largely by the low economic reality of new migrant communities.

> It was very difficult at that time, not a lot of money. People who came here, their families were back home. People were working here and sending money back home to their families to support them and in the future to get them into UK, into Bradford. Whatever support they could give they did. But we didn't get anything from the council between '76 and 1980—nothing at all. Every time we went for a grant they said, "Oh, we don't understand this," or, "You are not a properly constituted organization, you're just a bunch of students" and all this. We used to say, "At least we're doing something for the community!" But still, they had their criteria and policies, and we couldn't challenge them.[8]

Yet over the subsequent decade, the concerts organized by Oriental Arts became instrumental in cultivating South Asian music in Britain. Indeed, while Peter Gabriel's Real World Records is often credited with introducing Nusrat Fateh Ali Khan to the world stage at the WOMAD 1985 festival, it was in fact grassroots South Asian arts organizations such as Oriental Arts that first brought the renowned *qawwali* singer to Britain to perform at Bradford University in 1983.[9] These early concerts gave emerging generations, born in Bradford, a space in which to creatively explore, celebrate, and critique the South Asian heritage of their parents in response to their own experiences of growing up in multicultural Bradford.

In the early 1980s, *bhangra* emerged as a genre that spoke to the cultural heritage of young South Asians in Bradford but with their own imprint of electric keyboards, beats, and dance. Pioneering acts such as Alaap and Heera, the self-styled "Godfathers of Bhangra," cut their teeth in the city's large concert venues. It was also a period that saw the emergence of South Asian underground scenes in the city, with the rise of a disco culture that came to be known as Daytimers. These events were organized by lo-cal entrepreneurial music promoters who hired out nightclubs in the after-noons—at a discounted rate when they would otherwise be closed—and play hours of Bollywood music and *bhangra*. South Asian girls and boys would go to school at eight a.m. in their *shalwar kameez*, get changed into jeans and T-shirts in the school's bathroom, and then cut their afternoon classes to go to the Daytimers. The gigs would start at twelve noon and finish at four p.m. so that by the time it was over, the teenagers could go back to school, get changed, and go home as though nothing had happened. Champak recalled:

> The Council of Mosques was against it. Bradford City Parents Association was against it. But the thing is, these girls wanted to go and enjoy the music. Some of them only wanted to go and enjoy the music; they didn't want to go and fall into bad habits. Other girls fell into [bad habits], boys as well, boys and girls. Because this was an opportunity for them to meet in a club and cut loose, start drinking.[10]

Following pressure from the Council of Mosques, the Bradford City Par-ents Association, and the police, Daytimers began to disappear from the music scene in Bradford, but the underground movement continued, of-ten in forms ostensibly designed to address *and circumvent* the censorial anxieties of the Council of Mosques. By the early twenty-first century, for example, Ladies Only Nights began to appear in clubs across the city. These nights were hosted in medium-size venues and were, as the name suggests, open only to women. By being single-sex events, they were designed to be safe, *halal* (permissible) places where Pakistani women in particular were able to go without the perceived fear of losing honor. In February 2010, *bhangra* rap stars Jaz Dhami and Imran Khan played at one such ladies only night at Bradford City Football Club:

> Five hundred tickets—sold out! All girls. All women and girls. They were up to a certain age, I don't think married women, they were all single girls. This friend of mine told me: "Champak, the mischief these girls got into! Smoking, drinking like mad! They were let loose!" Jazz Dhami was saying, "Champak, so many Muslim girls! I've never seen them [like this], the mischief they're in!" So, I mean, these things are happening, Tom, and no one can deny it's not. I mean, if you go and speak to the leader of the Council of Mosques and some other councillors, they will probably deny it. But they haven't seen it![11]

For British academia during this period, the emergence of *bhangra* signaled "both an exciting example of musical fusion and the unexpected cultural expression of an 'Asian' identity in Britain" (Banerji and Baumann 1990, 137). For many commentators, *bhangra* even came to symbolize the fruits of migration and multicultural integration: "[Its] most exciting potential, that of a fusion of hitherto disparate styles, moreover, can be seen as the oldest virtue of Punjabi culture, rooted in a region characterized by immense cultural diversity and intense cross-fertilization for most of its history" (137). And speaking of the wider social context in which music scenes such as these flourished, Banerji and Baumann argued that "South Asian communities in Britain have remained invisible, and their music inaudible, for a surprisingly long time" (138). They argued that *bhangra* also marked the emergence of South Asian communities from invisibility.[12]

Yet throughout my research on the streets of Bradford, young Kashmiris appeared to have little interest in these academic critiques. They were not listening to the polemics of *bhangra* rap but a broad mixture of popular music, rap, and *nasheeds*.[13] Indeed, the somewhat celebratory narrative that surrounded *bhangra* rap in academic scholarship clashed with increasingly fraught debates about multiculturalism in the public sphere and the reality of life on the ground described by artists such as Fun-Da-Mental.[14] By the turn of the decade, the Kashmiri community in Bradford had been buffeted by intense public and academic scrutiny over the Honeyford affair, the Rushdie affair, and, in 1995, the Bradford riots: events that put pressure on multiculturalism as a policy and gave rise to national anxieties about cultural segregation.[15] Multiculturalism had to somehow reconcile the celebration of cultural diversity on the one hand with a desire for integration on the other.

In Bradford, at least part of the success of the concerts and discos described above lay in the way in which they provided the opposite of cultural and generational integration: safe spaces away from the intensifying glare of the media, parents, religious leaders, and everyday encounters with racism. They were, in this sense, deliberately hidden from public view. These early events were almost exclusively attended by the South Asian community and, in the case of Ladies Only Nights, were often specifically designed as gendered spaces.[16] Indeed, this deliberate hiddenness resisted the spotlight of both multicultural supporters *and* critics of the time, and for good reason. Against a backdrop of institutional and everyday racism and anxieties over how women should behave in public spaces, Daytimers and Ladies Only Nights instead provided protected spaces, away from the critical glare of public commentators.

Despite Kashmiris accounting for the largest South Asian community in Bradford, the publicly funded music and arts organizations that emerged during this period came to be dominated by members of the Indian community.[17] Indeed, as Champak explained, even with the best intentions, his organization, Oriental Arts, was set up in 1976 primarily for his own "Hindu community, who were made up of Gujaratis, Hindu-Punjabis, and Hindus. . . . They were from different backgrounds, you know, some from Kenya, some from South Africa, but [the] majority of them [came] from India." Other arts organizations in the city, such as Kala Sangam and Manasamitra, also became darlings of nationwide government grant agencies such as Arts Council England, who saw them as exemplars of their mission to foster "great art and culture for everyone."[18] As mentioned, these arts organizations, were highly adept at and effective in winning public grants and so came to dominate multicultural arts programming in the city. As we shall now see, the educational initiatives this produced suggest that cultural segregation can be as much a product of external processes (public arts organizations, schools) as geographic self-segregation.[19]

Mirpuri Music-Making in Schools

Mr. Khokhar's son, Muna, grinned toward the young men sitting in line to have their hair cut before flicking on his clippers. "I've got no interest in it whatsoever. I can't stand it." A small TV, mounted high in the corner, played a videotape of the Pothwari *sher* concert I had attended in Rochdale. The picture was fuzzy, and Urdu calligraphy streamed along the bottom of the screen, advertising a local taxi service. The barbershop smelled of hair oil. Muna's father, dressed in a traditional *shalwar kameez*, stood next to him, taking care of the barbershop's elder clientele, listening to our conversation.

"So what kind of music do you like?" I asked.

"I dunno, like R&B and that, you know, Tupac, hip-hop." I nodded along, unsure how to continue. My first question had been about whether Muna liked the poetry his dad and I had been talking about just moments before.

I persevered. "So where would you find Pothwari music in Bradford, if you had to?"

Under his breath, Muna replied, "Tokyo's." The bench of young men erupted into laughter. Tokyo's was a popular R&B nightclub in the city center: an unlikely venue for traditional Kashmiri folk songs.

Muna cut a different figure than his father. He wore a full sports track-suit, sneakers, a gold necklace, and a diamond stud earring that caught the light as he moved around his customers. He specialized in skin fades and shaving intricate patterns into tightly cropped hair.

The bell above the door rang. A young boy of around twelve entered the barbershop with his father. He slung his school bag down onto the floor next to me and spoke quietly to his dad. The boy did not have a locally defin-able accent, more that of a middle-England private school. He wore a blazer and, extravagantly, a cravat. The accent and attire felt oddly out of place in the barbershop, but nobody else paid any attention.

His father greeted me and asked what I was doing there, perplexed by my presence in a place otherwise exclusively patronized by the Kashmiri community. I told him about my interests. His boy looked up sharply and, in a crisp English accent, intoned that he played the classical guitar, and to grade 3 standard, no less.[20] I smiled just as Mr. Khokhar called out the day's punctuating phrase: "Next, please." The boy shrugged off his blazer and hopped onto the barber's chair. The crest sewn onto his jack-et pocket read "Bradford Grammar School"—the city's most prestigious private school.

There were three generations present in Mr. Khokhar's barbershop that day: Mr. Khokhar and his friends—first-generation migrants immersed in the world of Pothwari sung poetry; his son and his son's clients—born in Bradford, schooled in the city, attracted to a different kind of poetry: rap; and the young cravat-wearing customer, who distinguished himself through his (Western) classical guitar-playing abilities. The differing inter-ests in music were not, in themselves, completely surprising; teenagers and children often listen to different music from their parents. Until that point in my research, I had been fixated on finding Mirpuri music, as though there were such a definable thing. Younger generations of British Kashmiris, born in Britain, of course had their own musical worlds, their own histories, and yet their lives were something rarely included in scholarly and media ac-counts, unless as a focus of criticism.[21] Part of the reason for this, I would learn, was that local schools and arts organizations across Bradford simply did not know what to do with them and often saw them as a problem. Their perceived musical identities in these public organizations became inextri-cably indexed to their parents' despite the fact that they had been born in the city, and their education subsequently became shaped by the multicul-turalism debates of the late 1980s and early 1990s. Yet rap music, and what Adam Krims (2000) has described elsewhere as its "poetics of identity," was as much a part of Muna and his friends' lives as the Pothwari poetry of his father's generation. It follows that a poetics of migration might also be found in rap and that for Muna, its relationship to Pothwari sung poetry was perhaps closer than I anticipated in the barbershop that day.

∵

By the mid-1980s, there was an increasing awareness that Kashmiri students were being excluded from music-making in schools and public spaces, despite often listening to a wide range of music at home. As early as 1984, Patricia Jones observed that

> the children appear to be protected from live music situations. Very few of them play an instrument or have an instrumentalist in their family; very few of them ever learned any songs as small children, had any songs sung to them, or experienced any singing at home; very few of them are allowed to attend school discos. On the other hand, all the children listen to a considerable amount of music at home of various descriptions and watch films, as well as television programmes, which include dance.[22]

The sociologist Philip Lewis (2007) argued that one of the primary reasons that the Mirpuri community experienced slower socioeconomic development compared with other South Asian communities in Bradford was due to a disproportionately low level of educational achievement. This view was often also shared by Kashmiris themselves. In the town of Walsall, West Midlands, a prominent Kashmiri radio DJ, Changis Raja, explained to me that among young Kashmiris, there was a culture of education being "uncool," discouraged, and actively bullied against.[23] Local schools were failing to engage with young people, and parents were apathetic to raising aspirations or encouraging their children. Without a fundamental reformation in this area, Changis believed, young men would continue to turn to crime and prolong the cycle of underachievement. This view was supported by government reports that showed young Pakistanis in Bradford as significantly underachieving in schools compared to their peers and with distinct gender gaps within the community:

> In 1999, nationally, 22 per cent of Pakistani boys achieved five or more GCSEs [General Certificate of Secondary Education] (grades of A* to C) compared to 37 per cent of girls. The equivalent figure for white boys and girls was 45 and 55 per cent respectively (for Indians the figure was even better, 54 and 66 per cent). If these figures were not worrying enough, the Bradford statistics were truly disturbing: 17 and 28 per cent. In 2004

the respective national figures for Pakistan boys and girls were 29 and 39 per cent.[24]

These figures of relatively low educational attainment among Pakistani pupils came despite the several years of initiatives led by South Asian arts organizations described above. In the late 1980s, for example, Bradford's Local Education Authority (LEA) began to support South Asian music and arts in schools. With financial help from the Bradford Council and regional arts agencies, Oriental Arts began to run South Asian music education workshops in schools. Despite many schools in Bradford, such as those I attended as a child, hosting a majority of pupils with a Pakistani heritage, there had until that point been little provision for South Asian instruments. This was addressed when the head of the Bradford schools' music service, Brian Crier, acquiesced to providing peripatetic instrumental lessons on *tabla*, *dholak*, and *sitar* in a select number of schools in South Asian areas of the city. The services of four teachers were employed, and they began giving workshops and classes.

Champak was proud of these initiatives, yet they often spoke more to the multicultural policies of funding bodies than to the cultural differences and needs within the South Asian community. He described how, while students from a wide range of backgrounds took up these new music lessons, including young Mirpuri Muslims, it was the Sikh and Hindu children who tended to progress to more advanced playing. In Champak's view, this was largely due to greater support from their parents and the continuation of lessons for Sikh and Hindu children in *gurudwaras* and temples. Kashmiri children would sometimes take up instruments such as the harmonium, he said, but once the school program finished there were fewer pathways for them to take it forward.

These initiatives were not without scholarly input. The ethnomusicologist John Baily, who was conducting research with the Gujrat community in Bradford at the time, helped advise the council on these educational programs and observed that, within the Bradford schools' system, there were distinct reservations among teachers about the value of music felt by Kashmiris in the city (Baily 1990, 157). Yet these nuances often fell on deaf ears. By the mid-1990s a series of funding cuts ensured that provisions for South Asian instrumental lessons in school were stopped. Since then, the LEA has sporadically provided money for South Asian music in schools, channeled through arts organizations, but no coherent strategy has been developed to move students forward beyond a rudimentary introduction to North Indian *rāga* and a few instrument workshops. There was also surprisingly little attempt, at the city council level, to open dialogue with

students themselves to see what music they engaged with and might want
to perform or study themselves. As we shall now see, these reservations
among teachers and misfiring policy initiatives have continued deep into
the twenty-first century.

EDUCATION, EDUCATION, EDUCATION

In 1997, the Labour Party, led by a young and charismatic Tony Blair, swept
into power in Britain on the promise of "education, education, education."[25]
In the wake of this electoral victory, the Social Exclusion Unit (SEU) was
established to tackle a perceived disengagement with education among
young people in Britain, and Pakistanis in particular. Studies were commissioned by the SEU to try to establish why young Kashmiris experienced
slower upward social mobility compared with their peers. One such study,
by the Joseph Rowntree Foundation, "found significant numbers of [Paki-
stani] 16–17 year olds disengaged from education, employment and training" (Britten et al. 2002). A further study in 2004 found that a majority
of young Pakistani men left school with few or no qualifications and thus
suffered from reduced opportunities and employment.[26] The government
responded by pouring money into multicultural arts initiatives, yet due to
the cultural makeup of the South Asian arts organizations described above,
these projects often only compounded the problem.

Young Kashmiris' lack of engagement with music programs in schools
was exacerbated by two contributing factors. First, department heads had
general anxiety about the legitimacy of and hostility toward music in Islam.
Teachers described to me how they felt they were "treading on eggshells"
with regard to teaching music to Muslim students, which was part of a wider
fear of upsetting "Muslim sensibilities" and incurring recriminations from
parents. In particular, Bradford-based South Asian arts organization Manasamitra met resistance from several schools when holding music and dance
workshops. The organization was involved in a national program, in con-
junction with Education Bradford and funded by the central government,
called Sing Up. The program was designed to encourage more children na-
tionally to sing through a series of practical workshops and group events.
The director of Manasamitra, Supriya Nagarajan, explained to me that at
several schools in Bradford, teachers had vetoed the program because of
a belief that music was *haram* (not allowed in Islam). Head teachers even
began suggesting that Manasamitra's workshops should not contain any
reference to politics or religion for fear of upsetting religious leaders. For
Supriya, this was a relatively recent phenomenon, linked, in her view, to
the spread of Wahhabism and Salafism—which expressly forbid music—in

a number Bradford's mosques. Yet, despite this perceived proscription, Supriya described how, when discussing music and dance with Kashmiri pupils in schools, they would enthusiastically display extensive knowledge of Bollywood film music and *bhangra* as well as the latest US hip-hop artists. This suggests that anxieties among teachers were usually based on assumptive common sense and inflexible views that music is not allowed in Islam, rather than emanating from the students themselves or indeed a more nuanced knowledge of the important role music plays in many Muslim cultures.[27] Second, there was a general lack of encouragement from parents to treat music seriously or as a worthwhile academic subject. As Lewis (2007) has noted, when Mirpuri students did proceed to study for A-Levels and tertiary education, it was usually in subjects in the sciences or for vocational qualifications such as law. At Carlton Bolling College, as at many other schools across the city, this resulted in music as a subject being removed altogether from the curriculum.[28]

At Beckfoot School, meanwhile, these two factors combined and resulted in only two Muslim pupils, both of Mirpuri heritage, taking up music at GCSE in 2009 and 2010 out of a collective class size of seventy. Beckfoot lies approximately twenty minutes from Bradford city center and, at that time, catered to 1,593 pupils between the ages of eleven and eighteen.[29] It was also one of the schools I attended as a teenager growing up in Bradford. The head of music at Beckfoot, Matt Stimpson, explained to me that the uptake of students from a Muslim background for GCSE Music was disproportionately low. In year 7, Matt explained, Pakistani students would happily engage with music in the classroom on a practical level—such as in workshops, group performances, rhythm exercises, and so forth—but when it came to giving an after-school concert they would nearly always pull out. There was little or no uptake of instrumental lessons. To try to encourage more Pakistani students to take up music, the school began to offer peripatetic lessons on the *tabla*. However, Matt explained, the only students to register for these lessons were white; young Kashmiris showed no interest. Matt also ran a unit on Indian *rāga*s, but again, his Pakistani pupils showed no interest.

And yet, that was not to say these students were not interested in music. One of the rare success stories came when Matt offered the school's recording studio to the students to record their own rap song. Eleven Pakistani students took this opportunity with alacrity and demonstrated an ability to rap that was far beyond Matt's expectations. The group even performed their music in a school assembly. Since then, however, there has been little encouragement from teachers for these same pupils to continue using the recording studio as part of their pre-GCSE projects. The possibility that these rap songs could factor into the curriculum and were, in fact, a more appealing and accessible form of music than *tabla* and *sitar*s for young Mirpuris had not occurred to Matt, who instead diligently followed the advice of South Asian arts organizations. The marginalization of Kashmiri music-making in schools was therefore not due to a lack of interest among students or even enthusiasm from teachers: every year the school's head teacher, David Horn, would implore Matt to encourage more Muslim students to take up music. Rather, these efforts were hampered by perceived anxieties around music's position in Muslim cultures and guidance from arts organizations that privileged North Indian classical traditions at the expense of contemporary music that might actually appeal to students.

Broadly speaking, during my research, and indeed in my childhood, Kashmiri students at Beckfoot displayed little or no interest in learning the Indian classical tradition, practically or theoretically. Nor were they interested in learning instruments from the Western canon. Indeed, the only occurrence of musical engagement was the recording session in the studio. This suggests that at Beckfoot School there was a general lack of understanding among those who set the curriculum and external consultants as to what types of music were most likely to encourage more Mirpuri students to engage with music at GCSE. Furthermore, there was a clear undertone of anxiety when Matt asked me directly what music was allowed in Islam. His knowledge had been informed by things he read in the media and so-called commonsense assumptions made in the staff room—that is, that Muslims do not listen to music. These kinds of assumptions informed a broader climate within the school system in which the teaching of music to Muslims was felt to be a lost cause, despite evidence that, given the opportunity, these students actively performed and composed rap music. Beckfoot's lack of flexibility to recognize this positive interest and incorporate these forms of music into the curriculum suggested a need for more reflexivity and adaptability if more young Mirpuris were to engage with music education in schools.[30]

The above examples show that Kashmiris' experience of music education in Bradford too often involved them being lumped together into a wider South Asian community that was interested in advancing North Indian classical traditions. This was evidently met with limited success among Mirpuri students. Moreover, the experiences of John Baily, Manasamitra, and Oriental Arts show that a complex set of issues, understandings, and assumptions regarding the validity of music in Islam influenced how teachers approached offering music to Muslim students. Yet the idea of using rap music as a way to engage with young Mirpuris had not gone entirely unnoticed. Policies aimed at fostering multicultural integration did begin to shape Kashmiri music-making in Bradford, though not in the ways policy-makers expected.[31]

RAP WORKSHOPS

On July 11, 2001, the headline of Bradford's local newspaper, the *Telegraph & Argus*, asked, "What's Wrong with Bradford?" with the subheadline "A 'Virtual Apartheid' Divides the City, with Races Only Coming Together When Forced To" (fig. 17).[32] The double-page spread was the latest headline to hit the paper in the wake of riots in the city involving young Kashmiris. Over the next few days, readers of the paper answered its question in un-equivocal terms. One reader wrote to the paper that "Bradford Council's and the police authority's task has always been upper most and very appar-ent; a racially integrated city. But how is it possible to accept or recognize as co-nationals, a race of people who are Hell-bent on retaining their own cultural identity?"[33] Another reader took "exception with the rioters being referred to as Asians. . . . Nearly all the rioters were young Pakistanis. . . . Indians are far more willing to integrate, and our children achieve higher levels of academic qualifications."[34] Meanwhile, the chair of the Pakistan Christian Welfare Association Board lamented that "Bradford has now

FIGURE 17. A double-page spread in Bradford's *Telegraph & Argus* asks, "What's wrong with Bradford?" Wednesday, July 11, 2001.

become virtually the Muslim capital of Britain.... One of them was recently awarded an OBE. The responsibility of taking control of the youth lies with their parents. It appears they have lost control."[35]

The aftermath of the riots brought a renewed interest in the causes and consequences of ethnic segregation in Britain (Phillips 2006).[36] Multiculturalism was coming under pressure, and, in one government report written by the Community Cohesion Review Team, white and minority ethnic communities were said to be living a series of "parallel lives . . . that do not seem to touch at any point, let alone overlap and promote any meaningful interchanges" (Cantle 2001, 9).[37] Propelled by the ideological shift of New Labour toward integration, these reports effectively singled out Kashmiris as self-segregating, isolationist, and not sufficiently contributing to the wider society.[38]

In response, the city council commissioned a series of rap workshops aimed at bringing Bradford's communities together through music. Pipeline Productions, the organization that would run the workshops, was established by Philip Charles, a young Jewish man, born in Bradford, of African Caribbean heritage.[39] The workshops were run in schools and youth centers across the city and were specifically designed to address the kinds of concerns expressed by the readers of the *Telegraph & Argus*: segregation, integration, and out-of-control youths. During a workshop, Philip would initiate a discussion with the students about their perceptions of one another and their own experiences of living in Bradford. He would write down recurring themes on a whiteboard and start suggesting rhymes based on what the students were saying. The students would then start taking a more active role, suggesting new phrases and organizing the lines into verses. Philip would fire up his laptop, run some hip-hop samples, and prime the microphone. The resulting raps were a kind of hip-hop by committee. Flashes of violence were juxtaposed with sentimentality, as with the following example, recorded at Belle Vue Boys' School.[40]

> *Mo*:
> I wanna live a calm and peaceful life,
> Not going round streets stabbing people with the knife.
> I know how these Bradford streets are like,
> People going round doing drop offs all night.

> *Ash*:
> I wanna tell the world a little something about my mother,
> To let all of you know just how much I love her.
> No matter what I say I just want her to see,
> That I appreciate how she looks after me.[41]

Funded by public money, these rap workshops came with strings attached. They were shaped by an agenda of integration and mutual respect, so swearing was not allowed and certain topics, like Islam, were anxiously policed. Like the teachers at Beckfoot, Philip was at pains to circumvent any potential flash points during the workshops that might offend parents or religious leaders or, indeed, the source of his funding: Bradford Council. He had recently run a workshop at the MA Institute (an independent Muslim day school for boys and girls ages eleven to sixteen) on Lumb Lane.[42] Prior to arriving, Philip composed a selection of backing tracks for the teenagers that were purely percussive. His understanding, having Googled "music and Islam," was that drumming was acceptable, or *halal*, but melodic instruments were *haram*. "The funny thing is," he said, "none of these kids cared. They just wanted to rap and have a go."

Despite this enthusiasm, Philip was constrained by the conditions of his funding. In 2005, for example, he was asked by the council to run a rap workshop as part of their Skills for Success initiative. The program targeted the lowest achieving pupils across Bradford, bringing them together over twelve weeks with the aim of "raising educational aspirations." Philip's brief was to bring together youngsters from different communities across Bradford, get them in the same room, and encourage them to start talking to each other. The students were meticulously chosen to represent different ethnicities and genders: two students—a boy and a girl—from Holme Wood, a white working-class estate on the edge of the city; two Mirpuris—again, a boy and a girl—from Manningham and Girlington; a boy of African Caribbean heritage from Eccleshill; a white girl from Shipley; and a Mirpuri girl from West Bowling. All working-class areas on the geographic and economic peripheries of the city.

During the workshop, Philip encouraged the students to discuss their neighborhoods and how they perceived other communities in Bradford. The themes that emerged were shaped by Philip and led in a clear direction toward celebrating multiculturalism: no-go areas were challenged, racial stereotypes were broken down, and instead, above all else, diversity was to be celebrated:

Mirpuri boy:
Territories, yo, you know what I'm sayin'?
You know sometimes we're gonna have some pain.
People fighting because of their different colors,
We should all be praying, out and chilling with our brothers.

Holme Wood boy:
If you're black you can't go here, if you're white you can't go there,
People livin' in fear, we don't think it's fair.
We can't go anywhere, a change is overdue,
This racism needs to end, and this is true.

Chorus:
Why are people racist? Underneath we're all the same.
We're equal so face it, we don't all play that game.
Racist people think they're bad, but underneath they're just sad,
It's getting on my nerves, and it really makes me mad.

Eccleshill boy:
Racists—why do people act that way?
I'm afraid of the day when my children can't play.
So I say this nastiness needs to be stopped,
No more racist teachers, no more racist cops.

I think back to year 7, sat alone and reminisce,
I had such a bad childhood, everybody would diss.
I'd come home in tears, feeling angry and confused,
Thought it would last for years, being insulted and abused.

Stereotypes—one line per student:
They live on benefits, they have too many kids.
Their houses are dirty, I don't like how they live.
They think they're better than us, they smell too funny.
They take all our jobs, they get all our money.
They're taking over, their women are loose.

Stop, we need to remember, the myths become truths.
They are all lives, we know better than this.
Let's think about where we're from before we start to diss.
Let's celebrate our cultures, difference is cool.
Believe what other people say? You are just a fool.

What would it be like if we were all the same?
There'd be no different food or cultures, life would just be
    the same.
No different music, no different points of view.
No rice, chicken and peas, no chicken vindaloo.

As for me, I like the fact that we're a rainbow nation.
We think that this is cause for a celebration.

The rap is striking with its tone of multicultural optimism: stereotypes have been deconstructed, myths are demystified, and the "rainbow nation" is celebrated. The language of "us and them" is replaced by a seemingly inclusive "we." This was hip-hop from above, a project curated to "civilize" otherwise (perceived) out-of-control youth and bring them into the fold. Language was policed and moderated, themes identified, learning outcomes predefined. It was ironic that such tailored use of public money rarely addressed the actual experience that was in any way meaningful to young Kashmiris. Chastised at home for not being Pakistani enough and by imams for not being Islamic enough, and villainized by the media for not being British enough,[43] young Kashmiris were being squeezed from all sides and had few spaces in which they could express themselves creatively; now even rap was being mobilized by the state to try to entice them into being better citizens. It should not, then, have come as any surprise that in the face of these often overwhelming pressures to integrate, Kashmiris were instead turning to the street for musical and poetic expression. As it happens, generations of Kashmiris born in Britain were indeed actively writing songs and raps that critiqued life in Britain and the streets they lived in while also drawing on Islamic teachings. Just not in the sanitized space of rap workshops, as we shall now see.

The Street-Online Nexus

The Bradford Interchange was a modernist train and bus station built in 1973 on the site of the former grand Victorian rail station—nineteenth-century gothic giving way to concrete, steel, and glass. The building was designed to be a beacon of modernity, signaling Bradford's economic renewal after decades of industrial decline, and yet was destined to become part of it. For much of my childhood, most of the station shops had lain empty and shuttered; gangs of kids would prowl the concourse. At the time, Bradford had one of the highest inner-city crime rates in the country. On the day I returned during my research almost a decade later, much was still the same. Pigeons perched above me on steel girders caked in dust from diesel exhaust. Gregg's Bakery was doing a fine trade in piping-hot 70p pastries, and the smell filled the otherwise sparse hall. The pigeons swooped down to peck at the crumbs left by morning commuters on their way to Leeds or Manchester. Security guards in vivid yellow vests patrolled the concourse, wearily eyeing groups of teenagers in school uniforms. I bought my ticket from a machine at the top of the escalator.

Bradford Interchange is the end of the line, propelling people away from Bradford rather than through it. There was a small newsagent by the entrance, and I stocked up on water, potato chips, and fruit for my journey across the Pennine Hills to Walsall, on the outskirts of Birmingham. I was early and walked along the platform, to the end of the end of the line, and looked back at the Bradford skyline. The spires of churches and the minarets of mosques punctuated the horizon, exclaiming the city's multicultural history. Throughout my childhood, the bells of these churches had mingled with the call to prayer, time and space marked by sight and sound, giving anchorage to the rhythms and movements of daily life.

The train was quiet and smelled of warm dust. I had been invited to Walsall by Changis Raja, a prominent radio DJ and advocate of Kashmiri culture in Britain. "If you want to understand Mirpuris," he had written to me, "come here and I'll show you." The train pulled out of Bradford, and the engine strained against its weight on the way up toward Odsal Top. Car breakers and scrap metal yards passed beneath us. As we crested the hill, the engine died down to a low, steady rhythm, breathing out. The land grew green. Dairy cows chewed in fields crisscrossed with dry-stone walls. The contrast between urban industrialization and pastoral idyll swiped across my window. William Blake, at the dawn of the Industrial Revolution, wrote somewhat anxiously about whether, "among these dark Satanic Mills," a paradise had been lost. For Blake, industrialization not only came at a visible cost to nature but upended social orders, the mills standing ambiguously for power over morality and spirituality. Yet as the train led us on through farmland, the contrast between rural innocence and urban decay seemed less pronounced. Every arable inch was worked; the landscape was fully under control. Perhaps Blake needn't have worried. Change reimagines continuities. The textile industry had now left Bradford, yet Blake's "clouded hills" remained.

∵

Changis Raja and I met at Walsall station and got into his silver Vauxhall Corsa. The car's fan belt screeched as we set off. Changis was wearing jeans and a shirt, his hair graying slightly at the temples. Walsall felt like the same city as Bradford, its high street dominated by discount pound-stores, betting agencies, and pawnshops, markers of a town on the margins of its wealthier neighbor: Leeds in the case of Bradford, Birmingham for Walsall.

"OK, let me know a bit more about what you want to find out, because I don't want to just take you where I want; it needs to be specific to you." Changis scanned the street, looking for people to introduce.

"Well, whatever you want to show me," I replied.

"First things first," he said with a faint grin. "There's no such thing as Mirpuri identity." I waited and tried to absorb this statement made so early on in our friendship. It was clearly important, and Changis enjoyed its rhetorical gravity. Settling back into his seat, and into his theme, he gestured out across the street.

"When our people first came here, the passport office back home was located in this new city of Mirpur. The old villages and Old Mirpur were underwater because of the dam. Loads and loads of villages, hundreds. All gone. So when they applied for their passports and were asked where they were from, what did they say? Their villages were gone! Let me tell you. This is what happened: instead of spelling out all the different villages of origin, their real identities, when it asked for hometown, most just kept it simple and put Mirpur." He laughed.

This, for Changis, is how an imagined Mirpuri identity came into being. It is also something that he tries to resist. On his radio shows, Changis encourages his listeners to foreground their Kashmiri heritage, connecting them to longer and deeper musical and poetic traditions. Politically, it also connects them with a strong sense of a regional independence—*Azad Kashmir* translates to Free or Independent Kashmir—that also speaks to their cultural independence in a supposedly multicultural Britain.[44] He despaired that over in Bradford, there had been successful movements by otherwise well-meaning South Asian organizations for Mirpuri to be recognized as an official language. He thought this absurd, likening it to campaigning for Brummie, Cockney, or Yorkshire to be classed as distinct languages; "Mirpuri," he said, turning to look at me, "is just a regional dialect of Punjabi."

As Changis spoke, his head turned from side to side, scanning the pavements. "Ah!" he exclaimed, beeping his horn and abruptly pulling over to the curb, where three young boys were walking. He beckoned them over: "Get in, lads." Without questioning why, the boys climbed into the car, and we turned down a road of redbrick Victorian terraced houses. Wasim was the tallest of the three, and Changis immediately started asking him about his ambitions in life. The boy was visibly self-conscious. His friends sniggered beside him as he spoke, and it was only after much coaxing from Changis that Wasim said he held ambitions of becoming a policeman. "Good lad," Changis replied, nodding approvingly in his rearview mirror. We turned a corner and parked outside Changis's house. As we settled in his living room, with armchairs pushed back against all walls in the Kashmiri style, Wasim explained that he was teased by his friends for wanting a career in the police force; other boys had already started deriding him by calling him a "pig"—a slur on both his ambitions and his Muslim faith. Wasim's experience, Changis wanted to emphasize, spoke to a wider trend among

Kashmiri boys to energetically turn away from anything deemed academic or aspirational. Even having career hopes beyond being a taxi driver or warehouse worker was met with mockery and verbal abuse.[45]

I returned from the bathroom to find Wasim's friend Imran waiting for me in the hall. Through the doorway, we could see his friends laughing and punching each other boyishly on the sofa. "I do want to go to university," he said shyly, "but my friends call me dumb." He ran up the stairs and locked the bathroom door. I paused in the hallway. All the well-meaning multicultural arts educational initiatives I had encountered in Bradford did not touch the lives of young Mirpuris such as these. They were left out, at the end of the line in Bradford and the end of the road in Walsall.

Back in the living room, Changis asked the boys how many young men in their extended family had been to university. The boys stopped play-fighting for a moment and lapsed into thought. "My uncle went to uni," Wasim ventured. "He's an accountant now." The others stayed silent. In their extended families, Changis said, turning to me, there were probably around 150 men: only one had been to university. All the rest were taxi drivers or warehouse workers. I thought back to the Pothwari concert in Rochdale Town Hall and the streams of taxi drivers arriving after their shifts to listen to the sung poetry of Mian Muhammad Bakhsh. I asked the boys what a good and well-paid career looked like to them. Without blinking, an eleven-year-old boy, quiet until then, responded, "Drugs."

YOUTUBE AND THE CROFO BOYZ

Like Bradford, Walsall was a popular destination for Mirpuris in the postwar period, and like Bradford, it has since suffered from the decline of the textile industry and years of underinvestment. A town center once crowded with grand Victorian architecture and medieval buildings had, like the old Bradford Interchange, been demolished in the 1970s to make way for brutalist shopping centers and road-widening schemes. And like Bradford, the Mirpuri community lived on the margins of an already marginal town. The decline of industry and lack of available jobs saw Walsall become the second-most-dangerous town in the West Midlands, with a crime rate 82 percent higher than the national average.[46]

The boys in the room with me that day at Changis's house were part of the Crofo gang, whose territory extended across the local streets in this area of Walsall. Their territorial boundaries were in some respects marked by street names, beyond which lay their rivals—the Palfrey Boyz to the north, the Birchills Boyz to the west—yet their borders became further blurred and contested in the online world of social media.

"If one of those Palfrey *chodes* [fuckers] come over here, yeah, they'll get fucking stabbed. Check this out," said a grinning Nasir, the youngest of the boys, pulling out his phone.

We gathered around him on the sofa. On the small YouTube page on his phone was the green and white of the Pakistan flag; the crescent moon and star appeared to be painted by brushstroke. He pressed "play." The beats and melody of Ice Cube's "Why We Thugs" began, and dubbed on top came a muffled rap, the voice distorted:

"Yeah, yeah, it's Crofo . . . Crofo, Crofo, what the fuck? Fuck Palfrey, fuck your mum, fuck your sisters, fuck your dad, ha ha, fuck everyone, mother-fuckers, ha, listen."[47]

This was a Crofo rap, made on the streets we had just driven down, broadcast to the world on YouTube. Over the previous few months, there had been clashes between gangs. One gang member had been stabbed, Changis said, but instead of phoning the emergency services, the victim's relatives bundled him into a car and took him to the hospital themselves. He later died.

"You won't believe this, Tom, but these relatives who were helping were actually arrested by police! 'Why didn't you call us? Why didn't you call the police?' they kept saying. Well, Tom, why would they call the police? Who is going to believe them?"

This deep suspicion of public services, Changis said, was driven by years of racial profiling and prejudice toward the Kashmiri community. All the boys in the room had experienced racism firsthand; two had been called "fucking Pakis" by passing motorists over the previous few days.[48] The result was that social justice would be pursued within the community, often coupled with a sense of fatalism: it was Allah's will and his time to die, the victim's relatives had said at the time. Families of the victims of gang violence rarely gave permission for autopsies to be carried out and instead pushed for quick funerals and burials. There would then be the possibility of revenge attacks. Wasim pressed "play" again, and the rap began with a repeated chorus.

Chorus ×2:
Yo, go to Palfrey, let off two shots,
Fuck the feds 'cos Crofo won't stop.
Won't move till it gets on top
Suck your mum straight, we don't give a fuck.

Verse:
Yeah, we got your girl on lockdown,
Phone 'em up quick, tell me, wanna fuck now?
Yeah, she'll be down in five minutes,
Buck code tell 'em I'm down for anything she's givin'.

Yeah, because I spit lines over,
I'll leave your sister with one less brother.
'Cos I'm a killer like passive smoke,
You deserve it, you're on the crack and coke.

When push comes to shove we'll do a drive-by,
'Cos we don't stick out that fine line.
I mean this, it's my line.
Crofo's at the top, like a skyline.

[Chorus ×2]

Verse:
T pass me the MAC-10,
Strapped up, ski mask, on the attack then.
We've got it all locked off,
Blacked out, that's what you can class them.

Blacked out vans, CS gas,
We let off shots on a regular mass.
Shank, mask, stay on task,
On a last resort it's CS gas.

I hope you ain't afraid of the dark,
'Cos you'll get left in Green Lane Park.
And well, I'll leave holes in your chest,
And not just a bruising mark.

[Chorus ×2]

As the diss track played, the boys moved with the lines, pointing two fingers in the air at the words "pass me the MAC-10," a semiautomatic gun, "pop pop," the boys sang. They knew the area, Green Lane Park; they knew who the song was about; they knew what it was about. CS gas—more usually deployed by police as a riot control agent—was claimed for the street,

TABLE 1. YouTube comments for the video "The crofo song"

Published at	Author	Text
1/21/2018, 21:21	Kakarot	Wastemans haha.
3/21/2019, 7:42	SykunoX	Palfrey bang crofo anyday we land arena they to scared
6/20/2019, 18:30	B19 Addz	Pussio Crofo bastards
1/9/2019, 22:45	Usman Ulhaq	Crofo crew
8/9/2018, 11:06	Lukman Khan	Hard tune fam
3/5/2019, 16:10	Noneofyourbusiness X	Palfrey lads hairlines tell the story of jesus
4/14/2021, 20:21	SLIPZ	lmfao
7/30/2020, 16:10	Shakeel Khan	Big up CROFO pop pop

identities were hidden behind ski masks. And for a community in which family honor was considered sacred, insulting rival gangs' mothers and sisters hit the hardest. The rap—later published on YouTube in July 2017, but primarily shared via WhatsApp and Snapchat—watched while huddled with friends on a sofa or in a car, is street life presented online. Over the following years, the video accrued over twelve thousand streams while the comments underneath perpetuated the street feud online (table 1).

The Crofo rap and Zeshan Sajid's rap with which I began this chapter are in some respects two sides of the same coin. They are both diss tracks, aimed and directed within the community, and are observations of life on the streets of Britain. On one level, the comment section below the Crofo song relates what Forrest Stuart has described elsewhere as a "creative response to extreme poverty" (2020, 9). Hyperviolent and hyperlocal, the rap and the comments it attracted speak to their own lives in ways external agencies—schools, arts organizations, mosques—could never capture. It feels a far cry from the sanitized lyrics of the rap workshops described earlier. Yet the characterization of rap—and, in Stuart's case, Drill—as a creative response to extreme poverty does not always manifest itself as an expression of violence. The street-online nexus is a space of ambivalent publicness. As we saw with the satire of Zeshan Sajid, social media platforms such as YouTube, Instagram, and, most recently, TikTok—where Sajid also has a large presence—are an extension of the street, providing spaces away from the pressures of school and the gaze of parents for young Mirpuris to express themselves creatively and playfully: arenas where "the street" spills online, with all its ups and downs, complexities and contradictions, the crackle of crisp packets and the pops of imagined guns.

∴

After we watched the video on YouTube, Changis took us on a walking tour of the area with his daughter, Summa. "This primary school," he said, gesturing to our left, "was voted one of the country's poorest performing schools in England. It's been failing for the past ten years, but no one cares."[49] Yet when he tried to rally his community to campaign for better education, he was met with resistance and threats to desist. He blamed this on a general anxiety among Kashmiris about attracting the attention of the authorities; complaints might intensify the spotlight on a community already under pressure to change the way they live.

"What people don't understand is that these problems are faced by British *Kashmiris*, not *Muslims* like they say in the papers." While Indian communities were prospering through business, education, and music, Changis lamented that his own community was not tackling the primary problems they faced: education, crime, and health. Yet there was an alternative perspective to Changis's, and it came from his own daughter. After dropping the boys off, we returned to his house.

Throughout my time with Changis, his outlook had been downcast, and the young Mirpuris I had met and become friends with over the years were often the opposite: optimistic, full of humor, self-aware. Over cups of strong, sugary tea, Summa illustrated this generational gap in perspective and challenged her father's depiction of the community.

"You're just reinforcing stereotypes," she said. "Not all Kashmiris are like that. I'm not."

"OK, what's your ethnicity?" Changis asked her.

"Mirpuri . . . British Mirpuri, slash Pakistani, slash Kashmiri, slash British. I've been to uni. I'm almost an accountant. So you can't say we're all into crime and that." The real difference, Summa explained, lay in an educational gap between boys and girls driven by inequalities at home between genders: "Girls are locked up by their parents, and boys can do what they want. They can do no wrong," she explained.

Unlike boys, Kashmiri girls' movement in public was more closely observed and scrutinized by the wider community and by their parents. They were therefore much more likely, Summa explained, to stay at home than spend time on the streets. It was little wonder, she said, that they spent a greater amount of time studying for school. This translated into competition between girls as to who could achieve higher grades: the opposite of the boys, who would contrive to achieve the lowest. Summa was uncomfortable with her father's racialized portrayal of the area and suggested that the same socioeconomic problems could be found in any number of white working-class estates. For Summa, education, crime, and health were not issues unique to

Kashmiris. The problem lay in how they were being addressed. While the government was well versed in tackling poverty and unemployment in white communities, Summa could not see any efforts being made for dealing with the specific problems faced by Kashmiris, and boys in particular.

When Changis had picked me up from the station earlier that day, he had spoken wistfully about the great tradition of Pothwari poetry. Mian Muhammad Bakhsh, Munshi Muhammad Ismail, Muhammad Khalil Sawib. Sufi poets of the late nineteenth and early twentieth centuries. As he drove me back to the station at the end of my visit, we passed a row of empty shops. Takeout boxes littered the side of the road. He looked out the window and shook his head. Like in Blake's poem mentioned earlier, a sense of hopelessness at the changing times hung in the air. An imagined past in Kashmir, innocent and idyllic, gave way to a violent present in Walsall. Yet the poet Changis venerated most—Mian Muhammad Bakhsh—was also writing about changing times. The Industrial Revolution that transformed Walsall and Bradford—and inspired William Blake—was in part driven by the same forces that occupied Mian Muhammad Bakhsh's thoughts a century and a half ago: the British Empire. He wrote:

جنس اپنی تھیں وچھڑے جہڑے نا جنساں وچ اؤ
کاہدا سکھ سواد اوہناں نوں، دم دم دکھ سواؤ

Jins apnī thīn vichṛe jeṛe nā jinsāṅ vic aye,
kāhdā sukh sawād ohnāṅ nūṅ, dam dam dukh suwāe.

Those who desert their own people will never know true pleasure,
Their sorrows will increase with each passing moment.

Mian Muhammad Bakhsh was in a sense also writing about looking within one's own community in the face of enormous external pressures and iniquities, and about failures of those in power to protect the people. Wasim and his friends, like Muna and like Zehshan Sajid, may have been less interested in Pothwari poetry than their parents, but living in the industrial decline of Walsall and Birmingham, their poetics were connected across time and space. The poetics of rap—by turns violent and comedic, self-aware and observational—bound them together when outsiders wanted to pull them apart: other gangs, yes, violently so, but also the more subtle forces of multicultural policies driven by an integrationist agenda. They value the poetics of rap in particular because, lyrically, it often parallels their own story and experiences on the streets of Britain. More than that, it glamorizes an otherwise unglamorous existence. Rapping on street corners and calling out the hypocrisies of the world around them on YouTube is their thing. Not their parents' thing nor their school's. Rap affords a sense of unity when all else seems against them.

CHAPTER FOUR

Multicultural Harmony?

The greatest advantage of the melas was that the multicultural people could see you.

CHANNI SINGH, of *bhangra* ensemble Alaap[1]

The wind carries sounds of the festival to me in waves, muffling and revealing different musical migrations to the city. Bhangra, kimono drums, reggae, Irish traditional. The sounds throb and fade as though picked up on their long journey from Pakistan or Japan or the Caribbean and are now pushing to be heard. Children with vivid pink clouds of cotton candy dart between strollers, seemingly invisible to parents distracted by the food stalls. Sheesh kebabs sizzle over hot coals, their charred smoke mingling with the sounds on the wind and the exhaust of an auto rickshaw, covered in decorations and chrome, puttering its way slowly through the crowd, its megaphone blaring Bollywood sounds and *kulfi* vibes.

I walk along the upper edge of the great field and look down toward the main stage of the festival. Juggy D—a British Indian R&B singer from Southall, London—is rapping, microphone pressed close to his mouth. He has sunglasses on. His body arcs forward over the lip of the stage, craning toward the crowd below. The audience, tightly packed, gestures back toward the rapper, mimicking his arm movements to the beat of the bassline. The young lads at the front have Pakistan flags tied around their necks, the dark-green and white crescent and star draping down their backs like capes. The sound system is struggling to compete with the blasts emanating from their matching green vuvuzelas.

If I turn my back to the stage, I can see the house I grew up in, shrouded by trees. Between me and the house, women in niqabs push their babies along the park path. One of the children has a helium balloon in the shape of a superhero. The balloon trails above their heads, bobbing as though it too is dancing to the music, catching up with the children when they stop.

The vuvuzelas are overpowering the music now. Security men and women in yellow high-visibility jackets gather at the edge of the crowd, speaking into their walkie-talkies, pointing at the teenagers. People around me are shaking their heads, muttering that they can't hear the music, though I don't recall them paying much attention before. Most of the crowd are now watching the young men with the Pakistan capes and vuvuzelas, who seem entirely unperturbed. They are having a great time. As Juggy D's set comes to a close, the audience begins to radiate outward, and the men in yellow jackets move in, toward the teenagers. The boys look over their shoulders at the approaching security, laughing, bumping each other with their fists. They move as one across the front of the stage in search of more entertainment. One of the boys climbs onto his friend's shoulders, glancing back at the guards. He points to the sky as he blasts a rhythm on his horn, cape fluttering behind him. The security men track them, trundling along behind. They maintain a distance, slowing as the boys stop, speeding up as they move again, like the balloon tethered to the child's hand. As the main stage becomes quiet, stagehands dressed in black reset for the next artist, and waves of sounds from elsewhere wash over me again. Another fresh kebab hits the grill, hissing smoke in the air. The bass of stages across the festival site creates a low booming noise while snippets of melodies, vocals, high rhythms, and laughter flitter this way and that, following the smoke away on the wind.

∴

It is 2010, and by the end of the weekend the *mela* will have seen over one hundred thousand people visit a part of Bradford—Bolton and Undercliffe—otherwise untouched by tourism: an area that, for the rest of the year at least, is located on the economic periphery of an already marginal city. As described in chapter 3, this was also a moment of peak multiculturalism, when public arts funding was at its zenith and South Asian arts in particular were being held up by funding bodies as a panacea to the perceived scourge of segregated communities. Such bureaucratic optimism in the arts would not last much longer. Within just two years, the festival would see its budget slashed, its programming fully assumed by the city council, its duration reduced to one day, and its location transplanted to the city center; it would be rebranded and absorbed into a more generalized Bradford Festival. By this point, many Mirpuris had long since begun to turn their faces—and ears—away from a festival that had become unrecognizable to how they understood and experienced *mela*s in Azad Kashmir, especially in terms of programming and organization. Instead— and perhaps unsurprisingly, given what will unfold in the ensuing pages— the Mirpuri community fell back on what they could rely on the most: their own systems of cultural and financial support, not just in Bradford but in Mirpur, where, as we shall see, *mela*s remain closely tied, in terms of social and religious function, to the shrine of Mian Muhammad Bakhsh in Khari Sharif.

∴

In this chapter, I look at this particular form of cultural migration—festivals—through a comparison of a *mela* in Khari Sharif on the outskirts of Mirpur with the development of the Bradford Mela over three decades in northern England. The migration of the *mela* brings to the surface several observations. Building on Abner Cohen's (1993) work on a similarly grass-roots festival (the Notting Hill Carnival, also started by one of Britain's post-war migrant communities), we see the process by which Kashmiri cultural practices became co-opted, then excluded, by multicultural arts initiatives that were ostensibly there to promote and celebrate the very diversity they stood for. Moreover, as already hinted at by the vuvuzela-toting teenagers, the carefully curated multicultural harmony of the festival often drew a veil over what became tightly controlled and regulated environments of inclusion and exclusion.[2] Within this, we witness a narrative of public investment and disinvestment, led by the vagaries of multicultural politics, that only reinforced a perception of cultural segregation.

The Bradford Mela has been held annually, in various guises, since 1988, and its journey since then closely tracks the ups and downs of the multiculturalism debate in Britain. I was at that first festival as a five-year-old and have hazy memories of teetering on my dad's shoulders, overwhelmed by the glow of bonfires and the noise of the crowd. It was nighttime, and that is about all I can remember. But the feeling of the people and the sounds and the smells and the dark night sky came back to me many years later, unexpectedly, at another *mela* several thousand miles away in Khari Sharif, Azad Kashmir. The word *mela* stems from the Sanskrit verb for "to meet" and is widely used to identify gatherings and fairs held at harvest time across South Asia and, more recently, in Britain[3]—moments to exchange goods and food as well as times of religious and secular celebration.

That first festival in Bradford came at a moment when, as we have seen, the city was at the center of scholarly and national debates about multiculturalism in Britain.[4] In response to the negative images of the city portrayed in the press, a group of students and activists held a small music and arts festival on playing fields above the city's university.[5] The idea was to celebrate the city's South Asian communities—broadly defined—and to engage a wider public with aspects of multiculturalism beyond newspaper headlines, curry houses, and taxi ranks. Within a few years, the Bradford Mela had transformed into the city's flagship multicultural event and moved to the larger Lister Park, and then Peel Park, where this chapter began—both areas with large Mirpuri communities situated on the margins of Bradford city center. Yet as the event grew, so too did the involvement of Bradford Council. With this came not only increases in budget but an increasing awareness of the potential utility of *culture* to act as a driver of integration. Organized now by the local council, the event began to morph from being primarily a grassroots South Asian arts festival to one that attempted to represent Bradford's wider cultural diversity, and with it an ever-shifting interpretation of what multiculturalism is and whom it should include. In the process, and as this chapter explores, the Bradford Mela drifted further and further away from the community it was there to represent.

Yet against this backdrop, today there are signs of change, even optimism. While many musical gatherings—such as Pothwari *mehfils*—take place unadvertised and hidden to those outside of the community, there are strong indications that generations born in Britain are reclaiming the cultural heritage of Azad Kashmir for themselves and are more confidently (that is to say, independently) organizing public-facing events such as poetry gatherings, recitals, and forums. In 2023, for example, the poet Nabeela Ahmed and linguist Farah Nazir, part of the newly formed JAAG Collective, participated in what was described as the "first Panjabi and Pahari-Pothwari Language and Literature Festival in the world" in Handsworth, on the outskirts of Birmingham. The event, organized by the writer and academic Kavita Bhanot, was sold out, keenly attended by members of the Mirpuri community, and packed with talks on topics surprisingly familiar to those at the heart of the old multicultural debate: language and belonging, music and poetry, oral histories, and genealogies, to name a few.[6] Yet the fact that community-led events such as these are taking place—deliberately so—separately from more centralized and official multicultural initiatives is striking, and no coincidence. This strategy of keeping local government at arm's length is not incidental to their success: these events are organized and curated *on their own terms* and thus cut from the integrationist strings of public money.

The history and development of *mela*s from Pakistan to Britain thereby show that the relationship between Mirpuris and the state is riven with contradictory narratives: that integrationist approaches to multiculturalism, even when well meaning, often ignore the complex ways in which Kashmiris orient themselves within multicultural spaces and across national borders. This is, in many respects, at odds with orthodox readings of multiculturalism that celebrate and privilege cultural pluralism and integration.[7] Yet, as we shall see, it also exposes a kind of exceptionalism at the heart of multicultural politics. Azad Kashmiris, perhaps more than any other migrant communities in Britain, face particular pressures to integrate and consequently are deemed especially in need of the public funding that the *mela* attracts. But the question of what exactly they are supposed to integrate with or to is often left hanging in the air.[8] As this chapter shows, the binary of *integration or segregation* breaks down when seen from the perspective of those at the heart of the debate, and this is especially visible when contrasting *mela*s in District Mirpur with their progeny: the multicultural Bradford Mela.

The Mela at Khari Sharif, Azad Kashmir

My own experience of *mela*s happened as a kind of reverse migration—first in Britain, then in Pakistan. A few months after I arrived in Kashmir for the first time, Mr. Khokhar and I drove to Khari Sharif, the resting place of Mian Muhammad Bakhsh. We picked up my *ustad*, Zulfikar Ali Khan, on the way. It was dusk, the end of the working day for most of those heading toward Khari Sharif, but not for Zulfikar, who had his *shehnai* wrapped in his pocket, ready to perform. As we approached the *darbar*, crowds of people lined the side of the road, gravitating toward the shrine. There was dust in the air, kicked up from tires and sandals, warm from the day's heat; red taillights glowed and horns blared as the crowd weaved between car bumpers. We parked in a large field. The twin green domes of Mian Muhammad Bakhsh's shrine were lit up, drawing people to its center (fig. 18). I could hear a harmonium in the distance and the *tak-a-tak* of *dhol*.

"You see, this is a real *mela*," Mr. Khokhar said, breathing in, looking toward the green dome. He was smiling as we walked away, clicking the alarm button on his key ring; the car's horn sounded, and the amber lights flashed.

We had been to Khari Sharif many times before during the day, to pay respects and pray at the shrines of Pir Shah Ghazi Qalandar Damri Wali Sarkar and Mian Muhammad Bakhsh. Back then, I'd had to shield my eyes from the sunlight, reflected everywhere by the brilliant white marble floors, illuminating the inner sanctums. The space had felt vast and open and radiant. Now, as Mr. Khokhar led us down into the *mela*, the sun had just dipped below the horizon, leaving a spectrum of light blue to dark. I had a faint memory of my first *mela*, in Bradford, almost three decades earlier. Or perhaps more a feeling than a memory. All these people in one place, the smells of street food, the air charged with familiar sounds on the wind.

The courtyard of the shrines was surrounded by market stalls with brightly colored plastic toys, clothes, ornaments, and crockery for sale—items I

FIGURE 18. The shrine of Mian Muhammad Bakhsh at Khari Sharif, Azad Kashmir.

had also seen in my *ustad*'s house just a few hundred meters away. There were stalls of grains and spices. An elderly man with a long henna-dyed beard, dressed in a *shalwar kameez*, his head covered with a white *topi*, sat behind sacks of chili powder, ground cumin, turmeric, and coriander. He shoveled measures of each spice into a clear plastic bag for Mr. Khokhar. "This is the best *garam masala*," he said proudly. He was in his element.

The avenues of stalls were packed with people moving shoulder to shoulder. As we made our way along the path, the sounds of the harmonium and *tabla* grew louder. We could hear shouts of "*Wah wah*," just like at the concert in Rochdale. We were moving toward the *qawwal*s. There was a small stage on which sat the musicians: two harmoniums, two pairs of *tabla*, a *chimta* player. The singers' voices were drenched in reverb as they sang couplets written by Mian Muhammad Bakhsh, whose grave was just a few feet away. They appeared to be midway through the performance; the crowd were on their feet, pressing the front of the stage. The lead *qawwal* began to sing a different couplet from *Saif-ul-Malook*, and the air erupted with banknotes, thrown up and onto the heads and instruments of the musicians like paper snowflakes in a night sky. The tempo increased, and the backing singers repeated the couplet over and over. At the front of the stage, a man wearing a green *topi* and scarf, the color of Pakistan and a symbol of Islam, held a thick wad of rupees. He turned perpendicular to the stage, first spraying each *qaw-wal* with individual notes like he was dealing a deck of cards, then throwing the whole wad up into the air at the climax. Behind him, I could see pockets of the crowd with their arms aloft, moving up and down in time to the *tabla*.

Zulfikar cocked his head to me: "*Challo*." Let's go. We pushed our way through the gathering toward the fringes of the *mela*. Here, where the surrounding trees met the fields, were smaller groups of musicians, unamplified. I recognized Zulfikar's ensemble. We greeted one another, shaking hands and embracing. By then it was deep into the evening. Zulfikar pulled out his *shehnai* and began playing *Rāg Kāfi*. He was joined by two more *shehnai* and two *dhol*. There were no singers, but as the musicians played, Mr. Khokhar leaned toward me, cupping his hand to my ear: "This is Mian Muhammad Bakhsh. He is playing *Saif-ul-Malook*." The Sufi poet, Mr. Khokhar explained, was being voiced by Zulfikar's *shehnai*, its poetic meter embedded in Mr. Khokhar's mind through the countless performances he had attended here at Khari Sharif. The reed of the flute was no longer separated from the tree, as in Mr. Zuman's workshop—we were back to where it had begun. The use of *Rāg Kāfi* in particular was also rich in symbolism for how it connected Mian Muhammad Bakhsh not only to that other great Sufi poet Bulleh Shah but to the longer lineages of *qawwal*s who performed his poetry, including the late Nusrat Fateh Ali Khan.

The *shehnai* was in its natural habitat, outside in the fields and trees, the reeds and the soil. Its sound carried over a great distance, the waves bouncing back off the walls of the shrine. It drew people and pilgrims toward us. Before long, a small crowd had gathered and sat around the musicians. This was an ad hoc performance; there was no program of events, and the audience coalesced around what they heard and what they saw. The *mela* was governed by sound, its organization decentralized, dispersed, and diffused among those who were there. At that moment, the wood of the *shehnai*, rooted in Khari Sharif, carried the voice of the *mela*.

Zulfikar quickened the tempo, and the *dhol* accelerated their rhythms. A man sat cross-legged in front of the musicians, swaying from side to side, his eyes closed. He got up and moved into the small clearing in front of the musicians, his head wrapped in a loose white turban (fig. 19). His hands aloft, he lost himself to the poetry, dancing, moving quicker, lost to his surroundings, moving higher and higher, the ground falling away, searching for spiritual ecstasy, reaching for *wajd*. Rupee notes began to float down from the sky. The sound of the *shehnai* and the pulse of the *dhol* were all encompassing. The performance reached its peak, and the disciple was caught by the crowd and carefully lowered back down to earth. Zulfikar looked around at the banknotes covering the ground and pursed his lips. It had been a good night.

FIGURE 19. Ustad Zulfikar Ali Khan in a white *shalwar kameez* performing
with his ensemble at the Khari Sharif Mela.

The crowd began to disperse toward musicians elsewhere while Zulfikar and his ensemble collected their earnings. We retired to a small house just outside the *mela* and drank glasses of bright-green Mountain Dew. Music at the *mela* in Azad Kashmir was loosely organized in terms of time and space but tightly focused on Sufi spirituality. There was no set program; the choices of poetry and *rāga* were instead determined by the expertise and long experience of the musicians and *qawwal*s, taking their cues from the crowds and interpreting their spiritual needs. This freedom of time and space was important for the performers, who would travel here from far and wide. It allowed them to adapt and respond to their surroundings, shaping the sonic and spiritual environment while also maximizing their exposure to audiences—and remuneration—at the right time and in the right place.

As we drifted back through the market stalls, the air now buzzing with small insects, the crowd had begun to leave, carrier bags full of gifts and mementos, minds full of memories. The *mela* at Khari Sharif was part of the much longer and wider tradition of festivals across the Indian subcontinent—a place to meet and exchange goods and receive spiritual nourishment. Zulfikar and his ensemble sat somewhere in between, interceding between the worldly and the divine.

The prevailing sounds were now the horns of motorcycles and cars. As we got back into Mr. Khokhar's white Toyota Corolla, I thought back to the *mela*s I had attended in Bradford. Something had gone missing in translation, it seemed to me then. I began to see why Mr. Khokhar and many other Kashmiris in the city might not take the Bradford Mela particularly seriously, or at least seemed to keep their distance. If this was the real *mela* for Mr. Khokhar, what was the Bradford Mela supposed to be? Who was it actually for when it was supposed to be for Kashmiris? The memories and feelings of the *mela*s I had attended over the years mingled in my mind but remained distinct, separated by time and, I realized, by purpose. A few months later, I would find myself back at the 2010 Bradford Mela, surrounded by over one hundred thousand people, but the memories of the Khari Sharif *mela* seemed farther away—a peculiar inversion as my more recent experience in Pakistan faded from memory in the face of multicultural inclusion.

Migrating the Mela

The first *mela* in Bradford emerged during a period of intense public scrutiny for the city's Kashmiri community. A few years earlier, in 1984, the head teacher of Drummond Middle School, Ray Honeyford, wrote an article for the *Salisbury Review*—a relatively fringe periodical committed to the repatriation of ethnic minorities—that provoked a national debate about multicultural education in schools. The debate became a lightning rod for anxieties about cultural segregation and integration. At the core of his critique were the same children I was going to school with: Kashmiri Muslims, students who, in his view, were not being sufficiently integrated into British society. The media spotlight intensified again in 1989 with Ayatollah Khomeini's infamous *fatwa* against Salman Rushdie and public burnings of the author's novel *The Satanic Verses* in the city center.[9] For some observers, the "Muslim community had gone from being culturally and politically invisible" to being "suddenly projected as a dangerous fifth column, subversive of western freedoms: a trojan horse in the heart of Europe with a deadly cargo of fundamentalist religiosity" (Lewis 1994, 2). In what came to be known as the Rushdie affair, this "politically invisible" community suddenly found themselves on the front pages of national newspapers. Writing in the *Telegraph*, Fay Weldon declared that "these primitive folk up North, these mad fundamentalists" were to blame, and that "our attempt at multiculturalism is dead. The Rushdie affair proves it."[10]

It was from within this environment of hostility toward the Kashmiri community that a former art gallery curator, Allan Brack, and local artist Dusty Rhodes organized a small street festival. Their idea was to celebrate Bradford's history of migration and to reinvigorate an area of the city—Manningham—that had been heavily stricken by deindustrialization. Their motivation was also strongly influenced by the local peace movement and antiracist activism in Bradford.

We'd both been campaigners against racism and fascism and in a way, doing the Festival and then the Mela was a continuation of how we saw the city politically and what the threats to the city were—the constant fascist threat, not just the organised fascism but also the low level racism. We lived through a period where black and Asian people on the streets of Bradford were being physically attacked.[11]

The following year, Brack and Rhodes were asked by Bradford Council's Economic Development Unit to expand the event and make it a citywide celebration. They met with Champak Kumar, who at the time was also an activist of the Bradford Asian Youth Movement, which he had organized to challenge the growing threats of racism and to oppose the activities of the National Front.[12] Champak persuaded Brack and Rhodes about the popularity of live South Asian music and its potential for social cohesion.

> They said, "we want to do a huge outdoor event. What could it be?" And of course I said, "A mela!" When people in India and Pakistan celebrate Diwali or Vaisakhi or Eid, they always call it a mela. And I used to see a lot of Bollywood films, and when they mentioned a mela in the films, you would see a fair, you would see colours, and you would see artists dancing in the films, and I thought mela is the key word to use.[13]

The festival was thereafter reimagined as a multicultural celebration of music, dance, visual arts, theater, cabaret, film, and poetry. Artists who performed at the *mela* were a mixture of local musicians and established international acts.[14] Skinder Hundal, who had been involved in the organization since its inception, described the two events that were held in 1988 and 1989 as crucial because, for the first time, they created a public space that countered the growing backlash against multiculturalism:

> The communities were taking ownership of their own destiny in promoting the arts and culture and making sure there was something there for the communities to enjoy and be proud of. There were only the daytimers, or the commercial shows, but there wasn't a collective space where all the communities came together, of all Asian origins—Pakistani, Indian, Bangladeshi, Sri Lankan—that was the point of the mela. It was a connecting point for all the South Asian communities to come together as a creative voice.[15]

Following the success of the first *mela* in 1988, the event moved to the larger Lister Park in the Manningham area of the city.[16] Faced with limited funding, the organizers relied on local volunteers to help build the infrastructure, manage the site, prepare food, and, after the event, dismantle the stages and clean up litter. Local Pakistani-owned businesses, such as the Mumtaz restaurant and Bombay Stores, sponsored the event while Bradford College art students gave a hand or provided decorations. As Rhodes recalls:

> We used to go into [Lister Park] a week or two before the event and start building the thing, and people that we didn't even know would come with huge tubs of curry and feed us because we were working to build the Mela. These were spontaneous gestures. There was just a real sense that the event was by and for the community, and anyone who had an idea could come along and join in.[17]

Before that first *mela* in 1988, the *bhangra* concerts organized by Oriental Arts had mainly been attended by members of Bradford's South Asian community. The *mela* was, in this sense, one of the first instances of a curated multicultural public—a space of musical and cultural encounter. There was also money to be made. The *bhangra* band Alaap was one of the first groups to emerge out of Bradford's early *mela*s and achieve widespread recognition. The band's founding member recalls the impact that performing at the Bradford Mela had on his career:

> The big [*bhangra*] bands were all at melas so I used to watch every band from backstage to gain experience, to see how other people perform, how they interact with people. [But] the greatest advantage of the melas was that the multicultural people could see you. By that I mean not only Asians but people who can't even speak Hindi or Punjabi language [and] who had no idea what bhangra is. . . . The melas really helped to boost our publicity.[18]

In 1998, the *mela* relocated to Peel Park, away from the Kashmiri community in Manningham. It was now attracting over 150,000 visitors from home and abroad, making it the largest *mela* in the UK and one of the biggest in Europe.[19] Bradford had also by this point seen new migrations to the city, not just from Mirpur but from Eastern Europe, especially following the accession of Poland in 2004 and Romania and Bulgaria in 2007. Situating itself in step with local and national arts policy and funding, Bradford Council encouraged the Bradford Mela's producers to shift the event away from being a South Asian arts festival per se to one that represented a wider range of musical communities.[20] The *mela* was, by this point, becoming increasingly outward looking, a move that was tied to Bradford council's own bid to become a European Capital of Culture in 2008. Paul Brookes, who led the city's bid, situated the *mela*'s multiculturalism at the heart of his pitch:

> The Mela was most certainly seen as a demonstration of something that brought together communities in a celebratory way. "Europe's biggest and best Mela" is how we described it. The multiculturalism that the Mela represents, the way the Mela was a symbol of some of that multiculturalism, was absolutely at the centre of the bid.[21]

As we shall see, at the heart of this shift was a self-conscious framing of multiculturalism as something that should be not only abstracted but *experienced* as socially inclusive and integrationist. Over the course of a two-day *mela*, over sixteen hours of music and entertainment were programmed. The programming of the Bradford Mela developed to include, inter alia, Chinese ribbon dancing, Irish folk music, *qawwali*, punk rock, *bhangra*, fusion, rap, and Komodo drumming. Attendees of the *mela* were also meticulously documented by organizers to demonstrate the festival's appeal to a wide variety of backgrounds, ethnicities, and religions—a point celebrated in reports commissioned by Bradford Council, even while young Kashmiris were identified as "troublemakers" and a problem for social cohesion.[22]

The perception of young Kashmiris as troublemakers was an undercurrent at meetings I attended with funding bodies and stakeholders, Bradford Council and West Yorkshire Police, respectively. During these meetings, discussions took place as to the kinds of artists that should be booked to represent different cultural interests. More revealing were the discussions about what acts *should not be booked* for fear of attracting the "wrong" crowd. These meetings, particularly with the council and other funding bodies, were held under a rubric of multiculturalism—that is, a desire to curate musical diversity—with decisions made based on what acts, booked using public money, could best articulate multicultural policy. These discussions were guided by the city council's cultural strategy, the Only Connect manifesto,[23] and Arts Council England's NI11 target to engage communities with the arts.[24] This was a highly selective process whereby migrant communities in Bradford would be identified, and then music to be performed at the *mela* would be selected for them, on behalf of them, to *represent* them. Indeed, the 2001 Bradford Mela was explicitly promoted by its organizers as "The World in a City."[25]

The Bradford Mela, in this sense, had become an explicit implementation of top-down multiculturalism, over a fixed period of time, within a carefully designed enclosed space. The festival's producer, Ben Pugh, explained to me that the festival site itself was designed so as to be an idealized articulation of multicultural policy:

> From the moment they walk into the gate the audience should feel like they're being transported into a different world. They're at a festival, a celebratory moment. . . . So when they go from the Mango Stage, they walk through the avenue of stalls toward the Sunrise Stage. And along the way, they pass a samba band playing and they see in the corner a guy doing a plate balancing act.[26]

Meetings between the production team and West Yorkshire Police also had a deep influence on the types of acts that were booked, as well as the general layout of the festival. These meetings were shaped less by government policy toward multiculturalism and more by demands made by the police based on their experiences of past *mela*s. Their principal concern during these meetings, dressed in the language of "prevention," was maintaining public order. The police officers quizzed the production team on how they would prevent large groups of young Kashmiris from gathering in one place.

These kinds of meetings, in which the focus of the council was on not the inclusion of the Kashmiri community in their multicultural vision but their active exclusion, had a longer history in the organization of the *mela*. Having taken charge of the festival for much of its history, in 2002 the Bradford Council made the decision to pass the organization of the Bradford Mela to a private contractor. This represented a significant shift in the production of the event, a move that fostered a sense of resentment at grassroots level. Up until that point, local people such as Alan Brack, Dusty Rhodes, Champak Kumar, and Katherine Canoville had, for the most part, organized the production of the Bradford Mela. Yet once the production of the *mela* was handed over to a private contractor, many of the event's local community initiatives were discontinued. Instead, the contractor outsourced the organization to a team of programmers and organizers from outside Bradford and built a festival program that was more heavily centered on pop music and R&B.

While the Bradford Mela still attracted over one hundred thousand people during this period, complaints were made about the programming of the festival. The strong emphasis on contemporary R&B and rap was blamed for attracting larger groups of young Mirpuris. Ironically, the complaints were also dressed in the language of multiculturalism. The festival had apparently become "monocultural" in that its programming was focusing almost completely on Pakistani pop and rap. Reports in the media also alleged that, rather than representing the tastes of Bradford's various populations, the festival was pandering only to the tastes of young Pakistanis.[27] In this sense, people were concerned with it becoming not only monocultural but also monogenerational. In the eyes of the media, the Bradford Mela was, in effect, becoming increasingly partisan, reflecting one demographic rather than all.

The backlash against this new way of programming the Bradford Mela can be read in several ways. In one sense, it provides a counterpoint to the "multiculturalism backlash" identified by Vertovec and Wessendorf that has occurred in the UK over the past two decades.[28] The underlying framing of the complaint—that the *mela* was pandering only to the tastes of young Pakistanis—was one of a desire for more multicultural inclusion rather than any historical claims to the *mela*'s heritage as a South Asian festival: as far as the complainants were concerned, the *mela* no longer represented all of Bradford's cultures. Or, in other words, the event was not multicultural enough. This counters the prevailing discourses against multiculturalism by politicians and the media and demonstrates that, for people living day-to-day lives in multicultural cities like Bradford, the policies of multiculturalism are issues that shape, affect, and organize their social lives.[29] It shows that for people in Bradford who attend the *mela*, music plays a more generally important role in cultural representation. In a departure from its origins as a festival aimed primarily at celebrating the city's South Asian communities, now it seemed that a "good" Bradford Mela would seek to represent all of Bradford's cultures; a "bad" *mela* would represent only one. In this sense, multiculturalism came to be understood as an equanimity between, and impartiality toward, any given culture. Yet this could only come at the active exclusion of the Kashmiri community, who, ironically, were at the same time being blamed for not integrating into British society.

..

In Bradford, Mirpuris live both socially and economically on the periphery of the city. The neighborhoods that a large proportion of Mirpuris live in are inner-city suburbs that have traditionally suffered from lack of investment and underdevelopment. The main businesses that Mirpuris work in or own—such as restaurants, clothes shops, and taxi ranks—are not to be found in the town center but in areas such as Manningham, Girlington, and Little Horton (all on the outskirts of Bradford). In a cultural sense, too, they were not included in the planning process of the Bradford Mela and are not represented in the production team.

Festivals and community celebrations are particularly important to migrant communities, as they have the capacity to symbolically constitute a renewal of the past in the present. In a 1976 UNESCO report on festivals and intercultural dialogue, G. S. Métraux argued that festivals provide a space for recalling cultural heritage, whether mythical or historical: opportunities when cultural, religious, local, and national identity can be reasserted and feelings of self-awareness and participation in common experiences reaffirmed. On one level, the Bradford Mela self-consciously aspires to this functional description: "participation in common experiences" is one of the explicit goals of recent government policies of multiculturalism (often expressed as "common values")—a kind of world-building view not lost on the *mela*'s organizers, who described the event as "an opportunity for communities to come together to celebrate and share their cultures."[30]

Yet, while the city council promoted the Bradford Mela as a unifying event and a celebration of the city's cultures, the reality on the ground is that the festival is a space of exclusion as well as inclusion. For Abner Cohen (1993), the development of the Notting Hill Carnival from a grassroots festival to a large, council-run event represented a creative expression of shifting power dynamics, symbolizing and embodying a fundamental tension between subculture and dominant culture.[31] In the context of Swedish folk festivals, Owe Ronström (1991, 16) observed that "festivals reflect ideas, but also produce, distribute and dramatise ideas. . . . Festival organisers thereby become controllers of political and ideological power."[32] In this view, music festivals are seen as inherently limited and controlled spaces in which aspects of social engineering can be tested and forms of social behavior cultivated.[33] The Bradford Mela is an interesting case in point. The festival is deliberately promoted and funded by the Bradford Council as a "multicultural" event that intends to "represent all of Bradford's communities."[34] However, within this carefully planned space of multiculturalism, Mirpuris are poorly represented both in terms of programming and at management level, as we shall now see.[35]

The 2009 and 2010 Bradford Melas

The evening was wearing on, and most of Mr. Khokhar's customers in the barbershop had left. Mr. Khokhar disappeared downstairs to make tea, and I sat with two of his friends, Muhammad and Asif, who were leafing through books of poetry. The corner TV was playing grainy footage of a singer performing Pothwari poetry. Muhammad looked up from his book and pointed to the TV.

"You know, Tom, this is traditional music. From Kashmir. This is what we grew up on back home. This is what we like to listen to, not this modern rap—that's for the young ones." Muna, Mr. Khokhar's son, stood under the

TV shaving patterns into a young customer's hair. He smirked. I asked Muhammad where he listened to Pothwari music.

"I've got some CDs that I listen to in the car. I'm a taxi driver over in Keighley, you see, so I have a lot of time to listen to music." He laughed.

Mr. Khokhar returned from the kitchen holding a tray of steaming hot tea, served in a delicate china teapot and teacups decorated with the same gold leaf and floral patterns I had seen in Kashmir. As he poured the sugary tea, I asked whether there were many Pothwari music performers in Bradford.

"There are some," Mr. Khokhar replied, "but the best performers are in Pakistan. Sometimes, you know, they come over and we put on concerts. Not just here, but all around. Rochdale, Birmingham, Keighley—all over. If not, then there are maybe two or three concerts a year. But in Pakistan there are lots of concerts. All the time concerts."[36]

"How about at the *mela*? Do you get to see much Pothwari music there?"

"Oh yes, there's lots of music at *mela*. You know, in Pakistan, there are lots of *mela*, and always lots of music." He laughed.

"Ah, I see," I replied, "but what about over here? Do they have much Pothwari music at the Bradford Mela?"

"Over here, not so much. I think last time there was a Pothwari program at [Bradford] Mela . . . it was 2000," he said, nodding. "We had singer from Pakistan come over, and he give big performance at *mela*. I sponsored him."

"Did lots of people come to watch?"

"Oh yes, lots of people. [It was a] big performance."

"So that was quite a long time ago, ten years. Have you been to the *mela* since?"

Mr. Khokhar thought for a moment and rubbed his jawbone. "No, I don't think so. You know, I am working here all the time, every day [laughs]. I went for Pothwari music, but the rest aren't real players. I work here every day. Muna takes a day off. I work every day and save money for Pakistan. One month every year I go to Pakistan. Only top players are from Pakistan."

I asked Mr. Khokhar whether it was possible to compare the *mela*s in Pakistan with *mela*s in the UK, like the Bradford Mela. Mr. Khokhar and Mohammad exchanged glances and rocked their heads slightly. Mohammad answered.

"Not really. You see, Tom, in Pakistan the *mela*s are different. The music they have there. . . . It's music that people listen to—very traditional. Over here they have all different kinds of music, you know? Modern music, rap. . . . It's not really stuff we listen to."

I pointed out that for the past two years, there have been *qawwali* groups performing at the Bradford Mela that he might like to have seen.

He pondered this for a moment but then shook his head and said that these were not "real players, only people from London." He said that the best players were from Pakistan or, to a lesser degree, places like Birmingham, Keighley, and Rochdale.[37] Despite Mr. Khokhar's reputation as a musician in Bradford and the popularity of Pothwari music among Mirpuris, he had never been asked to perform at the *mela*. When asked why this was, Mr. Khokhar replied simply, "I don't know why. No one asked me."

A few months previously, I had put the same question to Champak at Oriental Arts while he was in the process of programming the 2010 Bradford Mela. Champak was seemingly surprised.

"They [Mirpuris] listen to Pothwari music," he had said before putting me in touch with Mr. Khokhar. Champak knew, in a broad sense, that Pothwari music was popular among Mirpuris and that Mr. Khokhar was the man to speak to, but he was not aware that Mr. Khokhar himself was a musician. Indeed, despite Champak's expertise in South Asian music, he was not clear exactly what Pothwari music was, nor what it meant for Mirpuris in Bradford.

Over a combined total of thirty-two hours of performance time, only four thirty-minute slots were allocated to music that might loosely be described as best identifying with the musical tastes of elder Mirpuris—namely, the Hussain Brothers and Haji Ameer Khan, both of whom are professional *qawwali* groups based outside of Bradford.[38] There were no Pothwari ensembles. This represents a great disparity—or inversion—between the size of the Kashmiri community in Bradford and their musical "representation" at the *mela*.[39] As we shall now see, Bradford Council's influence over the *mela* effectively served to exclude Mirpuris from its vision of multicultural Bradford. Drawing on meetings with the council and the festival production team, we see how the council's desire for the *mela* to in some way reflect "multicultural Bradford" by representing each of the city's cultures through music became destabilized, especially as Mirpuris, as we saw in the precious chapter, tended to avoid top-down multicultural policies, and for good reason. Looking back, it should have perhaps come as no surprise that Mr. Khokhar, on that dusty road to Khari Sharif, with the shrine of Mian Muhammad Bakhsh on our horizon, would describe our destination that day as "the real *mela*."

THE 2009 MELA: MULTICULTURAL HARMONY?

The 2009 Bradford Mela began at twelve noon on Saturday June 13. I had only recently begun my first period of concerted fieldwork in my home city. It was with no small sense of trepidation that I had arrived back in my childhood home. With a critical eye and ear, how would I see and hear the city? How would it differ from my childhood?

As I walked through the gates of the *mela*, memories of past experiences came flooding back. On my way to the festival, I had passed my old schools, the parks I had played football in, and the local newspaper shop—Mr. Sheikh's—where I had worked, first as a paperboy, then as a shelf stacker. An ice cream van was parked at the festival entrance, still playing the same theme tune of the popular TV program *Match of the Day* (although now, the slightly worn-out loudspeaker was eerily out of tune). The church bells tolled; the muezzin sent out the call to prayer. There were other memories too: of being attacked and heavily beaten up in the same park I was now heading to. Of my bikes being stolen, of my house being burgled on numerous occasions, and of being racially abused. I was aware at this early stage of my research that all these past experiences would play a part in my fieldwork, but to what extent I wasn't sure. Still, it felt good to be back in the city.

I kick-started my fieldwork by volunteering for the festival's production team, led by Ben Pugh. I was eager to make the most of the opportunity to conduct research at such a large event, one that had loomed so large in my own childhood and one that, after all, would occur only once per year. I was also still trying to formulate the right kinds of questions about Mirpuris, multiculturalism, and music in Bradford. My work with the production team encompassed a variety of tasks, including manning information points, assisting stage managers, transporting artists on golf carts between stages, distributing security passes, transporting equipment and water, and, more generally, liaising between the general public and the production team. Becoming involved with these tasks brought its advantages but also limitations. It meant that I built up a detailed familiarity with the layout of the festival site, including where the stages were, where the food area was, and how the markets were organized.[40] Once the festival began in earnest, this knowledge and familiarity allowed me, in an informed manner, to observe how people moved around the site in relation to what types of music were on offer at the different stages. In addition to this, I had continuous and close contact with the artists and the public as they moved around the site. As I sped the artists between the production offices and the stages, I was able to snatch conversations and insights about their backgrounds, histories, and performances.

But working for the production team in 2009 also revealed some of the more exclusionary aspects of the festival. I was struck by the absence of any Kashmiris on the production and programming teams—something, I realized, that was only exacerbated by my own presence. Responsibility for my duties also meant a lack of freedom to wander around the festival site and absorb the different music on offer in my own time and at my own pace.

By midafternoon on the first day, Ben agreed that I could take time off from my responsibilities and explore the site on the condition that I carry a two-way radio with me in case I was needed. As I walked around the festival, I had the surreal experience of seeing the *mela* in progress as well as hearing the constant structural organization of the event through my radio earpiece—a kind of augmented reality, top-down and bottom-up multiculturalism in action. While I watched a band perform, I could hear the production team indicating how long was left and what the progress of the succeeding artist was. Switching radio channels, I was able to stay in touch with site security and the conversations about crowds and any instances of trouble that took place.[41] Over the weekend, I would see steel drums, bagpipe ensembles, a one-man band, stilt walkers, dancers, a puppet show, and a Rajasthani circus.

One of the main stages at the festival was run and curated by the local South Asian arts organization, Kala Sangam, which I described in the previous chapter. The organization, which is based in Bradford and funded by Bradford Council and the Arts Council England, describes itself as "encouraging and promoting community interaction through South Asian art collaborations."[42] Outside of the festival, the center teaches classes in classical South Asian music and dance (in its broadest sense), promotes music and instrumental lessons in schools, and offers work experience for young people.[43] For the *mela*, the center had similarly curated a program of North Indian classical music, traditional *bhangra* dancing, comedians, workshops, and poetry recitals.

The Kala Sangam marquee was located in the middle of the festival site—center stage, as it were—and was popular over the weekend with families and elder generations. The entire front curtain of the tent was removed, creating an open space covered by a canvas canopy; people would drift in and out as they pleased. Most would sit on the grassy floor in front of the stage while those just outside the tent's perimeter could stand looking in. Yet the openness of the tent also encouraged participation from groups of people who might not normally be inclined toward a particular act or performance. An example of this came during a show by an Indian comedian. Sitting on the grass in front of the stage were families with their children. Halfway through the show, a small group of Mirpuri boys entered the tent, sat at the front of the stage, and began to heckle the comedian. At one point, one of the boys jumped up and shouted into the microphone. The audience shifted uneasily while the comedian said, "All right, lads, calm down now." After a few minutes, the boys jostled their way out of the tent and moved on. As they did so, the man next to me muttered, "Fucking typical," shaking his head. It was a response I would witness again soon after.

North of the Kala Sangam stage, the topography of the park sloped downhill to two more stages, sitting back to back in an area called the Valley. The largest of these stages—the Sunrise Stage—was the 2009 festival's only large open-air stage. The Sunrise was sponsored and run by the local South Asian radio station, Sunrise Radio, and throughout the weekend it was hosted and emceed by the radio station's DJs while being broadcast live over the radio and internet. Situated toward the top of the festival, facing away from the main site, the stage looked out toward a natural amphitheater with the valley rising away from it. Crowds would either stand on a flat area directly in front of the stage or sit high up on the banking that provided an ideal view. Performing on the Sunrise were predominantly young South Asian bands and dancers, including the *bhangra* dancers Nachda Punjab, alongside *bhangra* fusion artists 2 Steps Ahead.

Watching these performances was a mixed crowd: young families, groups of teenagers, passersby, and elder generations gearing up to go home for the evening. At one point, the young families and elder generations were sitting high up on the natural amphitheater that looked down on the Sunrise Stage, while immediately in front of the stage was a large crowd consisting mainly of young teenagers. During the performance, the crowd surged forward, bringing down three segments of the barrier. The crowd spilled through, and some of the boys climbed up onto the stage, interrupting the performance. Security quickly intervened and restored the barriers, and the performance continued.

In a physical sense, the brief episode was a subversion of boundaries between performer and audience. The physical barrier between the stage and audience had been crossed and, in the minds of those who stood around me, a social barrier had also been broken. The social rules that denote what behavior is acceptable and what is not were suddenly brought into discourse as various people around me condemned the actions of the teenagers. A mother with her young family at her side turned to me.

"I'm not racist, but they [the organizers] knew that if they let them [young Mirpuris] get together like this then this would happen, but they didn't stop it."

As news of the event spread around the site, and through my earpiece, the story of the teenagers changed and metamorphosed. At its most perverted, the drama was described to me as a full-scale riot with mounted police charging through the crowd to suppress the unruly teens. When I put this incarnation of the story to a security guard who had been at the front of the stage, he simply replied, "Nah, it was nothing. Some fences came down, that's all." The disparity between these interpretations is indicative of some of the low-level tensions that exist in Bradford but that are papered over at the festival by its multicultural positioning of "inclusivity." With little on offer for young Kashmiris at the festival, it is no small wonder that they began to express themselves in ways that transgressed social boundaries. And yet these transgressions served only to further perpetuate their exclusion from future festivals, as we shall now see.

THE 2010 *MELA*: MULTICULTURAL DISSONANCE?

The 2010 Bradford Mela took place on Saturday, June 12, and Sunday, June 13, and came at a time of economic crisis in the UK. The economy was pulling itself out of a recent recession with an unprecedented amount of fiscal support from public funds. A new Conservative-Liberal Democrats coalition government came into power and immediately began implementing deep spending cuts in the public sector. Bradford Council alone faced funding cuts of £67 million, over two years, to its budget. As the main financial sponsor of the Bradford Mela, this had an immediate impact on the budget for the 2010 festival.

During a planning meeting for the 2010 event, Ben Pugh explained that budgeting for the *mela* had always been a difficult process, but the newly introduced austerity measures would be acutely felt. In most years, the official budget would not be approved until April, some two months before the festival weekend. This created logistic problems as artists and site contractors required contracts to be signed by the production team well before this. Such late approval had always created a degree of uncertainty for the production team, but Pugh explained that normally the council would eventually approve a budget of approximately £300,000. This would then be augmented with title and stage sponsors and retail space hire.

The economic aftermath of the 2008 financial crash put pressure on the festival budget over the years that followed. By 2010, the city council indicated to Pugh at an early stage that he should expect cuts of 66 percent (£200,000), which would effectively reduce the festival budget to £100,000. Pugh explained that for an event that attracts an audience of over 150,000 people (over two days), simply putting the infrastructure in place would absorb much of that revised figure. Aware that more money would have to be found elsewhere, the production team went about finding ways to deliver the 2010 event with a vastly reduced budget. In a meeting with Bradford Council, the production team, and Oriental Arts (who were responsible for much of the music and dance programming), it was decided that there would have to be cuts in the music budget.

In the months after this meeting, it was left to Oriental Arts to decide how to implement these cuts and what types of music should be prioritized and that "big-name acts" would have to be dropped from the program. Such acts could cost up to £10,000 to book, and there simply was not enough money to accommodate these fees, Champak explained. Instead, it was decided that more emphasis should be placed on local music acts, as this would allow the production team to both save money and meet the council's NI11 targets. Despite this resolution, however, a number of big-name bands were booked, and it was striking to observe which genres of music survived the cuts versus the types of music that did not make it into the program.

The overall site size of the 2010 *mela* was significantly reduced compared to the previous year. The biggest spatial change was the removal of the Valley area to the north of the site, behind the Avenue. The loss of the Valley also spelled the end of the two stages that were situated there in 2009: the Sunrise Stage and the Sunset Stage. The loss of the Sunrise Stage, in particular, left a large gap in the programming as this had traditionally been the stage on which big-name *bhangra* rap groups performed. The children's area was also reduced, with the Hive being replaced by a smaller marquee.

It was with music, however, that the biggest changes were made. The loss of the Sunrise Stage meant that many of the genres that appealed to young Mirpuris were cut from the program. In 2009, a long list of big-name *bhangra* rap artists had performed on both the Sunrise Stage and the main Mango Stage, including Jazzy B, Adeel, AG Dolla, Bombay Rockers, Jaz Dhami, Integrity Beatz, and RDB. At the 2010 festival, not one big-name *bhangra* rap artist was publicly advertised.[44] The only artist to appear on the program who fit that genre was Sham D—a young, up-and-coming singer from London—who ended up performing on the small Kiwi Stage in the corner of the festival.[45]

In terms of programming, then, virtually an entire genre was cut from the 2010 Bradford Mela. This represented a marked change in programming compared with the previous year, particularly if one considers that this genre—*bhangra* rap—contains the type of music that most appeals to young Mirpuris. Interestingly, one big-name *bhangra* rap artist did perform at the 2010 *mela* (fig. 20). Late on Saturday afternoon, Preeya Kalidas feat. Mumzy appeared on the Mango Stage as a surprise guest. I asked the event's programmer, Champak, why Preeya Kalidas had not been advertised in the program.

> You know, Tom, we've had them booked for a while and Mumzy said he would play as a favor to me. But you see, Tom, if we advertise him on the program, then he would attract a big crowd of youngsters, and they thought that sometimes they can get a little over excited [laughs]. So we thought, "OK, we'll have him as a surprise guest."

I asked Champak who "they" were. He replied, "I think it's the council and the police, you know. They are always worried [laughs]!"

FIGURE 20. As police watch, a crowd of young Mirpuris await surprise guest
Preeya Kalidas at the 2010 Bradford Mela.

It was clear from pre-festival meetings that cuts to the programming had
to be made, but it was revealing that those cuts fell almost exclusively on music that appealed to young Mirpuris, especially in light of the previous years'
complaints. This was rendered even more stark when a number of more established *bhangra* groups were sustained over both years despite the decision to
move away from big-name acts. The 2009 *mela*, for example, saw a headline
performance by Channi Singh, lead singer of Alaap, a group who pioneered
the *bhangra* genre in Britain the late 1980s.[46] The 2010 festival again gave its
headline slot to this genre, with the return to the stage of Alaap's rivals from the
1980s, Heera. Mr. Khokhar's son, Muna, gave short shrift to these bands when
he described them to me as "old timers' music." This change in programming
toward what can roughly be described as music that appeals more to elder
generations, especially within the Indian community, was also reflected in the
timing of the acts. Whereas at the 2009 festival the program grew throughout
the afternoon, with the main acts performing in the early evening, the 2010
mela saw the headline act appear at three p.m. on Saturday afternoon. The
acts that followed were slower paced, with less broad appeal. This resulted in
crowd numbers gradually reducing as the late afternoon progressed.

The changes in programming from one year to another demonstrate a subtle move away from music that directly appeals to young Mirpuris. The move

was ostensibly made under the veil of cuts to funding, but the sustentation of other genres and big-name acts, such as Alaap and Heera, suggest there were also other factors. The reluctance to advertise the surprise guest, Preeya Kalidas feat. Mumzy, was motivated by a concern over what might happen should large groups of their fans—young Mirpuris—gather to watch. As Champak explained, this anxiety lay primarily with the city council and the police but also pervaded the production teams, who, as previous chapters showed, were more geared toward Bradford's wider South Asian community. This shift was then compounded by the police's fear of large crowds, which was based not only on incidents at previous *melas* but also on a kind of received wisdom that large groups of young Mirpuris would inevitably cause trouble, and panic would ensue. As Elias Canetti famously wrote, it is "the destructiveness of the crowd [that] is often mentioned as its most conspicuous quality. . . . It is discussed and disapproved of but never really explained" (1973, 19).

The public order concerns of the police raised in the wake of the 2009 *mela* seeped into the layout of the 2010 festival site. More stages were added and spaced out around the site with the public aim of encouraging more movement and diversity, but, as Pugh explained while showing me around the site, this was motivated by a desire to disperse crowds of teenagers.

> In recent years we've moved away from a large outdoor arena-type stage to something that is a more intimate environment. People don't want an event which is an intimidating pop concert/arena-type environment. You put a crowd of ninety thousand people in front of a stage, and however positive and happy they are, there's still something intimidating about that; it's not an environment for family audiences. So what we've done is taken away the big structures, made the structures less intimidating, and it changes the atmosphere on site.

Despite the language of intimacy and inclusion, the way in which the festival site was organized was deeply influenced by police concerns about large groups of Mirpuri teenagers.[47] Such crowd engineering demonstrates that within a multicultural rhetoric of "openness" and "inclusivity" are hidden concerns about how people move around the site. The move from large, open stages to smaller but more numerous tents stems not only from the council's desire to include more communities but also from a fear of large groups of young Mirpuris gathering in one place. As this aspect of festival design was put into effect, festival organizers used a kind of doublespeak to describe the layout. It became less about young Pakistanis hell-bent on causing trouble and more about being part of the council's broader multicultural policies of inclusion and "something for everyone" approach. It shows how, in many ways, the concerns of the police and the concerns of the council's multicultural policy coincided.

Crowd engineering at the *mela* highlighted the tension between the council and organizers' ambition to create multicultural spaces within which people of different ethnicities and faiths could congregate, and their fear of what might occur when they did. It shows that despite the overtones of inclusivity and openness emanating from the production team and council, there was, nevertheless, a clear idea of how people were expected to behave, interact, and move around the site. Indeed, it could be argued that the layout of the site was specifically designed to encourage a kind of cultural world tour whereby festivalgoers moved around and sampled little tasters of Bradford's different cultures. Implicit in this layout, then, was an ordering of culture. Music from a wide variety of cultures were neatly placed at various points around the site, ready to be encountered by the general public. The inclination to fragment and disperse Mirpuri youth in the name of "multicultural harmony" demonstrates a more fundamental essentialization of culture and faith that was manifested through increasing methods of control.

From a young Mirpuri's point of view, the Bradford Mela was still an event to go to and, with its overtones of inclusivity and "something for everyone," they would be justified in thinking that the *mela* was also something for them as Bradfordians. Champak was aware of this tension, even as he felt there was nothing he could do to address it.

"You see, Tom, the problem is, whatever you are programming, they [young Mirpuris] will still come, but there is nothing for them! So they go around, cause trouble. It's sad."

The "trouble" that Champak referred to was the visible and often audible teenagers with whom I began this chapter. These young Kashmiris—mostly boys but also a number of girls—wandered around the site carrying their vuvuzelas and air horns, the flag of Pakistan tied around their necks, stopping in front of stages and assessing the music on offer (fig. 21).

Whereas at the 2009 *mela* a number of teenagers were heavily criticized by festival attendees for transgressing the physical barrier between stage and audience because they interrupted a *bhangra* rap performance, the same teenagers now came under renewed criticism for a different type of transgression. With a lack of music that appealed to them, young Mirpuris expressed their dissatisfaction by interacting with performances with the loud, resonant, monotone of the vuvuzela, cutting across the crowd and the stage—in some cases overpowering the sound system—before then moving on.[48] The antagonistic way in which the public reacted to the teenagers was reinforced by the presence of a significant number of police officers, who stood nearby. On several occasions the police, holding large

FIGURE 21. Teenagers with the Pakistan flag at the Bradford Mela.

video cameras, followed the teenagers around the site, recording their behavior. While there was little on offer for young Mirpuris onstage, they
nevertheless remained the focus of attention offstage—be it through the
watchful gaze of the police or through the castigation of other members
of the audience.

Centralizing the *Mela*

More recent years have seen further transformations of the *mela*. Since the
2008 financial crisis, arts organizations in Bradford, and elsewhere in the
UK, continued to suffer massive funding cuts. Traditional sponsors and
programmers of the festival, such as Kala Sangam and Oriental Arts, not
only have endured cuts to their funding but were also squeezed out of the
festival's organization. In 2011, the Council reassumed full control, reducing
the festival to a single day rather than its traditional full weekend. To make
matters worse, following a torrential downpour of rain, the plug was pulled
on the 2012 *mela* the day before it was due to begin. The financial losses sustained through this late cancellation provoked the local council to rethink
its cultural strategy.

During this period (2011–12), the city center's Centenary Square—an area directly in front of the grand Victorian Town Hall—underwent a £24 million transformation and became rebranded as City Park. Gemma Wilkinson, Bradford Council's major events organizer, explained to me that while central government funding cuts had fallen in other departments and areas, the major events budget in Bradford had remained stable. Despite this apparent stability in funding, the previous two years' trouble with rain and the newly redeveloped City Park meant that centralizing the festival (both organizationally and geographically) became a priority. In 2013 and ever since, the Bradford Mela moved further away from its roots and was restricted to a single day in City Park, preceded now by the newly reintroduced Bradford Festival—a move that took the festival away from its traditional home in Peel Park. There has, in other words, been further political and geographical centralization of the festival. The impact of this centralization rippled down through the arts organizations and was felt at the grassroots level. As Wilkinson explained to me,

Our [new] festival is a mishmash. We've retained a music element, so there's a stage and music. Street theater is a big element. We've gone for the street theater and music, foods on offer, and potentially an arts market as well. And other activities, fringe activities. . . . Just to give you an example, we had Demon Barbers. They recently won the BBC 2 Folk Awards. We had Edward Niebla, who's a flamenco guitarist. We had a calypso band. A real mix that kept people down there for the afternoon. On the Sunday, on the *mela* day, we had a "world" kind of feel, so we had the Taiko drummers. We did have the Bollywood Brass, but we had the Taiko drummers, and a whole mix of things.[49]

This steady dilution of South Asian music at the festival—even while retaining the name *mela*—left the local arts organizations reeling, a feeling acknowledged by Wilkinson:

There's a sense of, with some of those organizations, of "Why is the council running the festival and why aren't we running the festival?" And there's a whole history there. The council is the major funder, at the end of the day.[50]

Large, publicly funded South Asian arts organizations, like Kala Sangam and Oriental Arts, who interact between the state and communities in Bradford have dominated the South Asian musical landscape in the UK's cities over the past two decades. These organizations—set up by South Asian communities who, in Bradford, have often distanced themselves from Mirpuris and are generally considered better integrated—have enjoyed substantial funding through the Arts Council and Bradford Council. The examples above provide a brief insight into the role of local government as it attempts—successfully or otherwise—to create multicultural spaces in Bradford. Entwined within these discussions are competing narratives of money; centers and peripheries; agency and affect; and undertones of a general distrust of power. This is not a unique position for arts organizations in the UK, and it is certainly not the first time the arts sector in general has experienced funding cuts.[51]

What the discussion above brings into focus are some of the nonfinancial implications of funding cuts for tertiary (i.e., nongovernment and noncouncil) arts organizations, which have previously played a key role in state-led community cohesion initiatives. Public funding in the form of government subsidies allowed the *mela* to expand and attract internationally renowned artists while, importantly, retaining a policy of free entry for the public. The rise and success of the *mela* also coincided with the Mirpuri community becoming more firmly established and culturally confident in Bradford's social landscape. Yet, this success also brings with it a sense of disempowerment and disenfranchisement for those at the grassroots level, particularly Mirpuris, as musical programming and organizational autonomy are taken out of their hands by those holding the purse strings.[52] And so the issue of public funding is full of ambiguities and often viewed suspiciously by many Mirpuris. Public spending cuts have focused attention on the *mela* and contributed to a discussion and argument about what the event is for.

Cultural Self-Sufficiency

Ironically, some of the external prejudices directed toward the Mirpuri community—that they are self-segregating, isolationist, and generally not integrating into society—have meant that they escaped relatively unscathed from the kind of funding cuts experienced by broader South Asian arts organizations such as Kala Sangam and Oriental Arts.[53] As one moves through Bradford today, Mirpuri musicality is both audible and visible: the city's curry houses have the constant hum of Bollywood music in the background; a mixture of Imran Khan and the late Nusrat Fateh Ali Khan often accompanies a late-night taxi ride;[54] barbershops in Manningham form a nexus in which musicians coalesce to organize Pothwari poetry evenings; on street corners, rap music is used to mark out territories from rival gangs; in schools, despite a growing anxiety among teachers about music's permissibility in Islam, young Mirpuris are utilizing recording studios to create their own musical theater in the form of "hip-hoperas"; and in youth centers, rap workshops are organized by social workers to discuss crime, education, racism, and religion.

As seen in the previous chapter, the latter of these examples—rap workshops—are complex spaces of music-making because, like the *mela*, they also involve heavily mediated interactions between young Mirpuris and the state. Like the *mela*, these rap workshops are carefully designed spaces and are seen by the city council and the Local Education Authority as a way to engage with perceived "problem teenagers." Rap music in this context, then, is not just about subaltern resistance (as is often thought to be the case) but represents a civilizing project. The council utilizes rap music as a social force to "connect" young Mirpuris with other young people across the city, with an agenda of countering the kind of racial segregation highlighted in antimulticulturalism discourses.[55]

Lacking any particular representation among local arts organizations, elder Mirpuris have instead long organized their own concerts outside of official channels—arts organizations, NGOs, the *mela*—such as those described in chapter 2. Pothwari poetry gatherings are funded with Mirpuris' own structures of finance, visa support, marketing, and venues. Incidentally, financial self-sufficiency, volunteerism, and community-led organization are all virtuous hallmarks of the kind of big-society/small-state cosmopolitics of the UK government around the time of the 2010 *mela*.[56] From the perspective of elder Mirpuris like Mr. Khokhar, patronizing performances of Pothwari sung poetry (*sher khavani*) is important because it establishes and reaffirms ties and senses of belonging with Mirpur, not with grand visions of multiculturalism. For musicians who are visiting from Pakistan, many of whom will have performed and been recruited at the kind of Kashmiri *mela* described above, the degree to which they are looked after and patronized means that they will return to Kashmir and the Punjab with stories of their host's generosity. These stories circulate widely, affecting the host's standing in both Pakistan and England.

And yet this patronage is not primarily about economics but a poetics of the migratory experience that finds no voice in official policies of multiculturalism. During a Pothwari performance, for example, Mirpuriness is continuously performed through the audience members showering the musicians with banknotes for all to see. The showering of money, followed by the reading out of patrons' names and the emotional cries of approval (*Wah wah!*), are all part of asserting levels of cultural connoisseurship under the constant scrutiny of those who are there. Pothwari concerts, as we have seen, are intimate, cosmopolitan spaces of Mirpuri male subjectivity in which levels of status are won and lost, the ramifications of which are felt across the city and beyond, in Azad Kashmir.

Yet, despite these diverse examples, ignorance of Mirpuri cultural practice runs deep elsewhere in the city in a political climate dominated by anxieties surrounding Muslims. Notwithstanding the fact that Mirpuris possess strong senses of community and fiscal responsibility, give money to charity as a matter of course (*zakat*), and look after their elderly at home, they are Muslim and are thus defined in public debates by the negative, stereotyped connotations that label brings. They are consequently deemed to be particularly in need of the kind of connections and articulations with the outside world that events such the *mela* supposedly brings, and with it civility, integration, and cultural status. We have already seen how selective and partial such multicultural civility is and how exposed it is to the vagaries of funding (and its sudden withdrawal). Mirpuris evidently have had good reasons to keep their distance from the *mela*, or not to participate energetically. And this distance may not simply be about a desire to remain isolated and traditional. In fact, music, along with sport and cuisine, suggests quite the opposite: that Mirpuris live highly cosmopolitan lives. But this is a cosmopolitism that is not always easy to see, at least to eyes conditioned by the conventional multiculturalism model.

∵

Since 2013, the British government's Department for Digital, Culture, Media and Sport has run a nationwide competition, once every four years, to elect a new UK City of Culture. The stated mission of the program, and bear with me here, is to "level up opportunity across the UK—using culture as the catalyst for investment in places to drive economic growth and regeneration, promoting social cohesion and instilling pride in places and making them more attractive to live and work in and visit."[57] I will attempt to parse that in just a moment, but the upshot is this: the city that most compellingly makes the case that it needs "leveling up" is rewarded, for one year, with the title of UK City of Culture. It is also granted exclusive use of the competition's trademark and branding. As an indication of how deep cuts to arts funding have been in the years since the 2010 Bradford Mela, however, government guidance for potential bidders makes it clear that while "the title itself does not come with automatic funding," they will help with "brokering relationships with arms-length bodies from the BBC to Arts Council England."[58] It is up to host cities, in other words, to make the most of the invitation to "level up." At the heart of their proposals—and indeed the scheme itself—prospective cities are asked to set out their "vision for culture-led regeneration." On May 31, 2022, Bradford was announced as the winning city for the 2025 title, amid much well-deserved fanfare in the local and national media. Speaking to the BBC, the artist Shanaz Gulzar, who led the bid, described the award as a "huge opportunity" and a moment for Bradford's "young, ethnically diverse population . . . to become leaders and changemakers and begin a new chapter in our story."[59] It was once more unto the culture-as-integration breach.

While the wording in the quotes above may have changed (slightly) since the days of the Bradford Mela, the well-worn formula of mobilizing "culture"—fuzzily defined—as a means of "promoting social cohesion" should be strikingly familiar by this point in the chapter. (My choice of words here is not incidental: in its guidelines for the competition, the government explicitly states, "We do not want to prescribe what constitutes culture and we encourage each bidder to define their own culture").[60] As ever, it will be up to local government and publicly funded arts agencies to deliver on the promise of urban regeneration and articulate what it understands "culture" to *look and sound like* as it does so. We have already witnessed Bradford Council and its chosen arts organizations' attempts at trying to engage with—and represent—its largest minority community through this thing called "culture": indeed, we have seen that an agenda of multicultural integration has often led to the opposite outcome. At the time of writing, it remains to be seen what effect the UK City of Culture 2025 title will have on Bradford and the Mirpuri community. There are some reasons to be optimistic. The track record of previous awardees has been impressive, at least in economic terms: since Hull was awarded the title of UK City of Culture in 2017, the BBC reported that five million people attended events, generating £200 million of investment and 800 new jobs.[61]

And yet the specter of previous experiences—like those described above—never seems too far away. In the aftermath of the JAAG Collective's festival celebrating Punjabi and Pahari culture in 2023, I spoke with Awais Hussain, a young British Mirpuri from Bradford. Hussain, who is about to embark on a PhD at the University of York, is working (along with the Pakistani scholar Saeed Ahmed) on the first full English translation of *Saif-ul-Malook*: a work comparable in size and scope, Hussain proudly pointed out, to Homer's *Iliad*. Hussain is also the founder of Mirpur Heritage, an organization, founded in 2019, with over four thousand members and focused on preserving and celebrating the history and cultural heritage of the Mirpur region, especially among Mirpuris in places like Bradford. Young Bradfordians like Awais Hussain, and the work he is doing, are precisely the kind of citizens and initiatives one might expect to be foregrounded during Bradford's year in the cultural limelight. But not so fast. Awais and I were reflecting on the success and popularity of the JAAG Festival among British Mirpuris, and I said, almost in passing because it seemed so obvious, "This must be an absolute shoo-in for the Bradford City of Culture 2025." To which he replied,

"I don't know much about that really, to be honest with you. No one's been in touch."

ENGLAND

History is now and England.
T. S. Eliot, "Little Gidding"

We all have lives that go on without us.
I've a cricket-me who didn't stop—like that
was that, when my bat had felt as heavy as England
and I took no wickets while the coach stood in my net
in the second and final trial for Warwickshire.
A bear and staff on my jumper, perhaps later . . .
But those butterflies. Life forks and stops
where another follows on. England's Moeen
Ali went to my school. His dad's from Dadyal.
Mine's up in the village over the bridge.
I don't know if he knows what I do now.
Dad I mean. We all have lives that go on
without us. Unwritten. I have history on grounds

I've not played on. Grace Road. The Oval. Eden
Gardens. We all have lives that go on without
us. It matters where the line breaks. I knew
I should pursue this future—that was almost
behind me, at the woods' edge, a realm between
weathers, where losses and times fold, at the crease—

clueless as to what it was. Or for who.

ZAFFAR KUNIAL

CHAPTER FIVE

New Poetics

When I went to visit Zaffar Kunial in late 2019, it was just a few days before Christmas. He was living in Hebden Bridge, a bucolic market town in the Upper Calder Valley in Yorkshire. Hebden Bridge is only about fifteen miles from Bradford but in many respects feels a world away. The town, known for its bohemian atmosphere and socially activist community, sits at the bottom of a sloping green valley, surrounded by woods and fields. Flowing through its center is the Hebden Beck stream, which passes under old stone bridges on its way to the River Calder and the Rochdale Canal. The stream is a quirk of the town's geography and supplied the clean and continuously running water that helped drive its nineteenth-century textile industry. Like in Bradford, the town's industry declined in the latter half of the twentieth century, and, like Bradford, the area saw the arrival of new migrants during the 1970s and 1980s. Unlike Bradford, however, Hebden Bridge's new arrivals were primarily white, lower- to middle-class artists from within England: writers, hippies, musicians, alternative therapists, and smatterings of New Age activists. Today, during the summer months, Hebden Bridge is home to folk festivals, arts fairs, and lively open-mic nights. It's a close-knit community; people tend to know one another.

On the day I took the train from Bradford, over and under the Pennine Hills, passing through the similarly postindustrial town of Halifax, Christmas festivities were already well underway. It was late afternoon, already dark, and the town was draped in the soft tones of Christmas lights. Shoppers, buried under scarves and hats, laden with bags, bustled over cobbled streets in search of a restorative drink. A choir sang in the town square, and I could see my breath in the night air. Zaffar met me in a small bar away from the main drag, chosen primarily as one of the few places free from Christmas decor and shoppers. He ordered us two pints of ale, and we settled into a corner table. I had first contacted Zaffar over Twitter only a couple of weeks earlier. I'd been in Qatar at the time, meeting with

Kashmiri migrant workers. Sitting in a small café in Doha, Zaffar's poem "England" (overleaf) had appeared on my Twitter feed and stopped me in my tracks.[1]

The poem struck a chord with me in the Gulf for three reasons. The first was thematic. I had just finished playing cricket on a dusty construction site in Doha. The men I was playing with had, like Zaffar's father in *England*, traveled far away from their homelands in search of greater economic fortune. The game of cricket had begun at 5:30 a.m., before the heat of the sun hit and before the men would begin their shifts constructing Qatar's sporting infrastructure ahead of the 2022 Football World Cup: seven days a week, low pay, barely any rights.[2] These early, break-of-day cricket sessions constituted one of their few moments of escape from the hardship of work and the emotional pain of being separated from loved ones back home. Like in Zaffar's poem, their lives had, in their own ways, also forked, away from families left behind in Pakistan. Yet I felt in Zaffar's verses an almost inverted sense of distance. Of being left behind in England, remaining in *his* homeland, where he was born, just as another life—his father's—carried on in *his* homeland, Pakistan, a different world on another continent that may as well have been another planet, without his son. Reading the poem in that small café after the game of cricket, I felt a lasting sense of "what if" running throughout the verses. What if he had been selected to play for Warwickshire County Cricket Club? Would his father have stayed? Would he have opened up more about his life in Kashmir, the world he could not resist returning to? His father's life has gone on without his son just as Zaffar's own unlived life, like a ghost, plays on at the Oval cricket ground in England. A kind of unlived memory. What if it had played out differently, he seems to ask, if time were to unfold itself, and its losses reversed?

The second reason arched back to the poem's title and epigraph. It reminded me of my own invocation of another one of T. S. Eliot's poems that, at that moment, I was incorporating into what would eventually become chapter 2 in this book: "One of the low on whom assurance sits; as a silk hat on a Bradford millionaire." In Zaffar's *England*, he opens with a line from Eliot's "Little Gidding": "History is now and England." The line comes from a passage of "Little Gidding" that deals with moments of destruction and renewal. The passage begins, "What we call the beginning is often the end; and to make an end is to make a beginning. The end is where we start from." Eliot was in one sense writing about the destruction—cultural, physical, and spiritual—wrought by World War II, the same destructive loss of life that eventually led to the migration of so many men like Zaffar's father from Azad Kashmir to Britain. Yet Eliot's sense of loss is framed by an emergent tinge of hope: that the twentieth century's darkest moment—when history itself was on the eschatological brink—should instead precipitate new ways of being; when, in Eliot's words, the fire and the rose are one. This thematic allusion—of beginnings and ends, decline and renewal—runs through Zaffar's own sense of England, becoming intertwined as a kind of poetics of migration. To leave and to arrive. To leave again. For Zaffar, cricket appears to offer its own kind of spiritual escape, or at least echoes the kind of hope at the heart of Eliot's work, its own path out from inner turmoil. In Zaffar's poetics, the cricket bat—his path of hope out of all this—nevertheless felt *as heavy as England,* an idea more than a place, where belonging is ambiguously understood, jealously guarded, and poetically concealed. The sense of a home away from home, I could see, was more complex, more often at cross purposes, more charged, than I had perhaps been assuming in my current thinking about Kashmiri migration.

The third reason spoke to me in the eighth line of the poem. His father was from a village near Dadyal, an area I had visited just a few years before. In the poem, his dad was now "up in the village over the bridge" from Dadyal. As I reread the line, memories of traveling through this area, just north of the Mangla Dam in Azad Kashmir, came back to me. I had been with my *ustad,* Zulfikar Ali Khan; I had crossed that bridge. I distantly remembered the blue sun-bleached steel girders high above the Poonch River. We crossed it, I remembered, from the Dadyal side because we were on our way to Islamgarh to play at the wedding I described in chapter 1. But the poetics of Zaffar's bridge seemed to lead both there and elsewhere; away from himself, away from England; it was a bridge his father had crossed, away from his son. "Here, the intersection of the timeless moment," Eliot wrote elsewhere in "Little Gidding," "Is England and nowhere. Never and always." These lines—of love and loss, journeys and paths—reminded me of the poetics of that other great Kashmiri poet Mian Muhammad Bakhsh, something Zaffar's father would surely have recognized. Yet for his own epigraph, Zaffar had reached instead for the enduring Englishness of T. S. Eliot. I wondered about the significance of this—whether it had also been on Zaffar's mind.

I sent him a message on Twitter suggesting we could perhaps meet up when I returned from Qatar. He responded immediately and warmly. I put down my phone and quickly bought up as many of his public works as I could find, then spent my own journey home reading it all as closely as possible.

∵

Zaffar Kunial is a British poet, born in Moseley, a suburb to the south of Birmingham, to a Mirpuri father and an ethnically white British mother. His father migrated to Britain from the Mirpur area of Azad Kashmir along with many other men of his generation, such as Mr. Khokhar and Shakoor. Yet Zaffar's father had returned to live permanently in Kashmir, leaving his family in Britain behind. Zaffar had only faint memories of his father's village in Kashmir, a place he had visited as a child. On the final page of his collection of poems, *Six*, is a grainy photograph of him as a young boy, dressed in white *shalwar kameez*, playing cricket. Zaffar is running in at the peak of his bowling action, left arm raised to his chin, right arm raised above his head, eyes fixed down the pitch. His body is sideways to the camera, left leg off the ground. You can sense the movement and the momentum. In the right side of the frame are three *gharay*—clay pots used in performances of Pothwari sung poetry but here lying in wait for cooking. The photograph— the last word in this collection of poetry—is captioned "Barefoot in Kashmir, holding a stone wrapped / in cloth." What one sees isn't always as it appears, and what looks outwardly soft and delicate can sometimes shroud a hardened core.

Zaffar is an acclaimed poet, published by Faber & Faber and short-listed for numerous international awards.[3] On the day we met in his hometown of Hebden Bridge, he was generously welcoming and inquisitively shy. As we sipped our pints, he wanted to know about my travels and time in Azad Kashmir. I showed him the silver one-rupee coin given to me by my *ustad* on top of the Kashmiri mountain. I described the Mangla Dam, how the waters recede each year to reveal the sunken town of Old Mirpur. I described traveling through Dadyal and crossing the bridge over the Poonch River. I showed him a photograph of what I thought was his father's village, taken from the other bank, looking across the water. He smiled, then frowned, then said, "Yes, maybe." We looked at some photographs of me in my *shalwar kameez*—just like the ones he wore as a boy in Kashmir—playing cricket on a dusty field by the same river. I told him more about my *ustad* and how we would travel around Azad Kashmir playing at weddings, often those of British Kashmiris. I told him about my own childhood in Bradford. He told me about growing up in Birmingham. I described my trip to Walsall and meeting the young rappers. I showed him the photographs from the Belle Vue Studio, images of Kashmiri men his father's age, posing in their bus drivers' uniforms while holding crisp five-pound notes. I described to him, essentially, the contours of this book, without really knowing that was what I was doing.

I told him about Mian Muhammad Bakhsh and his shrine at Khari Sharif, and I showed him some of my clumsy translations. We thought through the ambiguity of words and meanings. Something in Zaffar became activated. He had listened attentively to everything I had said before getting up to fetch our second pints. He had been interested in what I was saying, the places I described, the pictures I had taken. But it also wasn't *him*. For so much of his life growing up in England, because of his name, because of his complexion, so many people—teachers, friends, colleagues, strangers in the street, his own father—had assumed it was. But it wasn't. His life had to a large extent been shaped by these outside perceptions while, in his words, the "memories that seem to hold me the most are in green pockets, in gardens, parks bits of woodland. Perhaps it's time's green pockets, as much as Moseley's."[4] Not Kashmir, but England.

This dynamic—between surfaced and concealed meanings, memories, migrations past and present, memories of hope and loss, the feeling of presence and absence—drive much of Zaffar's own poetry and became animated when we started talking about poetic translation. By pulling apart these forces in his work—word by word, playing with their ambiguities, revealing their contrasting meanings—Zaffar is writing about himself, but he is also writing about England, a place, as we have seen throughout this book, with a muddled purpose, unsure of how to reconcile all these competing identities, its multitude of cultures driven by migrations from near and far; a place at turns haunted by and proud of its colonial past.

∴

In his poem "Hill Speak" (overleaf), Zaffar takes this linguistic and historical curiosity and applies it across his own native language—English—and the language of his father, Pothwari. He examines words, exploring their multiple meanings to imaginatively explore his multiple pasts and unlived futures. Poetry, in this sense, bridges the distances between different cultures, different histories—the forks in the road driven by migrations gone by. I read the poem for the first time on the airplane back from Qatar, just as I was trying to make sense of all the materials I had gathered over the previous ten years in Pakistan and Britain, all the people I had met, their lives across continents, across cultures, across histories. Somewhere deep in my subconscious, I was formulating how to structure this book, and as I read "Hill Speak," these wonderings began to percolate to the surface. The poem, from his collection *Us*, is on one level about the difficulties of trying to pin down the connection between language and place. But it is also about a longing to understand—and locate—oneself through language.

"What is Pothwari?" Zaffar, through his poetry, asks. Even his father, a taxi driver like so many other Mirpuri migrants in Britain, and who speaks the language so fluently, struggles to articulate exactly what it is: ". . . So was Dad's speech some kind of Dogri? / Is it Kashmiri? Mirpuri? The differences are lost on me."

The title of "Hill Speak" is itself a play on just one variation of how the language is referred to: Pothwari is also sometimes called Pahari (mountain or hill speak). As I read and reread "Hill Speak" on the plane back from Doha, its poetics spoke to the experiences of so many of the people I had met over the previous ten years. I remembered listening to Mr. Javid sing *Rāg Pahari*—mountain or hill *rāg*—in that same language, which I explored in chapter 1. I remembered sitting in the shrine in Kashmir, hearing his voice, with the high mountains surrounding us. The highness of that poetry also brought to mind the opposite way in which those outside the community often see Mirpuris: I remembered the Karachi music producer recoiling in surprise when I told him about my research. "You're writing a book about MPs [Mirpuris]? I've seen everything now!" His contempt for the lowness of this language—of these people—was written across his face. "This mountain speech is a low language," Zaffar's father retorts, yet it is still "ours." I thought of the long conversations in Walsall with Changis Raja and his aversion to the idea of Mirpuri as a placeholder for identity: "There's no such thing as Mirpuri," he had told me enigmatically. I thought of the hours I had spent trying to translate *Saif-ul-Malook*, a labor rendered all the more challenging because, as Zaffar recognizes in his opening to "Hill Speak," "There is no dictionary for my father's language." I thought of being in Mr. Zuman's *shehnai* workshop, up the creek from Khari Sharif, and him poetically explaining the instrument's connection with the soil, with the land, something that was beyond language: "too earthy and scriptless to find a home in books," Zaffar writes. The poetics of "Hill Speak," in other words, speaks to the ambiguity of Kashmir and migration and how an attempt to locate its meaning is also a bid to locate oneself.

HILL SPEAK

There is no dictionary for my father's language
His dialect, for a start, is difficult to name.
Even this taxi driver, who talks it, lacks the knowledge.
Some say it's Pahari—"hill speak"—
others, Potwari, or Pahari-Potwari—
too earthy and scriptless to find a home in books.
This mountain speech is a low language. *Ours.* "No good.
You should learn speak Urdu." I'm getting the runaround.

Whatever it is, this talk, going back, did once have a script:
Landa, in the reign of the Buddhists.
. . . So was dad's speech some kind of Dogri?
Is it Kashmiri? Mirpuri? The differences are lost on me.
I'm told it's part way towards Punjabi,
but what that tongue would call *tuwarda*,
Dad would agree was *tusaanda* -
"yours" -

truly, though there are many dictionaries for the tongue I speak,
it's the close-by things I'm lost to say;
things as pulsed and present as the back of this hand,
never mind stumbling towards some higher plane.
And, either way, even at the rare moment I get towards—
or, thank God, even getting to—
my point, I can't put into words
where I've arrived

ZAFFAR KUNIAL

More broadly speaking, the teasing apart of linguistic meaning that occurs throughout his collection of poetry—*Us*—also points to the wider complexities, and indeed tensions, at the heart of multicultural politics, tensions that ultimately are also about coming to terms with contexts of cultural and linguistic diversity. Throughout "Hill Speak," we see glimpses of the challenges and misunderstandings that surface when a multitude of cultures and languages come into contact and live in one place, from the father who struggles to connect with his son in English to the son who longs to recognize his own past in the English countryside.[5] This tension is pulled apart by Zaffar through his playful use of dialect—Pothwari, Urdu, and various forms of northern English dialect—which, taken together, serve as productive markers of cultural and geographical haziness. Through this use of dialect, Zaffar explores the ways in which language and culture can be both deeply intertwined and also mobilized to draw boundaries around groups of people—not so much in a geographic sense but as epistemic interfaces between worlds.[6]

"I have a mad theory," Zaffar writes at the end of *Six*, "that the old forest of Arden has left an imprint somehow, zipped into the air, small pockets that fold worlds in. There was a hazy, wooded feel to the worlds I lived in, whether concreted over or not. I like how poetry can hold this mossy sense of folded-in worlds."[7]

Zaffar's world was here in Hebden Bridge, yet zipped into the air and folded into his poetry are the places elsewhere, the times gone by, the memories unlived. As I sat on the train back to Bradford later that evening, reflecting on this book, it became clear that hidden within Zaffar's poetry was a poetics of migration that I scarcely understood—how could I?—but that this was also perhaps the point. This was not the poetics of migration from Kashmir to Britain but of someone who had migrated nowhere but within England. Within and through England's past. Its hiddenness was biographically understood and yet also spoke to the wider messiness of migration. From Birmingham to Hebden Bridge, Zaffar was also navigating how England imagines itself. It is not about us and them, he suggests, but the affective consequences of overlapping histories and futures. A kind of collective and often conflicting memory of the past. The poetry had resonated with me in that café in Qatar and on the plane back to England because this sense of collectivity had touched upon so many of the things I was trying to get at and understand in this book. His legacy is that of both the England of T. S. Eliot and the Kashmir of Mian Muhammad Bakhsh. And yet it is also distinct from these lineages. "Life forks and stops / where another follows on." Continuing Zaffar's cricket metaphor, it occupies its own crease, which is to say its own path—one that he, and only he, journeys along.

Diverging Poetics

As I sat in his barbershop one evening in Bradford, Mr. Khokhar opened his small notebook to read verses of his own poetry, penned in the same language Zaffar was trying to poetically unpack: "Some say it's Pahari—'hill speak'— / others, Potwari, or Pahari-Potwari— / too earthy and scriptless to find a home in books," Zaffar had written. "Too scriptless," yet here it was, scripted in its own kind of book—Mr. Khokhar's notebook—hidden from view and away from the public gaze, like "a stone wrapped / in cloth." Page after page of neat cursive script. Before reading the poem, I asked Mr. Khokhar about when he had first arrived in Bradford.

"Oh, it was very different, you know, not like today. Work was very hard. I missed my family back home, you see."[8]

Upon arrival, at the age of fourteen, Mr. Khokhar joined his father, who had already moved to Bradford some years earlier in 1971.[9] He had lived his life until that point in Takipur, ten kilometers away from what was then the still new city of New Mirpur. Despite its proximity to the city, Takipur was, and remains, a rural area. The family lived in proximity to their relatives, in small one-story houses often consisting of just one or two rooms, with livestock in the courtyard. His childhood was spent playing with his cousins in the fields nearby and on the banks of the Jhelum River—the same fields where I had recounted playing cricket to Zaffar. They kept pigeons and goats and fighting dogs.

Compared to this pastoral scene, Bradford was a shock. The city was still heavily industrialized, though the textile industry, as described earlier, was already in a terminal decline, undercut by cheaper manufacturing in East Asia and South America. Early globalization was giving way to new.[10] Aged fourteen, Mr. Khokhar was still required to go to school, but the main motivation behind his arrival in Bradford was to contribute to the money that his father was sending back to the family in Takipur.

"I told my dad, I don't like it here. I want to go back home. And my dad, he said, 'OK, let's see after three months; if you still don't like [it] I'll buy you a ticket [home].'"

Mr. Khokhar didn't remember very much about his school days, he told me. He couldn't speak English very well, and the school system in Bradford at that stage was ill equipped to deal with such an ethnically and religiously diverse student body.[11] But then again, he wasn't enrolled at school for very long. After three months he turned fifteen, left school, and went to work in Buttershaw Mill: "I learned what I had to at the mill. I didn't have any other education." What he did know, however, had been learned from poetry and music. Growing up in Takipur, Mr. Khokhar had been in the shadow of Mian Muhammad Bakhsh and surrounded by musicians. The elders in his village would regularly sit around the courtyard together, reciting passages of *Saif-ul-Malook* and other local Sufis.

"Whenever you had a problem," Mr. Khokhar explained, "or if you were naughty, you would get a slap, but you would also hear a lesson. Whenever something happened there was always a *ghazal* to explain it or say what you should do." At a time when many people from his village were emigrating to Britain, the poetry of Mian Muhammad Bakhsh was always at hand to offer wisdom and advice. He pointed to the wall, which bore an inscription:

آپنے دیس دیاں وَلاں نالوں تُے کھو کھو کھایئے

غیر مُلک دیاں باغاں آندر، میوے کھان نہ جایئے

Āpne dēs diyāṅ wallāṅ nālōṅ tume kho kho khāyi'e,
ghair mulk diyāṅ bāghāṅ āndar, mewe khān nah jāyi'e.

It is better to eat even the bitter fruits of your own land's gardens,
than go to foreign gardens to eat sweet fruits.

Saif-ul-Malook, as we have seen throughout this book, is full of caution-
ary tales such as these, stories about roaming far away from home and the
perils one may face. But they are also read by Kashmiris as advice on how
to cope with migration when marriage or work takes you abroad, far away
from family, friends, and loved ones. With little or no formal schooling in
either Mirpur or Bradford, these encounters with Sufi poetic traditions
constituted, for Mr. Khokhar and many others of his generation, a formative learning experience. The ethical and moral tales imparted by these
poetic traditions not only are enacted through musical performances
today but are imbibed through everyday life, evident in family relations
and in how Mirpuris orient themselves in Britain and navigate a changing social and economic landscape in Mirpur.[12] As we saw in the previous
chapter, during the multiculturalism debate of the 1980s and 1990s, Kashmiris from Mirpur were often accused of living segregated lives, of not
integrating properly into British society.[13] Yet if we understand migration
less through the prism of ethnicity or religion and more through musical
and poetic practices, a more nuanced and complex picture of multiculturalism emerges.

Early migrants to Britain such as Mr. Khokhar and Shakoor were quick
to open shops that stocked spices from home, restaurants to prepare familiar foods, and fabric stores to stitch traditional clothing. In Bradford,
many of these stores carried signage in both Urdu and English. In figure

FIGURE 22. The Khari Sharif General Food Store on Whetley Hill in Bradford.
Photograph by Tim Smith (2002).

22, for example, a stretch limousine can be seen outside the Kharri Sharif General Food Store on Whetley Hill in Bradford. The store is named after the town Khari Sharif, just outside Mirpur, famous as the resting place of Mian Muhammad Bakhsh. The Urdu calligraphy seen in in this photograph is a transliteration, rather than a translation, of the English words to its right—something only those who could read Urdu would know. Visualizations of a foreign culture such as this, however, drove much of the backlash against multiculturalism in places like Bradford in the years that followed.[14] Yet many of those early migrants spoke and read little or no English, and so signs such as these show, on the contrary, a concerted effort to communicate across languages. Moreover, viewed through the moral teachings of *Saif-ul-Malook*, we come to understand some of the ethical and spiritual reasons Kashmiris chose to orient themselves in this way.

Mr. Khokhar's memories of these early months and years in Bradford were a mixture of hardship and nostalgia, something, as we shall see, reflected in his own poetry. Working at the mill was tough, the hours were long, and conditions were cramped, noisy, and dangerous. The work was low-paid manual labor, and he would often sign up for extra shifts to earn more money to send back home. He remembered his overseer, a man called John. The young workers in the factory would often be asked to work overtime, he explained.

"I would always say yes [to overtime] because I knew that, a few hours into the shift, John would say, 'OK Abdul [Mr. Khokhar's first name], you've done well, you can go home now.'" He would always remember John kindly for that, he said.

After work, Mr. Khokhar would return home with his father. The men would stick together and take turns cooking. They had a common purpose here in Britain: the prosperity of their family back home. The mills may have been hard work, but the value of that work brought more than just economic benefits. By sending the majority of what they earned back to Takipur, they projected an image of prosperity that elevated their family's status back home. The money could buy material goods, but it also sent a message of movement: of both moving away and moving up in the world. Mr. Khokhar and his dad, huddled in their room on Oak Lane, looked after their family back home, providing them with food, clothes, and, as the years wore on, new houses, cars, and weddings. They became great patrons of musicians back in Kashmir, musicians such as my own mentor, Ustad Zulfikar Ali Khan. Such patronage was itself a sign of prestige and status, conjuring images of the great Mughal courts of years gone by. For a community that values family relations and status so highly, patronizing music and performances of *Saif-ul-Malook*, as well as the quotidian

FIGURE 23. Mr. Khokhar's barbershop, with his handwritten poetry in the foreground. To the right, an amateur musician tunes his *sitar*.

invocation of couplets,[15] connected memories of the past to the lived experiences of the present.[16]

As I listened to Mr. Khokhar speak, memories flooded my mind. Hebden Bridge, Qatar, Kashmir, the *darbar* in Old Mirpur where I first heard Mr. Javid sing Mian Muhammad Bakhsh. By that point it was early evening in the barbershop; the customers had left, and the workplace was poised to become a temporary *mehfil*, a space for music and poetry. We were joined by half a dozen of his friends. Instruments appeared: a *sitar*, a *dholak*, and, of course, the voice. *Rāg Pahari* again filled my ears—acoustically this time—and I was transported again back to the shrine in Kashmir (fig. 23).

As I opened my eyes, it began to make sense to me why the walls and coffee tables of this barbershop in Bradford were inscribed with quotations from *Saif-ul-Malook* and Mr. Khokhar's own poetry (fig. 23). Outside the window was Bradford, but in between the buzzing of hair clippers and the chatter of customers was the memory of a time before, a land elsewhere, easily at hand, there on the wall, just a glance away. I picked up his handwritten notebook and read (fig. 24):

کہڑی جگہ نہیں جا کے دعا منگی

اس دل دی بنجر زمین خاطر

Kehṛī jagah nahīṅ jā ke du'ā maṅgī,
is dil dī banjar zamīn khāṭir.

Which place have I not been to and prayed?
For the sake of my heart's barren land.

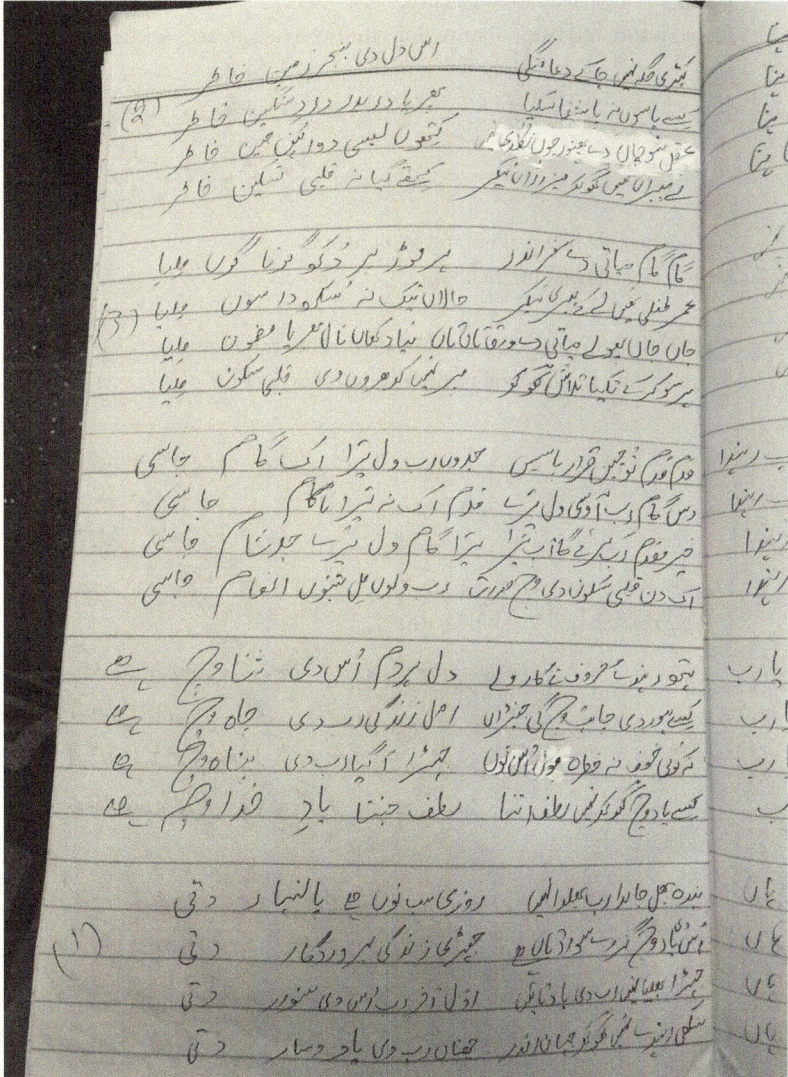

FIGURE 24. Mr. Khokhar's handwritten poetry.

کسے پاسوں نہ پا شفا سکیا
پھریا در بدر دردِ سنگین خاطر

Kisē pāsoṅ nah pā shifā sakiyā,
phiriyā dar badar dard-i sangīn khāṭir.

From no side have I found a cure,
I have wandered from door to door for my heavy heart's sake.

عقل سوچاں دے بھنور چوں نکلدی نہیں
کتھوں لبسی دوا ہُن جین خاطر

'aql sōciyaṅ de bhanvar cūṅ nikaladī nahīṅ,
kithōṅ labsī dawā huṇ jīn khāṭir.

My mind cannot escape the whirlwind of my thoughts,
From where do I find the remedy to just live my life?

لے پیراں تھیں کھوکھر میزاراں تیکر
کتھے گیا نہ قلبی تسکین خاطر

Le pīrāṅ thīṅ khōkhar mizārāṅ tīk,
kithe gayā nah qalbī taskīn khāṭir.

From pirs and to shrines, oh Khokhar!
Where have I not gone for the sake of my heart's peace?

گام گام حیاتی دے سفر اندر
ہر موڑ پر دُکھ گونا گوں ملیا

Gām gām ḥayātī de safar andar,
har mōṛ par dukh gūnā gūṅ miliyā.

With each step of my life's journey,
At every turn I was met with various sorrows.

عمر طفلی تھیں لے کے پیری تیکر
حالاں تیک نہ سُکھ دا سون ملیا

'umr ṭuflī thīṅ le ke pīrī tīk,
hālāṅ tīk nah sukh dā sōṅ miliyā.

From youth 'til old age.
I have not found one moment of relief.

جاں جاں پھولے حیاتی دے ورق تاں تاں
نیا دکھاں نال بھریا مضمون ملیا

Jāṅ jāṅ phūle ḥayātī de waraq tāṅ tāṅ,
nayā dukẖāṅ nāl bhariyā maẓmūn miliyā.

While I opened the pages of my life,
I found every entry filled with new sorrows.

ہر سو کرکے تکیا تلاش کھوکھر
پر نہیں کدھروں وی قلبی سکون ملیا

Har sū karke takiyā talāsh Khōkhar,
par nahīṅ kadhroṅ vī qalbī sakūn miliyā.

I have looked and searched in every direction, oh Khokhar!
but I have not found peace of heart from anywhere.

قدم قدم تُو چین قرار پاسیں
جدوں رب ول تیرا اک گام جاسی

Qadam qadam tū cīn qarār pāseṅ,
jadōṅ rabb val terā ik gām jāsī.

But you will find peace at every step you take,
when you take one step toward your Creator.

دس گام رب آوسی ول تیرے
قدم اک نہ تیرا ناکام جاسی

Das gām rabb āusī val tere,
qadam ik nah terā nākām jāsī.

He will come ten steps toward you,
No step you take will ever go unsuccessful.

خیر مقدم رب کرے گا آپ تیرا

تیرا گام ول تیرے جد شام جاسی

Khair maqdam rabb karē gā āp terā,
terā gām val tere jad shām jāsī.

He will welcome you Himself,
The day the flame of your life comes to an end.

اک دن قلبی سکون دی وچ صورت

رب ولوں مل تینوں انعام جاسی

Ik din qalbī sakūn dī vich ṣūrat,
rabb valōṅ mil tainūṅ in'ām jāsī.

On that day you will be filled with true peace and fulfilment,
That will be the gift from the Creator.

ہتھ رہندے مصروف نے کار والے

دل ہر دم اُس دی ثنا وچ ہے

Hath rahnde maṣrūf ne kār vale,
dil har dam us dī sanā vic haī.

My hands are busy with work,
but my heart is every moment busy in His praise.

کسے ہور دی جانب وچ کی جینڑاں

اصل زندگی رب دی چاہ وچ ہے

Kisē hōr dī jānb vich kī jīṇṛāṅ,
aṣl zindagī rabb dī cāh vich haī.

What is a life spent for someone else?
True life lies in the love of God.

نہ کوئی خوف نہ خطرہ مول اُس نوں

جہڑا آگیا رب دی پناہ وچ ہے

Nah kōī khauf nah khatrah maul us nūṅ,
jeṛā āgayā rabb dī panāh vich haī.

Neither fear nor any danger will come their way,
The one who has come under God's protection.

كسے یاد وچ کھوکھر نہیں لطف اتنا

لطف جتنا یادِ خدا وچ ہے

Kisē yād vich Khōkhar nahīṅ luṭf itnā,
luṭf jitnā yād-i khudā vich haī.

No thought holds such bliss, oh Khokhar!
As the joy in God's remembrance.

بندہ بھل جاندا رب بھلدا نہیں

روزی سب نوں ہے پالنہار دتی

Bandah bhal jāndā rabb bhaldā nahīṅ,
rozī sab nūṅ haī pālnahār dī.

People forget but God never forgets,
The Nourisher has given sustenance to all.

أُس دی یاد وچ گزرے سواد تاں ہے

جہڑی زندگی پروردگار دتی

Us dī yād vich guzrē sawād tāṅ haī,
jeṛī zindagī parvardigār dī.

True pleasure is time spent in His remembrance,
about the life God has given.

جہڑا بھلیا نہیں رب دی یاد تائیں

اوّل آخر رب أُس دی سنوار دتی

Jeṛā bhalyā nahīṅ rabb dī yād tāṅ,
awwal ākhir rabb us dī sanvār dī.

For the one who has not forgotten remembering Their lord,
Their beginning 'til the end, God has imbued with beauty.

سکھی رہندے نہیں گھر گھر جہان اندر

جنہاں رب دی یاد وساردتی

Sukhī rahnde nahīṅ ghar ghar jahān andar,
jināṅ rabb dī yād wasār dī.

At unease in the houses of this world
Are those who have forgotten God's remembrance.

Like Zaffar's poetry described earlier, Mr. Khokhar's verses present a kind of interface between worlds—a meditation on the hardships and sorrows he has faced, a reflection on his own life in lands far away from Kashmir, a path to the divine. As the poem's narrator, he sees a person damaged by the troubles of life, the hardship of migration, who goes everywhere to find a cure. The wanderer travels to faith healers and shrines, seeking council from those along the way, journeying everywhere to find solace. Peace of mind is nowhere to be found. Until, that is, the day he starts walking toward God. From then on, everything changes. He takes *just one step* in His direction and—in a powerful moment of poetic metaphor—God takes ten steps toward him. The final two sections of the poem focus on how he is finally healed, spiritually and emotionally, through this journey toward God.

The use of these metaphors reflects the deep connection between spiritual and worldly paths in the context of Mirpuri history and migration. As in Mian Muhammad Bakhsh's epic poem *Safar ul-Ishq* (*The Journey of Love*), Mr. Khokhar situates himself in the role of narrator and guide (*murshid*), looking down on his life and his own journey, offering the wisdom of experience to others, ready to be passed down to those who follow.[17] Mr. Khokhar's own journey of love is written into every verse, and the Pothwari vocabulary he uses, as I often saw and heard in his barbershop, would be easily comprehensible—and relatable—to those Kashmiris who came to his barbershop and sought his services. A true interface between worlds: Bradford and Mirpur, the worldly and the divine. And so it was not just hairdressing that Mr. Khokhar offered in his barbershop but also spiritual nourishment for a community bound together through the poetics of migration.

∵

Sociologist of memory Barry Schwartz argued that collective memories should be understood semiotically in relation to their surrounding, more or less discrete, cultural systems (1996). He was drawing on Clifford Geertz's definition of collective memory as a "pattern of *inherited* conceptions expressed through symbolic forms—such as poetry, music, and other aspects of culture—through which people imagined, rehearsed, and articulated their knowledge of and responses to their lived environment" (1973, 89, emphasis added). Reflecting on what this might mean for a poetics of migration, the operative word here is *inherited*. For Geertz, these inherited conceptions, passed across and down generations, act as a means to understand society and one's place within it.[18] Collective memory, in this view, is a way of representing deeply rooted cultural values—spanning generations as well as geographic distance—and so render present experiences meaningful.[19] In performances of *Saif-ul-Malook*, in the verses of Mr. Khokhar's notebook, in the collections of Zaffar Kunial, with their themes of spiritual and worldly journeys, Kashmiris' and Britons' collective memory of migration is enacted in narrative form, encapsulating key values of family, kinship, and honor, and indeed moments of disjuncture, within the wider spiritual "grand narratives" of Sufism.[20] In this sense, the unknowability of migratory experience to those outside the community is illuminated not in relation to what the verses might explicitly mean but in how they ambiguously map onto people's memories, both lived and unlived.[21]

As he swept up the hair clippings from his final customer of the day, Mr. Khokhar recited lines from *Saif-ul-Malook*. I asked Mr. Khokhar what the couplet meant. Rather than translate the words—which, naively, is what I had been asking—he instead told me a story of how his brother had died suddenly in Mirpur many years ago, leaving his wife and children behind. While still grieving, Mr. Khokhar had assumed the responsibility of looking after his sister-in-law and her family. The responsibility marked Mr. Khokhar's moment of ascension to family patriarch. It also entailed substantial economic and social burdens. The couplet he recited from memory reminded him not just of that moment in history and the familial pressures that ensued but, crucially, bestowed both with an honor that connected his worldly duties to the poetic divine of *Saif-ul-Malook*. Its vocalization by Mr. Khokhar was an expression of the sorrow he felt *and* the honor of responsibility that was his to bear, the duality of which gave his daily laboring in the barbershop meaning. Meaning in poetry, in other words, was indexed against memory, and sung poetry connected the quotidian to the performative to the divine.

Conclusion

Or, Un-ending . . .

I would like to know how I can prove that I'm a Muslim and I have integrated into society. Look at me. I wear British clothes. I speak broken English but, still, I speak English and I have got a beard. That gives away my identity. Some people would recognise who I am. Now, people ask me "Why don't you integrate?" and I say, "How do you mean?" And they can't answer me back because I go to schools, give talks about how to deal with racist incidents and very often the teachers ask me, "Why don't Muslims integrate?" I say, "What do you mean? I pay tax. I obey the laws of the land."[1]

In 2005, the Runnymede Trust hosted a conference to support the government's Improving Opportunity, Strengthening Society strategy. The conference was attended by many of the key politicians and academics who had shaped the multiculturalism debate over the previous two decades.[2] Amid much handwringing over how to conceptualize diversity, inclusion, and the perceived failures of multicultural policies came the question from Mr. S, above: a characteristic response to a debate that had become preoccupied with questions of integration and had little regard for what that actually meant to those on the ground. By that point there had been an implication that immigrants must "opt in" to the obligations of Britain's multicultural citizenship.[3] In the media, a language of "us" and "them"—separating migrant groups (them) from host societies (us)—culminated in an almost Europe-wide denunciation of multiculturalism.[4] Indeed, in 2011 the then British prime minister, David Cameron, declared that in Britain, "We have failed to provide a vision of society to which they feel they want to belong. We have even tolerated these segregated communities behaving in ways that run counter to our values."[5] Over ten years later, these tropes still dominate debates about migration in Britain: In July 2023, Suella Braverman, then the British home secretary—the ministerial position ultimately responsible for immigration—told an American think tank that multiculturalism "has failed because it allowed people to come to our society and live parallel lives in it."[6] It is no small irony that Braverman herself is the daughter of parents who migrated to Britain from India (via Kenya) and who served under Britain's first Hindu prime minister, Rishi Sunak.

As we have seen, framing multiculturalism negatively through the language of segregation and integration ignores the complex ways in which Kashmiris orient themselves in Britain, often in the face of a hostile media and a succession of governments with only a limited understanding of the nuances of Mirpuri life and culture. Kashmiris are fully, often painfully cognizant of their position on the margins of British politics and the double standards by which they are held. It is hardly surprising in these circumstances that they instead turn to their own community for support and ethical guidance. We have seen throughout this book how reliance on government support often leaves public arts organizations exposed to the vagaries of funding and the ethical consequences of it coming with strings attached or being suddenly withdrawn. Meanwhile, concerts such as those at Rochdale Town Hall—organized by and promoted within the Kashmiri community—are self-reliant not through a willful policy of negative self-segregation but through a more positive embrace of community values and relationships; virtues, incidentally, that many politicians were signaling at the time.[7] Sticking closely to Kashmiri poetics rather than multicultural politics is an attempt by the organizers and musicians at these events to navigate memories of migration both past and present away from the glare of a hostile media. That these poetics remain largely hidden from public view has less to do with self-segregation and more to do with performative acts of self-preservation.

Anxieties about ethnic and religious belonging are of course not unique to Britain but are at the heart of debates about national borders across the world. Kashmir today is in the middle of one such debate, playing backdrop to both Indo-Pak and Sino-Indian border tensions. The recent rise of ethnonationalist politics in South Asia has also seen renewed interest in the consequences of Partition in public discourse. A series of current (refugee) and ongoing (climate) crises suggest that along with more conventional forms of economic migration, nation-states will need to continually rethink how they respond to increasing levels of diversity within their borders. Historically, this has been the work of multicultural politics. Yet narratives surrounding multiculturalism have stalled. Multiculturalism—as a policy and a lived practice—must, if it is to be effective, bridge this plurality of cultures on the one hand with the singularity of the nation-state on the other. Given the likelihood that globalization and climate change will produce ever-increasing levels of migration, the need for a more nuanced understanding of the relationship between diversity and nationalism is becoming ever more urgent.

As I have tried to show in this book, understanding migration only through the prism of race or ethnicity can also obscure the more intimate and hidden means by which people orient themselves within and across borders, and how they situate themselves as belonging to longer histories of movement and displacement. A poetics of migration can take us some of the way there but not all the way, nor perhaps should it. One of the points of a hidden poetics of migration—its mystical unknowability to outsiders—must surely be that it remains just that: hidden. It is clearly not for me to decide what something means, nor what should be revealed. But by extension, it is surely not for anyone to decide what it means to "opt in" to British society beyond, as Mr. S. put it, paying your taxes and obeying the laws of the land. My principle aim in this book has been to find a way of talking about migration that cuts through the posturing of nationalist politics and a multiculturalism debate that became unmoored from the lives of those at the heart of it: the people who make Britain their home. Poetry, in its enduring ambiguity, opens up space for multiple meanings—and understandings—to emerge, and to focus on it is to resist reaching for easy answers.

∴

It is a tricky thing to write a conclusion about something that is ongoing. I began *Journeys of Love* with a story about a silver one-rupee coin gifted to me by my mentor, Ustad Zulfikar Ali Khan, and I will close the book with another. Almost a decade after that moment on a Kashmiri mountainside, I was confronted with a near identical coin, minted around the same time, in 1884. This one was housed in glass display case in the Qatar National Library. Here was Queen Victoria's head again. The label behind the coin told me that "the Indian rupee was the dominant, and later official, currency of Kuwait, Qatar, the Trucial States and parts of Oman from the late 19th century to the 1960s CE, a reflection of India's financial importance to the region." On display elsewhere in the exhibition were beautiful examples of Kashmiri shawls, "one of the most obvious examples of Indian influence on Gulf material culture." The exhibition was there to illustrate, through objects, the historical and cultural ties between Qatar and India, but in doing so it also seemed to be self-consciously turning its face away from the legacies of the British Empire, even while Queen Victoria's face remained frozen within the glass display case. The exhibition was instead there to situate—and celebrate—contemporary migration to Qatar within a much longer, and seemingly distinguished, history of cross-cultural pollination across the Arabian Sea. I would soon learn that this wasn't quite the full picture.

Until 2019, virtually all my research for this book had taken place in Britain and Azad Kashmir. But my recent travels in Pakistan had taught me that Kashmiri economic migration today mostly points in other directions, principally toward the Persian Gulf and, tragically, as victims of attempted migrant boat crossings to Europe.[8] It was December—dark and wet when I left London—and as I stepped out of the airport in Doha, I was greeted with a warm blast of desert heat. I had no contacts to meet up with, no networks of musicians I could plug into, no sense, really, of what migration in this part of the world looked like beyond what I had read in the media. And what I had read painted a bleak but not completely unfamiliar picture of what has been described in the preceding chapters: that Kashmiri migrants had come to Qatar to fill labor shortages in the construction industry; that they were there at the invitation of the government, yet treated as de facto second-class citizens; that they faced dangerous working conditions, with few civil rights; that many were living in shared dormitories, segregated away from a society hostile to their presence; and that most were men, there to send remittances to their families back home.

As I stepped out of the air-conditioned airport and into the desert air, I wasn't sure where to start, but as it turned out, I didn't have to wait too long. I ordered an Uber and, as we pulled out onto the wide boulevard toward Doha, the driver, Shahzad, switched on the stereo. The sounds of Coke Studio Pakistan filled the car.[9]

Shahzad and I met up several times over the following week. He had been in Qatar for five months and had another six to go before he would, "*inshallah*," God-willing, in his words, return to Pakistan. Prior to arriving in Qatar, he was based in Riyadh, Saudi Arabia, for ten years, where he also drove taxis as a subcontractor, sending most of what he earned back to his young family in Lahore.

"I came to Qatar because, last three years in Riyadh, I did not get paid. [I was owed] 192,000 Riyal [approximately 50,000 USD]. They did not pay me, but I could not do anything."

"Could you not go to the police?"

"No no, you can't go to the police. You cannot go to the court either because there, one Saudi and one foreigner are not equal." He chuckled to himself. "It's no problem." He smiled, turning to me, pointing upward. "God is great!"

Shahzad's story, I would learn, was not unusual among workers in Qatar, yet there was both a familiarity to how he philosophically dealt with what seemed to me like enormous setbacks in his life and a clear distinctiveness to his experiences compared with those of postwar migrants to Britain described throughout this book.

"I am lucky," he explained, gesturing out the window at the numerous buildings springing up out of the desert in anticipation of the FIFA World Cup in two years' time. "I have my car; I control my own journey."

As we drove around Doha, sand blew up from the roads, dusting his white car in a desert hue. We were effectively driving around one huge construction site. According to the Qatari government's own figures—posted on a website specifically designed to counter the perception that migrants were being exploited—30,000 workers had been invited to the country to build the upcoming soccer tournament's stadiums (not counting the many other construction and infrastructure projects).[10] Most of these migrant laborers, like Shahzad, came from South Asia. When Shahzad said he was "lucky," it was because he was not one of the construction workers: he did not have to live in the labor camps, in rooms with dozens of other men; he was not shuttled from the dormitories to the construction sites every morning and evening; he was not exposed to working conditions that, by conservative estimates, would claim the lives of over 6,500 migrant workers.[11] Relatively speaking, Shahzad felt free—"blessed"—insofar as he was able to begin and end his daily shift when he chose to do so and make his own decisions about working conditions—that is, he could play Coke Studio all day on his car radio and communicate with his family back in Lahore via WhatsApp more or less continuously. Yet the reality was that, legally speaking, he shared the same status as a migrant worker, which, in the eyes of the Qatari state, placed him in the same bracket as the construction workers. His work visa was sponsored by a third-party limousine company that handled his earnings on his behalf and held a veto on whether he was permitted to leave the country.[12] His freedom, in other words, was tightly controlled and framed in narrow terms.

The effect of all this, Shahzad explained, was that he and his fellow migrant workers felt at once desperately needed by the state—indeed, the huge infrastructure projects entirely depended on them—and eminently disposable, easily replaced by any one of the many other economic migrants drawn to Qatar by the promise of new wealth. It was a feeling of being at once fastened to the shifting desert sands and lying prone to destabilizing geopolitical winds. And it was through this kind of depressed legal status—as noncitizens, non-Qataris—that migrant workers were deliberately hidden by the state: on carefully guarded construction sites and in fenced-off worker accommodations, far away from the glare of the tourists Qatar so hoped to attract, and excluded from the new buildings and infrastructure those migrants had themselves erected. In light of this, Shahzad's mission was clear: work seven days a week and earn as much as possible so that he could return to his family in Lahore and open his own shop. In some respects, it was a dream I had heard and read about many times before: what Mohammad Anwar described in the British context, back in 1979, as "the myth of return."[13]

Yet looking around, and hearing Shahzad and his friends describe the Qatari state's attitude toward migrant workers, I was inclined to believe him. There was a key difference, it struck me, between the recent Gulf migration from Pakistan and the migration to Britain in the decades after World War II. If the multicultural politics of Britain that the postwar migration produced was a messy means of trying to find ways for multiple cultures to harmoniously coexist within a nation-state—equal under the eyes of the law, less so in real terms—then the approach of the Qatari state seemed deliberately to be about pursuing the opposite: treating migrant workers as not just de facto second-class citizens but actual second-class residents and enshrining that status in law—indeed, denying the very possibility, now and at any point in the future, of citizenship. They would never *be* Qatari in the way so many of those featured in this book are legally and culturally entitled to think of themselves as British, even when ambiguously so. Not integration, then, but deliberate segregation. For Shahzad, the kind of chain migration that meant the families of Mirpuri migrants would join them in Britain was not only *not an option* but also, given the political climate he witnessed as he drove around Doha, manifestly undesirable. His migration to Qatar was a means to a clear end. His mind and his heart were oriented straight ahead, through the windshield of his car, down the long road back to Pakistan.

Not long after my arrival, Shahzad introduced me to his friend Yunis, who had also moved to Doha to work and save money to buy land in Lahore and build a house for his family. Yunis also spoke of the iniquities of the visa system, which tied migrant workers to their employers.

"If you want to leave the country for whatever reason, your employer, who is also your visa sponsor, must first approve your exit visa, else you will be turned away from the airport. If you want to leave your job for another, you can only do so if your current employer provides you with a certificate!"

It was a system open to abuse, as Yunis, like Shahzad, knew only too well. Deciding he wanted to leave his current employer, Yunis explained that he was due a 32,000 Riyal bonus for working overtime. His employer withheld the payments "for one month, two months, three months. No payment, no certificate." Eventually, he gave up. He received his certificate but not his bonus, which amounted to the equivalent of six months' salary. As in Saudi Arabia, there would be no recourse in the law.

"Do you know how many Qataris there are in the country? The country has two point three million people in total. How many Qataris do you think there are? There are three hundred thousand. It's a joke to even call us a minority!"

Only native-born Qataris, Yunis explained, receive the benefits of full citizenship. Everyone else is just a worker, with correspondingly curtailed human rights. For Yunis, there was little point in complaining to the employment office or the police. He was a Pakistani migrant—they wouldn't be interested in pursuing his case.

"First," he explained, "you have the Qataris, second you have good passports—Canada, America, UK—then you have Pakistan, Sri Lanka, India, Bangladesh."

∵

As Shahzad and I drove around Doha, we would take turns playing excerpts from *Saif-ul-Malook* on his car stereo and continued to do so via WhatsApp long after I returned to England.[14] As with Shakoor, whom we met in chapter 1, the narrative lessons of *Saif-ul-Malook* provided Shahzad and Yunis with what they described as their "path" home, even when a return may have been many years away. It also provided a spiritual resilience to absorb the blows they faced on their long journeys away from home and the seemingly endless days journeying around Doha, ferrying people between air-conditioned offices and malls in their Ubers. New digital technologies have made this journey more bearable, as the drivers interact with family members continually throughout their days via messaging services such as WhatsApp, through which they share YouTube clips of sung poetry. Driving through the city's streets, often working twelve to fifteen hours per day, the poetry reminded them that while they may be meandering down foreign roads in a place where workers' rights are severely restricted, their spiritual path remained true.

The enduring patience and perseverance—not to mention entrepreneurialism—of Yunis and Shahzad reminded me of many of the Kashmiri migrant workers I had met elsewhere and described throughout this book: I thought of Shakoor, standing calmly on the roof of his soon-to-be-submerged house on the edge of the Mangla Dam, and Mr. Khokhar, nostalgically describing the hardships he had encountered when arriving in Bradford.[15] In the face of adversity, far from home, the first thing they reached for was not anger toward local iniquities, or officials indifferent to their plight, or a system designed to exploit them, but Sufi wisdom.

∵

I will finish this book by returning to where it began, on a hillside in Azad Kashmir. Zulfikar had brought me to the top of the mountain that morning to witness a juncture of land and history, to where many of the threads discussed in this book became intertwined. Looking across to Indian-controlled Kashmir that day, I felt not only a sense of arbitrariness and regret at this legacy of empire but also a deeper feeling of permanence. Not so much of the politics but of the land. Those vast mountains. My late trip to Qatar showed that the politics and reality of migration are precarious and ongoing. But the land of Kashmir itself—and the feelings of belonging it affords—stretches beyond disputed borders, beyond multicultural politics, beyond construction sites, and through the window to the future, in the poetics of Kashmiris here and thousands of miles away.

As the silver rupee and the empire it represented were laid to rest—in a graveyard in Kashmir and as a relic in a library in Qatar—the poetry of Mian Muhammad Bakhsh thrived above, traversing the land, giving anchorage to feelings of home and longing to those who needed it the most. His shrine in Khari Sharif is today a site of pilgrimage for Azad Kashmiris wherever they happen to be in the world. It is there that Mirpuris return for spiritual nourishment, to reflect, receive blessings, marry, ask for intercession. The poetry of Mian Muhammad Bakhsh, so full of lyrical metaphor for home and belonging, is central to many Azad Kashmiris' spiritual and cultural identity, especially as these identities become unmoored from the physical geography of this part of Pakistan through migration. While home may become Bradford, Rochdale, the Gulf states, or wherever Kashmiris migrate to in the future, a part of them, if needed, can remain in that landscape, its memory kept alive through the performance and patronage of music and poetry. And so the political upheaval during the midnineteenth century that gave rise to this poetry still reverberates in the act of migration to and from Kashmir today.

Zulfikar's gift of the silver rupee coin seemed startlingly generous at the time. "This is part of your history, you can take it home with you," he had said. Perhaps the coin was an invitation for me to look in the mirror and confront my own country's past; or maybe it was simply a means of dissolving one kind of history and beginning another: "What we call the beginning is often the end; and to make an end is to make a beginning. The end is where we start from," as T. S. Eliot, the poet so close to Zaffar Kunial's heart, wrote. The late David Graeber, reflecting on Marcel Mauss, suggested that such gifts are there to "create alliances and obligations between individuals or groups who might otherwise have nothing to do with one another" (2001, 27). A good point to reflect upon as we think about multicultural societies going forward.

The coin ended up traveling back to Britain with me, an awkward kind of reverse migration: Queen Victoria returning home from the country she famously never set foot in. I have the coin here on my desk as I type these final words. More than that, I have what it affords: memories of poetry shared on a Kashmiri mountainside. The exchange of the coin had created something I couldn't quite put my finger on, something unknowable, between Zulfikar and me. I wasn't sure what I would be reciprocating, but with Mauss in mind, I knew that whatever it was would unfold over time. If we look at it through the morals of *Saif-ul-Malook*, it was a reminder that journeys of love—like books about migration—rarely have a clear beginning or end. The value of the coin lay no longer in its currency but, as with the poetry of Mian Muhammad Bakhsh, in what it revealed about the past and a promise it held for the future.

Acknowledgments

A book about journeys of love can only be written with the love and generosity of a great many people.

The journey began in earnest when I was a graduate student at Oxford, where Martin Stokes took me under his wing and guided me along the meandering path of doctoral study and beyond. He has been my friend and intellectual north star ever since. It is no stretch to say that I wouldn't be where I am today without Martin's unfailing support, and I will forever be grateful.

I was supported at Oxford by a St. John's College Lamb and Flag Scholarship, which funded my first forays into ethnographic research in Bradford and Mirpur. I was also fortunate enough to receive a Gerry Farrell Travelling Scholarship, which saw me through a three-month trip to the Himalayas to learn Urdu. A great many friendships were forged during this period. The likes of Ian Ashpole, Elizabeth Chatterjee, Bryn Harris, John Jenkins, Kate Leadbetter, Nastassia Maritzova, John McManus, Struan Murray, Laura Pitel, Edward Posnett, Katherine Rundell, Anbara Salam, Richard Sowerby, Rachel Wilson, and Mikey Wood were, without exception, a constant and welcome reminder of how little I really knew. It was also during this time that I began playing the trumpet in two bands, The Yarns and Stornoway, which led to experiences that never ceased to provide a much-needed musician's perspective on my work. Thanks also, then, to Brian Briggs, Jon Ouin, Oli Steadman, Rob Steadman, and Susie Attwood. A British Academy Postdoctoral Fellowship at King's College London subsequently gave me welcome breathing space, including a second extended period of fieldwork in Pakistan. It was during these travels that I first met many of the people who feature in this book.

My research in Bradford owes a great deal to two people in particular—Champak Kumar Limbachia and Mr. Khokhar. Champak's knowledge and wisdom were informed by a lifetime's experience of South Asian music in Bradford, which opened me up to an entire history and network of musicians across the city and beyond. He is responsible for introducing me to Mr. Khokhar, whose friendship and extraordinary hospitality in Bradford and Pakistan made this book what it is. It was also Mr. Khokhar who, in Pakistan, first introduced me to Zulfikar Ali Khan, the *shehnai* master who would later become my *ustad*. It is hard to express the kindness and hospitality afforded to me by Mr. Khokhar, Zulfikar and his family, who took me into their homes and fed and watered me over many months and years. My enduring memories of Azad Kashmir are those spent with Zulfikar, zipping around Kashmir on the back of his motorbike. This book, and the world it describes, is in no small part thanks to him.

I returned to King's College London to work in 2018, and I am thankful to all my colleagues and students there for giving me that perfect mix of collegiality and friendship. For all those conversations in the corridors, in research seminars, and in the pub, I would like to thank John Baily, Emma Dillon, Jo Fort, Andy Fry, Matthew Head, Radha Kapuria, Daniel Leech-Wilkinson, Fred Moehn, Wajiha Naqvi, Edward Nesbit, Roger Parker, Katherine Schofield, Martin Stokes, and Flora Wilson. My own journey then swerved full circle when I returned to teach at Oxford in 2020. There, I was lucky enough to work with students and colleagues who continued to expand my thinking. For all their kindness and unending intellectual stimulation, I would like to thank Suzanne Aspden, Georgina Born, Michael Burden, Eric Clarke, Jonathan Cross, Sam Dieckmann, Laurance Dreyfus, Daniel Grimley, Adam Harper, Martyn Harry, Sarah Hill, Elizabeth Eva Leach, Alison Shaw, Jason Stanyek, Christian Leitmeir, Gascia Ouzounian, Laura Tunbridge, and Jenny Walshe.

No journey is complete without its twists and turns, and, geographically at least, the most unexpected came with a move to UCLA in 2022. It was here that this book was finished, and thinking about it now, it's hard to imagine being able to have done it anywhere else. Yet again I landed on my feet and found myself in the company (and debt) of extraordinary friends and scholars—Joy Calico, Nina Eidsheim, Cesar Favila, Bob Fink, Jenny Johnson, Mark Kligman, Ray Knapp, Elisabeth Le Guin, Mohsen Mohammadi, Anna Morcom, Tiffany Naiman, Dan Neuman (who generously lent me his cabin in Idyllwild to write these words), Tim Taylor, Helen Rees, Catherine Provenzano, Jessica Schwartz, Eileen Strempel, and Elizabeth Upton. I am grateful, too, for the generous reading and feedback on an early draft of this text by my graduate students Austin Ali, Maddie Barrett, Morgan Bates, Xavier Brown, Luka Douridas, Kate Hamori, Emmie Head, Molly Hennig, and Michele Yamamoto.

Two anonymous reviewers at the University of Chicago Press provided critical (and crucial) insights and suggestions, which have only strengthened this text, and I completely lucked out to have been shepherded through the editorial process by the expertise and sharp eye of Mollie McFee. A long overdue thanks must also go to Philip Bohlman, who, at an inaugural PhD workshop in Hannover way back in 2010, brought me together with the likes of Gavin Steingo and Nico Higgins, and in doing so energized—and validated—our fledgling ethnomusicological interests.

I am hugely in debt to Awais Hussain, who not only provided feedback on my full draft but patiently steered many of my translations toward their true meaning. The musical transcriptions herein could also not have been possible without the work of Austin Ali, whose sensitive ear to both Western and Hindustani modes of listening helped make sense of what I was hearing. Any ensuing errors in translation and transcription are mine alone.

(Almost) Finally, I would not have been able to write a book about Bradford without the friends I grew up with. Amar Benkreira, Rory McKeating, Tom McArthur, Adam Clark, and Andy Robinson—my best friends and brothers. And for their endless enthusiasm for a late-night Bradford curry, I must also thank Alex Dallas, Chris Marshall, John McLear, and Simon Whitley.

And so here we are. At the beginning and end of every journey of love will always be my family. To my wife, Andreea, who has journeyed with me to the ends of the earth and sacrificed so much. And, at the end of it all, to my mum, dad, brother, and sister—Sarah, Alan, Matt, and Em—without whom I would be nowhere at all.

Thomas Hodgson
Los Angeles, 2024

Notes

1. The *shehnai* is a kind of wooden shawm, the significance of which I explore in more depth in chapter 1. For a more general overview of the *shehnai* in South Asia and how it was debated in ethnomusicological circles, see Jairazbhoy (1970, 1980) and Deva (1975).

2. In *Saif-ul-Malook*, Mian Muhammad Bakhsh indicates his age in poetic form: عمر مصنف دی تد اہی تن دا ہے تن یکے (The writer was thirty-three years old when he wrote this book).

3. *Safar ul-Ishq* translates more literally to "The Journey of Love." The translated word for "love" here—*ishq*—does not really do it justice (a point one could say more broadly about poetic translation that I will return to repeatedly throughout this book). *Ishq* relates more closely to divine or transcendent love and is something felt often as a burning desire or ecstasy. The word *safar*, meanwhile, is more properly translated in the singular form—that is, "The Journey of Love," but I have transposed it into the plural for the purpose of my own book's title and to refer to the multiple ongoing journeys of Mirpuris between Pakistan and Britain.

4. For Maurice Halbwachs (1992), history is often seen as "dead memory," removed from our experiential relationship with the past. In contrast, collective memory is theorized as a continuously evolving bond, connecting individuals and communities to their past. The notion of "sites of memory," for Halbwachs, represents attempts to historicize memory, salvaging fading collective memories that transform into history. In this view, collective memory is experienced and internalized individually while history is an artificial reconstruction and representation of the past.

5. While there has been a great deal of attention paid in ethnomusicology and anthropology to music and migration (Lomax 1959; Allen 1971; Gross, McMurray, and Swedenberg 1996; Baily and Collyer 2006; Toynbee and Dueck 2011; Stokes 2021a and 2021b), there has been surprisingly little consideration afforded specifically to how music, and those who practice it, might contribute to understandings of multicultural politics. Increasing levels of migration and technological communication in Europe and elsewhere in the world have led to a growth in anthropological inquiries into how states regulate and respond to diversity (Goldberg 1994; Bennett 1998; Baumann 1999; Modood 2000; Kosnick 2007; Vertovec and Wessendorf 2010). Scholars have frequently interpreted these processes through the various prisms of cosmopolitanism (Turino 2000; Stokes 2007; Werbner 2008), diaspora (Slobin 1993) and globalization

(Stokes 2004). On the ground, however, diversity is still frequently discussed *as* multiculturalism. See also Thomas Turino and James Lea's (2004) volume on the topic of identity and arts in diasporic communities.

6. This is not necessarily the case with respect to the wider role of Urdu poetry recitation for South Asian Muslims (see, for example, Mahmudabad 2020).

7. A notable exception here is Jürgen Wasim Frembgen's (2012) beautifully written ethnography about Sufi music in shrines on the Potohar plateau. His evocative and sensitive ethnographic description also reminds me of that other great "pure" ethnography, Bernard Lortat-Jacob's *Sardinian Chronicles* (1995). I return to Frembgen's work in more detail in chapter 1. For more on the wider Sufi music of the Indus valley, see also Peter Pannke's (2014) coffee-table book and accompanying CDs *Saints and Singers: Sufi Music in the Indus Valley*. Meanwhile, scholarship on Mirpuris in the UK has tended to subsume Mirpuris into a wider South Asian diaspora. Notable exceptions to this are Sean McLoughlin and Muzimal Khan's (2006) work on Pir Shah Gazi's and Mian Muhammad Bakhsh's shrines at Khari Sharif near Mirpur (which I discuss more in chap. 1) and Christopher Shackle's (1990, 2007, 2012) work on the latter's poetry (though Shackle is primarily concerned with linguistics rather than migration).

8. See, for example, Pasha Mohamad Khan (2013). As Khan identifies, Mian Muhammad Bakhsh explicitly sang the praises of his contemporary Punjabi poets— such as Ahmed Yār—in his verses: "Then Aḥmad Yār took up the government of poetry; He made an assault and sat upon the throne, and received the region of the Punjab" (159).

9. In her excellent monograph, Radha Kapuria explores how, in pre-Partition Punjab, there was an "effortless organicity in the choice of folk music and dance to represent Punjab to outsiders" (Kapuria 2023, 3). Kapuria in fact turns this fetishization of "the folk" on its head to reveal the deep history of classical performance and performers in colonial Punjab and thereby situates it within the wider tradition of Hindustani art music. As she goes on to argue, however, a persisting factor here may well also be the longer history of hereditary musicians (*mirasi*) being treated with contempt—and borderline fear—by both the colonial British and higher caste contemporaries (159).

10. By *regulated* I am alluding to the changing dynamics of immigration laws and multiculturalism, which I explore more fully in chapter 3.

11. There are parallels here to what Michael Herzfeld has theorized elsewhere as "cultural intimacies" (2005). Yet, as we shall see, the Mirpuris in this book are rarely "embarrassed," in Herzfeld's term, by their poetry and music. If anything, we will see a strong indifference to what others might think of them—an indifference that is self-consciously fashioned as a means of resistance in the face of pressures to integrate.

12. For more on the wider impact of Partition, and especially the role of music among refugees in West and East Bengal, see Carola E. Lorea (2018).

13. Funded by the World Bank and the Asian Development Bank, the dam was designed by a British firm, Binnie & Partners of London, and its construction was carried out by a consortium of eight companies from the US, who in turn hired engineers from Pakistan, the US, Canada, Britain, Germany and Ireland to carry out the project. At its inception, it was an international project, funded by global capital.

14. I explore the significance of this moment in more depth in chapter 1.

15. For more on land acquisition and involuntary displacement in South Asia, see Somayaji and Talwar (2011).

16. See Imran and Smith (1997, 18). This quote is from an oral history of Mirpuris by the anthropologist and writer Irna Qureshi (née Imran). Along with the Bradford photographer Tim Smith, she published a number of wonderful coffee table books on Mirpuri culture in Britain and Pakistan, including the 1997 book *Home from Home: British Pakistanis in Mirpur*. I have taken inspiration for the title and themes of chapter 2 of this book from Irna and Tim's works.

17. See Shaw (2000).

18. Imran and Smith (1997, 19).

19. While it may appear from this that "music" and "poetry" are distinct categories, this is not the case on the ground in Azad Kashmir. As we shall see in chapter 4, the lines between music and poetry are blurry: my *shehnai* teacher, for example, would often perform Mian Muhammad Bakhsh's poetry on his instrument, the *shehnai* giving melodic and metrical voice to the verses. Conversely, everyday micro performances (*mushai'ra*) of poetry by amateur musician-poets, such as those we encounter in chapters 2 and 5, are enacted with no formal musical training. It is, rather, the process by which acts of musical performances connect the poetic with the affective that I focus on here, and describe below as a poetics of migration. See also Carola E. Lorea (2018) and Abha Chauhan (2021), whose work I cite more fully in chapter 1.

20. Schwartz was drawing on Clifford Geertz's definition of collective memory as a "pattern of *inherited* conceptions expressed through symbolic forms—such as poetry, music, and other aspects of culture—through which people imagined, rehearsed, and articulated their knowledge of and responses to their lived environment" (see Geertz 1973, 89, emphasis added). The key word here, for the conceptualizing the relationship between memory and migration, is "inherited." For Geertz, these inherited memories, passed across and down generations, serve as ways of understanding society and one's place within it. Collective memory, in this view, is a means of representing deeply rooted cultural values, that may span generations as well as geographic distance, and so render present experiences meaningful.

21. These grand narratives are realized during performances of sung poetry through a process of what Berger (2009) has described elsewhere as "auditory perception . . . intimately enmeshed with bodily action" (Berger 2009, 13, quoted in Chávez). Action, in this sense, is taken to mean not only bodily movement in the present, but how such corporeality embodies collective memories of migration through what Chávez terms "aesthetic labor" (2017) and what Walter Andrews and Mehmet Kalpaklı have described in other contexts as "undocumented emotional histories" (2005, 8), moments when poetic themes of love and the beloved become enacted. See also Deborah Kapchan (2007) and Richard C. Jankowsky (2021) for more on the relationship between Sufi trance rituals and their relationship to worldly experience.

22. Other studies of poetry among working-class cultures come to mind here, and in particular Aaron Fox's (2004) ethnography among rural Texans in *Real Country*. There are strong, though not always visible, parallels between how Fox locates a kind of poetics-of-the-voice among rural, working-class musicians, and my own observations of how musicians in Kashmir and Britain call upon poetry in everyday life as a means of navigating life on the margins (of Britain, of Pakistan). In this regard, see also Steve Caton's (1990) *Peaks of Yemen I Summon*.

23. I discuss this in relation to Herzfeld's (2005) "social poetics" in more depth in chapters 2 and 3 and again in the conclusion. In particular, I am drawn to the idea that poetic metaphors of spiritual journeys—as they become recited and enacted—are indexed against the act of migration as a way of rhetorically coming to terms with often unimaginable pain and hardship.

24. Gloria Anzaldúa describes this emotional liminality across and between borders through the term "borderlands" (1987, 3)—dividing lines that are understood more symbolically than materially.

25. In some respects, the marginalization of Mian Muhammad Bakhsh relates to a sharpening of nationalist sentiments in Pakistan that have foregrounded *qawwali* as the music of the nation par excellence (see also Shackle [2007] for a more focused discussion of poetry and Pakistani nationalism). This positioning has been reinforced by scholarly writing on *qawwali* that has tended to focus on its performance in urban centers in Pakistan and India and its subsequent emergence as a world music genre in the West (Ernst and Lawrence 2002; Frishkopf 2008; Asher 2009). Such changes to this music's social positioning reveal the extent to which music and its social status are exposed to the vagaries of politics and economics, especially as they become entwined in nation building (Neuman 1990).

26. I am reminded here of Fredrick Barth's (1969, 408) influential treatise on how social groups orient themselves within and across ethnic boundaries: "Categorical ethnic distinctions do not depend on an absence of mobility, contact and information, but do entail social processes of exclusion and incorporation whereby discrete categories are maintained *despite* changing participation and membership. . . . One finds that stable, persisting, and often vitally important social relations are maintained across such boundaries and are frequently based precisely on the dichotomised ethnic statuses. In other words, ethnic distinctions do not depend on an absence of social interaction and acceptance but are quite to the contrary often the very foundations on which embracing social systems are built." Inherent in Barth's writing is the assertion that because social boundaries are continuously being permeated by people both from within the social group and from without, it is increasingly problematic to distinguish and define a person as belonging to any one unchanging ethnicity.

27. "From some perspectives," Richard Wolf has argued, "music that transcends locality is more interesting and lucrative than so-called traditional music of a particular place" (2009, 5). See also Wolf's (2013) article about how the poetics of Sufi practice relate to questions of agency. Through such emphases on the "global hierarchies of value" (Herzfeld 2004, 2–3), Wolf argues, the significance and importance of local-level music practice for people or groups is often lost. Wolf discusses the renowned *qawwali* singer Nustrat Fateh Ali Khan as an example of an artist who has come to symbolize Pakistan both within South Asia and beyond. In the world music marketplace, Nusrat has become the example par excellence for Sufi music performance. Indeed, in many respects, Nusrat has come to symbolize "Pakistani-ness"—a kind of "assumed shared aesthetic," as Wolf puts it.

28. See also Jürgen Wasim Frembgen (2012, 21).

29. The name of Mian Muhammad Bakhsh's collection—*Safar ul-Ishq*—itself contains its own ambiguity: '*Ishq* can be taken in Sufism to mean both "love" and "burning passion" and relates to the desire to obtain the beloved.

30. While I indicate my own terminological preferences in the main body of the text, I will outline here some of the scholarly debates that surround these terms.

Philip Lewis, for example, has noted that in Britain, "the category 'Pakistani' encompasses distinct regional and linguistic groups: Pathans distinguish themselves from Punjabis, with young Mirpuris—a group to which some two-thirds of all British Pakistanis belong—re-categorise themselves as 'ethnic Kashmiris' to distance themselves from Pakistan" (2007, 22). See also Uzma Anjum and Ahmed Siddiqi (2012) for a discussion of Pothwari across generations. In the introduction to her book, *Diaspora Youth and Ancestral Homeland*, Gill Cressey (2006) runs through and dismisses a list of academic terminology that is used to describe the identities of British Kashmiris and Pakistanis. For Cressey, "hybridity" (Hall 1996) won't do, as it "implies a binary starting point and it [is] too easy to fall into the trap of contesting binary models whilst continually [imputing] them with choices of language and metaphor" (Cressey 2006, 4). The idea of "new ethnicities" (Hall 1988; Back 1996) is also seen as problematic, as it is believed by Cressey to be "associated with categorisation and minority status within the nation state" (2006, 4). These terminological debates were characteristic of much writing on identity politics in the 1990s. In what follows, I have deliberately set them to one side and tried to focus instead on how Mirpuris understand themselves through and by poetry and music, rather than racial or ethnic categories.

31. When I use the umbrella term *Kashmir* in this book, I am referring specifically to Azad Kashmir—that is to say, Pakistan-Administered Kashmir. This is an important clarification not least because of the division of Kashmir between Pakistan and India but also because of the ensuing cultural differences between the two partitioned states.

32. See Lothers and Lothers (2010) for a linguistic survey of the Pahari/Pothwari language. It is notable that only around 5 percent of the population of Azad Kashmir speak actual Kashmiri, a language that is more commonly spoken over the Line of Control on the Indian side of the Kashmir valley (Jammu and Kashmir). The claiming of a Kashmiri identity by Mirpuris is thus multilayered and complex—something I explore in more detail in later chapters.

33. See Farah Nazir (2014). See also Bhatti (2013).

34. The Kashmiri Arts and Heritage Foundation, for example, is an energetic advocate for Kashmiri identity and culture in Britain and regularly organizes public-awareness events. See https://www.kashmiriarts.com (accessed January 12, 2023).

35. This reference to Mirpur as *Little Britain* has also found its way into mainstream news outlets in the UK. See https://www.bbc.co.uk/news/magazine-17156238 (accessed January 12, 2023).

36. Philip Lewis has noted that "the category 'Pakistani' encompasses distinct regional and linguistic groups: Pathans distinguish themselves from Punjabis, with young Mirpuris—a group to which some two-thirds of all British Pakistanis belong— re-categorise themselves as 'ethnic Kashmiris' to distance themselves from Pakistan" (2007, 22).

37. Bradford Congress (1996, 94). The notion of duality, in terms of both identity and music, is one that fell from favor in the 1990s, with scholars instead adopting terms such as *syncretism, creolization, bricolage, cultural translation,* and *hybridity* (Vertovec and Cohen 1999) to describe a range of cultural phenomena and processes that shaped what Hall (1988) coined "new ethnicities." The idea of South Asian migrant youth being "between two cultures" (Watson 1977), or that their sense of identity was mediated by duality (Banerji 1988), was challenged by the recognition that facets of culture, identity, and religion are selected, often self-consciously, from multiple heritages (Vertovec and Wessendorf 2010) and that, importantly, these new ethnicities were

contextual, transitional, and always subject to change and evolution (Stokes 1994). For further context, the term *Jat*, mentioned in this quote, refers to a Punjabi agricultural community, an ethnosocial caste.

38. This is a point that was made repeatedly by the anthropologist Gerd Baumann (1996, 2004), which I follow in this book. Baumann stressed the importance of paying particular attention to the minutiae of individual and group behavior when considering broader societal concepts, such as multiculturalism, and their implications.

39. The value of the cultural diversity brought about by postwar migration was famously critiqued by Charles Taylor (1994) in his study of multiculturalism. Taylor identified two fundamental contradictions in the way multiculturalism was conceived by politicians in the late twentieth century. The first, he argued, lay in a tendency toward treating people in a "difference-blind" fashion, which pushes against the second: a liberal need to recognize and foster particularity. Inherent in this duality were, for Taylor, several issues—namely, that "the reproach the first makes to the second is just that it violates the principal of non-discrimination. The reproach the second makes to the first is that it negates identity by forcing people into a homogeneous mould that is untrue to them" (1994, 43). Taylor went on to state that in practice—and this is what is particularly relevant to Mirpuris in Britain—only the minority cultures in a society are expected to submit to these formulations, which ultimately serve to render them as "alien." Taylor questioned Dworkin's (1978) claims that a liberal society is one that adopts no particular substantive view about the ends of life (i.e., about what constitutes a "good" life): "The society is, rather, united by a strong procedural commitment to treat people with equal respect" (1994, 56).

40. For more on the Honeyford affair, see Foster-Carter (1987), Dermaine (1993), and Lewis (1994).

41. It is a debate that periodically bubbles back to the surface. See, for example, *The Daily Telegraph* (February 8, 2012) and *The Daily Mail* (February 20, 2012).

42. Since 2009, my fieldwork continued more-or-less uninterrupted over the following decade, and widened to include other cities in the UK, as well as three extended stays to Pakistan, and, more recently, in 2019, Qatar. In Bradford, some of the primary sites of my research included volunteering for local South Asian arts organization Oriental Arts, founded and run by Champak Kumar Limbachia, and for Festival Director Ben Pugh at the 2009 and 2010 Bradford Melas; working with music teachers in schools across the city; spending many a day and night in the barbershop of Mr. Khokhar on Oak Lane, where between the buzzing of hair clippers we listened to music and recited poetry, and where, after dark, musical instruments would appear; at gatherings of Pothwari *sher* (sung poetry) held across Bradford and Rochdale; in late night curry houses and in taxis. In Pakistan, most of my time was spent in the home of my *ustad* in Khari Sarif, or else travelling with him and his ensemble around Azad Kashmir and northern Punjab to play at shrines, and at the weddings of British Mirpuris. An important focal point (and privilege) during this period were the lessons Zulfikar gave me on the *shehnai*, which were philosophically enriching as much as they were musically challenging. These lessons culminated in my own *ganda bandhan* ceremony, attended by the crème-de-la-crème of the local music scene: an auspicious occasion during which Zulfikar formally accepted me as his *shagird* (student); a lifelong commitment.

43. There are striking similarities here with John Baily's (2006) study of Gujarati Muslim musicians in Bradford, who would regularly tell him that "music is in our blood."

44. In some chapters, there are exceptions to this general rule, and I have indicated in the text when I have quoted conversations that were part of a more formal interview. For the most part, I have instead relied on my daily ethnographic journal (in which I would recall, transcribe, and translate conversations, often immediately after they took place or else at the end of each day) in addition to the hundreds of photographs and videos I took throughout this period and continuous correspondence over WhatsApp.

45. The politics that regulates the movement of people across national borders seems to be moored to the changing tides and iniquities of globalization—the ebb and flow of people and capital. The global financial crash of 2008 resulted in a decade of austerity measures that reshaped the political landscape. One of the ironies in the years since 2008 has been how, rather than seeing an increase in regulation of the global banking system, much political and public blame has instead been directed toward the people at the opposite end of the economic spectrum: immigrants. The flow of global capital, facilitated by neoliberal market economics, has been maintained while politicians have sought new ways to constrict the flow of people. This is a curious slippage of logic and shows that while the financial crash may have been economic, its fallout has been deeply political. After a decade of austerity and rising inequality following the financial crisis, the political language of North America and much of Europe has become increasingly marked by immigration. In the UK, the EU referendum of 2016 was fought largely along these lines: that above arguments about legal sovereignty, the real issue facing the country was uncontrolled immigration. We must break away from the EU, the argument went, in order to take back control of our borders. There is a historical relationship that bears relation to the discussion here between the vagaries of global flows of capital and the movement of people: as one has increased, often the other has contracted and vice versa.

46. This has arguably been a tendency in the multiculturalism debate on both sides of the political divide. For government reports, see Cantle 2001; West 2005; Phillips 2005. For a useful summary and analysis of the "multiculturalism backlash," see Phillips 2006; Vertovec and Wessendorf 2010.

CHAPTER 1

1. *'Urs* are moments of commemoration on the anniversary of a saint's death. *Biraderi* refers to the endogamous network of close kin to which a person belongs, and it continues to play a crucial role in Mirpuris' lives, both in Kashmir and in Britain (for more, see Shaw 2000).

2. See also Carola E. Lorea (2018). Lorea has similarly described how, for Bengali migrants to the Andaman Islands, the "circulation of performers, song texts, and music instruments represents a strong connection that maintains ties with a perceived homelands" (2018, 52).

3. Music and musical instruments in Kashmir play a key—one might say instrumental—role in the formation of collective memories because the sensory experiences of music-making plug into and inform various other spheres of migratory experience. The organological history of the *shehnai* (what Bates [2012]

and others might describe as its social life) is one of physical movement: its relatively small size, durability, and portability are likely reasons why it is found in so many parts of South Asia, with local variations in length, finger holes, mouthpieces, and materials.

4. I draw here on scholarship that takes sound seriously as a means of understanding physical environments and the way people move through them: what Stephen Feld famously termed "acoustemology." Often these studies have worked to destabilize the primacy of the printed word in the formation of knowledge, particularly as a means of mapping history. As the previous chapter showed, performances of sung poetry play an important role in the production of these cultural memories. Elsewhere, Feld and Basso (1996) interrogate the connections between landscapes, places, and unspoken memories, showing how environments become intertwined with personal and shared acts of remembrance. Through their research, they show how physical surroundings shape and influence our memories, both individually and as a community.

5. At this point, I should probably say a few words on scholarship on the *shehnai*, not least because it was written about so insightfully by Nazir Jairazbhoy, beginning in 1970, with his paper "A Preliminary Survey of the Oboe in India." In many respects, the 1970s were the *shehnai*'s moment in the global limelight. Only a few years earlier, in 1966, the instrument's most famous player, Ustad Bismillah Khan, was sent to Britain by the Indian government to perform at the Edinburgh Festival: the *shehnai* was sounding India on the global stage. In 1975, B. C. Deva responded to Jairazbhoy with his own take, "The Double-Reed Aerophone in India," which included a number of suggestions and corrections. Then, in 1980, Jairazbhoy responded with his own rebuttal, "The South Asian Double-Reed Aerophone *Reconsidered*." The debate was animated by contrasting views of the instrument's etymological and organological history across South Asia and Persia. What's apparent in this decade-long conversation is how contested the *shehnai*'s history and etymology came to be within ethnomusicology; and yet, since then, surprisingly little has been written about this important instrument.

6. My previous training on the trumpet proved surprisingly useful during my own *shehnai* lessons, as my ability to control the air as it passed through the instrument meant I could pick up Zulfikar's initial instructions quickly, despite the differences between the instruments. ("You have a gift from God," Zulfikar somewhat overgenerously remarked before handing the instrument over to me as a gift. By the following day, his wife, Maqsood Begum, had made a simple case for the instrument from leftover cloth. The thin, brightly patterned cloth fit snugly over the instrument but offered little protection, except maybe from dust. I realized that the fabric matched that of one of the blankets on the *khat* [rope bed] inside.) During my time in Kashmir, I spent a good part of each day sitting with Zulfikar, learning from him and practicing the *shehnai* in his small courtyard. His children played around us; visitors came and went. During our lessons, he would chastise me for writing down what I was supposed to learn by memory: "Music is in your heart and mind," he would remind me, "not on paper."

7. Our companion, Mr. Khokhar, would also often use this proverb, though in its Urdu version: *Jaisa bogay, vaisa kaatogay.*

8. Indeed, as Rekha Chowdhary (2021, 6) notes, a great many Punjabi and Pahari speakers across the border with India—and beyond the immediate Mirpuri community—revere the poetry of Mian Muhammad Bakhsh and are drawn to his shrine at Khari Sharif. See also Chauhan (2021) and Kapuria (2023).

9. Jayson Beaster-Jones (2016) has written about this proliferation of meaning through Peircian semiotics—that is, the capacity for any given sign (an instrument, a voice, a song) to relate to a plethora of objects (memories, beliefs, feelings) that hold together as a form of cultural memory.

10. There are strong parallels here with Deborah Kapchan's (2007) ethnography of Sufi spirituality and trance among Moroccan Gnawa.

11. I am also reminded here of how Denise Gill (2018) describes listening practices (*muhabbet*) in Istanbul and their role in cultivating gendered emotional aesthetics.

12. The opening lines to Rumi's *Mathnawi* utilize the metaphor of the reed flute's separation from its natural state to symbolize the pain of separating from a beloved: "Listen to this reed how it complains, telling a tale of separations." He was also, as Pasha M. Khan (2013) has shown, well connected to other contemporary poets in Punjab, in particular at the court of Rajit Singh. There are many parallel examples of this across the Persianate world, in which the poetic metaphor of pain and longing are expressed through the reed flute. For further examples, see Annemarie Schimmel's (1975) *Mystical Dimensions of Islam*.

13. For more on Mian Muhammad Bakhsh's biography and wider literary relevance, see Nabil Syed Ali (2010) and Christopher Shackle (2007).

14. For more on Punjabi poetry more broadly, see Rakshat Puri (1997), Shackle (1990, 2012), Pasha M. Khan (2013, 2019), and Abha Chauhan (2021).

15. As listed by Christopher Shackle (2007, 127), the principal modern editions of *Saif-ul-Malook* include Muhammad Bakhsh, *Qissa Sayf al-Mulook*, edited by S. H. Zaygham (Lahore, 1993); *Safar al-'Ishq ya'nī Qissa Sayf al-Mulook ma'i Sawānih-'uMr.ī -yi Musannif* (Muzaffarabad, 1994); *Sayf al-Mulook*, Urdu translation by Z. Maqbool (Lahore, 2000); and *Sayf al-Mulook* (*Safar al-'Ishq*), edited by Sh. Sabir (Lahore, 2002).

16. See also Sean McLoughlin and Muzamil Khan (2006), who, citing Werbner and Basu (1998), describe how, for Mirpuris, the story of *Saif-ul-Malook* draws connections among Sufi cosmologies, ritual practice, organizational forms, and ethical ideas.

17. The *dhol* is a large double-skinned barrel drum found across much of South Asia; the *chimta* is a long steel tong with small metallic cymbals running down both forks, also common in many Punjabi folk traditions such as *bhangra*.

18. There are striking similarities here to how Frembgen describes musicians performing in shrines in the Potohar Plateau. He shows how these musicians also mobilize *Rāg Pahari* as a means of connecting audiences—experientially and spiritually—to the surrounding landscape (2012, 16–17). While Frembgen primarily relates the significance of this "coupling" to the landscape of the Pohotar Plateau, as we will see, for Mirpuris, the invocation of landscape through *Rāg Pahari* becomes especially magnified when living in diaspora.

19. See Neuman (1990). See also Bor et al. (2010).

20. See Bhatti (2013).

21. For more on cousin marriages and chain migration, see Shaw (1988, 2000). See also Charsley et al. (2020).

22. For more on Mirpuri remittances, see Ballard (1994; 2003).

23. For Kashmiris, first-generation migrants to places like Bradford were soon joined by spouses and children, and subsequent marriages within kinship groups (*biraderi*) created a rhythm of chain migration (Shaw 2000). In the late 1970s, Verity Saifullah Khan's (1977) contribution to James Watson's edited volume *Between Two Cultures:*

Minorities and Migrants in Britain was one of the first anthropological studies of Mirpuris in the UK. The volume approaches the study of migrant communities by comparing their lives in Britain to their countries of origin. For Khan, this dual-site analysis spans and connects British Mirpuris in Bradford with Mirpuris in Azad Kashmir. Through comparison, Khan is able to demonstrate how some of the Pakistani village's institutional and social structures have not simply continued in the UK but have adapted and developed in new surroundings (often through the perpetuation and strengthening of the *biraderi*). This nuanced and in-depth study provides critical insights into socioeconomic development, patterns of settlement, and experiences of racism that, as McLoughlin (2006, 118) notes, is "so often missing from contemporary accounts of 'segregation' in Bradford." See also Shaw 2000; Anwar 1979, 1986; Baumann 1996; Lewis 1994; Modood 1997; Werbner 2002. For government reports, see The Runnymede Trust 1980, 2000.

24. While this verse is often attributed to Mian Muhammad Bakhsh, it is not actually found in any of his written manuscripts. That it has become so tightly linked to Mian Muhammad Bakhsh shows the importance, and indeed ambiguity, of oral traditions. Of particular interest here, however, was Shakoor's easy code-switching. Code-switching such as this had been a familiar part of my childhood in Manningham, Bradford. As a child at school, my Mirpuri friends had frequently switched between English and Pothwari, often within sentences. Working as a paperboy at Mr. Sheikh's newsagent, I also heard him code-switch depending on the customer, and he came to address me affectionately as "Tom *beta*"—Tom, my son. As Farah Nazir (2020) has brilliantly written, "Code-switching is not random but rather is motivated by social discourse functions, such as formality or informality, solidarity, group identity, lexical need, and topic. For instance, someone from the British South Asian diaspora may insert *yaar/yara* (friend or brother) in their English utterance as a symbol of their group identity, solidarity, and familiarity." Code-switching, in this sense, acts as both a marker of identity and a cipher against outside hegemonic forces. Rather than seeing such bilingualism as an indication of two worlds, we might more productively understand it as indexing a specifically Kashmiri identity—indeed, an *azadi* (free) identity, independent from the twin polarities of Britain and Pakistan, or what Homi Bhabha (1994) famously described as the "third space."

25. For more on musicianship and status in South Asia, see Clayton and Leante (2015) and Schofield (2010).

26. It was clear during my fieldwork that bagpipes were at the lower end of the hierarchy—an observation that was evident in the lower remuneration bagpipers received when performing alongside other instruments such as *shehnai* and *dhol*. For a wider historical overview of hierarchies of instruments in South Asia—at the apex of which sits voice—see Wolf (2014, 10–13).

27. I am reminded here of Jane C. Sugarman's (1997) ethnography of Prespa Albanian weddings, in which moments of performance "embody" multiple aspects of the performers' and audience's senses of self and community.

CHAPTER 2

1. This quote is from Irna Imran, Tim Smith, and Donald Hyslop's (1994, 23) fascinating coffee-table book *Here to Stay: Bradford's South Asian Communities*.

2. This has also been noted by Katy Gardner (1993) in her study of Bangladeshi migrant communities in Sylhet, northern Bangladesh.

3. There are resonances here with Paul Oliver's (1990) *Black Music in Britain*, which looks at the various forms of Black musical cultures that emerged in Britain, particularly since World War II. Oliver asks how this music might contribute more broadly to our understandings of "Britishness." Looking at the emergence of reggae, calypso, and bhangra in Britain in the late 1950s and '60s, Oliver uses music to ask questions about the relationship between identity and music.

4. There is a violent historical irony at play here in how the textile industry in places like Bradford benefited significantly from the British Raj banning textile exports from India in the nineteenth century, thus driving production (and, later, migrant workers) to Britain.

5. As Alison Shaw (2000) has identified, these early migrants were the first in a four-part process of migration from Pakistan to Britain. The first migrants, known as *pioneers*, were followed by the second stage of a chain migration. These pioneers were generally unskilled male workers. Throughout this phase the impermanence of the migrants in Britain was dispelled, and so a third phase of migration began when wives and children began joining the men. The fourth and arguably continuing phase comprises generations of British Mirpuris who were born in the UK.

6. See Phillip Lewis (1994, 2007) and Marta Bolognani (2007a, 2007b).

7. See Cantle (2001); West (2005); Phillips (2005).

8. Over the past decade there has been a widespread denunciation of multiculturalism by politicians across Europe and in the press. This debate has been well discussed in anthropology, sociology, and political science, particularly under the terms of (super)diversity and transnationalism (Cohen 1997; Gidley 2007; Vertovec 2007); in multiculturalism and the regulation of diversity (Taylor 1994; Baumann 1999; Back et al. 2002; Parekh 2006; Vertovec and Wessendorf 2010); and in diaspora studies (Tölölyan 1996; Turino 2000; Werbner 2002; Cohen 2007; Knott and McLoughlin 2010). Barely heard in all the debates and discourses cited above, however, are the voices and opinions of Mirpuris themselves. They are, in this respect, an absent presence. This is surprising when one considers that Mirpuris account for over two-thirds of all Pakistanis living in Britain (Lewis 2007).

9. For a counterargument to the parallel lives perspective, see Deborah Phillips' 2006 article "Parallel Lives? Challenging Discourses of British Muslim Self-Segregation." Phillips shows that British Muslim "self-segregation" is largely a myth mobilized by politicians to advance an integrationist agenda. Instead, her study reveals that people choose to live in particular areas because, as one respondent put it, "you feel safe, comfortable. . . . You're with your own kind" (2006, 33)—a sentiment surely shared by everyone, everywhere. It is also the case that areas such as Manningham experienced significant "white flight" whereby ethnically white British families moved away as migrant communities moved to the area. To frame segregation as necessarily negative, and to then lay the blame solely at the feet of Mirpuris, is somewhat disingenuous.

10. From the Bradford Mechanics Institute: "As an international centre of the worsted cloth industry there was a huge demand in Bradford for education in technical and commercial subjects, chemistry (for the dyeing industry), building construction and industrial art and design. Modern languages teaching was also important: it was said that on the Bradford Wool Exchange it was possible to hear every European language on any morning of the week." "History—Bradford Mechanics Institute Library." Bradford Mechanics Institute Library, https://www.bradfordmechanicsinstitute.org (accessed March 5, 2019).

11. Alison Shaw (1988, 9) noted that in Mirpur, the average weekly wage was the equivalent to approximately thirty-seven pence, whereas in Birmingham the average weekly wage for a Pakistani was thirteen pounds.

12. Imran and Smith (1997, 23).

13. It is estimated that in the eighteen months prior to the introduction of the 1962 act, fifty thousand people migrated to Britain, compared to the seventeen thousand who had entered between 1955 and 1960. For an excellent analysis of this period of migration from Mirpur to Britain, see Alison Shaw, *Kinship and Continuity*. In his book *Race and Politics*, Muhammad Anwar suggests that the 1962 immigration act had a large bearing on the pattern of migration from the Indian subcontinent to Britain: "It turned a movement of workers, many of whom were probably only interested in staying temporarily, into a relatively permanent immigration of families. Also the voucher system initially reinforced the kinship and friendship bonds and therefore reinforced the pattern of settlement" (1986, 9).

14. While the postwar period saw the most significant and sustained period of migration from Mirpur to Britain, they were by no means the first migrants to make the journey. Many strong communal and familial ties were maintained and perpetuated when the early recruits to the merchant navy, known as *lascars*, began to form shifting and semipermanent settlements in British ports, notably Cardiff, Liverpool, South Shields, Hull, and London (Lewis 1994, 11).

15. Because of the relative political enthusiasm for immigration over this period, British Pakistanis became the second-largest ethnic minority community in Britain, of which Mirpuris represented some 60 to 70 percent of the total population. It was estimated that in Bradford, 16.1 percent of the overall population were British Pakistanis. See 2001 UK Census; see also Pnina Werbner (2008).

16. Today, these photographs are held by the Photography Archive of Bradford District Museums and Galleries. See https://photos.bradfordmuseums.org/view-item?i=207579&WINID=1727735382383, accessed July 3, 2023.

17. Imran and Smith (1997, 12).

18. In *Camera Lucida*, Roland Barthes discusses the lasting emotional effects of photographs, which act upon the body as much as the mind. He was interested primarily in the viewer—or spectator, in his terminology—as opposed to the photographer and the object being captured. Barthes develops two concepts to describe how the spectator responds to a photograph. The first, "stadium," relates to how the spectator interprets the photograph in relation to their own linguistic, cultural, and political surroundings. The second, "punctum," connects the object or person(s) depicted in the photograph to the internalized emotional response of the spectator.

19. See Anwar (1979).

20. One customer described having his photograph taken at Belle Vue Studio thus: "So you have to choose one of the ties, or shirts, or a jacket, just for the pose. You put it on and then they will give you a comb and there's a nice mirror if you want to apply any lotion on your face. Then you make yourself comfortable. And this fellow will do his best to make you look brighter, fair in colour, smart-looking, and with expensive stuff; they might give you a watch to put on just for the photograph. So it helps you know, when the person looks at the photograph he thinks that all these belongings are yours, you are a man of substance!" (Imran, Smith, and Hyslop 1994, 27).

21. Imran, Smith, and Hyslop (1994, 38).

22. See, for example, my discussion with Shakoor in chapter 1.

23. Imran, Smith, and Hyslop (1994, 37).

24. *Biraderi* refers to the endogamous network of close kin to which a person belongs, and it continues to play a crucial role of Mirpuris' lives, both in Kashmir and in Britain (Shaw 2000). One result of this close-quarter living and interaction is a strong communal sensibility. Members of the household will, more often than not, eat together, work together, and sleep together under the stars. In such small pockets of housing, this communality extends beyond the courtyard to the degree that most people know one another, sometimes through working relationships but more often through *biraderi*. Interactions take place on a daily basis, with frequent visits to houses of other members of the *biraredi*. These guests will receive food and, often, a bed for the night with the assumption that such gestures will reciprocated, or they have already been. All these factors combined result in tight-knit family units in the sense that there is a strong sense of intimacy among all family members.

25. As the previous chapter showed, cousin marriage is also a crucial means by which kinship groups are strengthened across Britain and Pakistan.

26. Whenever I traveled to Mirpur, I would carry two suitcases packed with gifts for Mr. Khokhar, which weighed twenty kilograms each. The politics of these gift exchanges, or *lena-dena* ("take and give" in Urdu), has been explored in detail by Shaw (2000).

27. In his famous formulation, Marcel Mauss (1925) defined gifts as "prestations which are in theory voluntary, disinterested and spontaneous, but are in fact obligatory and interested."

28. As I explore more in chapter 5, other goods also circulated between Mirpur and Bradford that helped cultivate the feeling of a home away from home and all the emotional connotations that brings. Mirpuris in Bradford, for example, were quick to open grocery stores that stocked spices and other commodities that, at the time, would have otherwise been difficult to acquire—quintessentially Mirpuri ingredients that, through the labor of combining through cooking, would activate the smells and tastes of home, carrying enormous emotional value while these Mirpuris were physically separated from loved ones.

29. Imran, Smith, and Hyslop (1994, 171).

30. For example, while in Mirpur during the summer of 2010, I spent several evenings watching cricket on the television with Mr. Khokhar and his family. During my stay, both England and Pakistan were competing in the ICC World Twenty20 finals. After the initial group stages, England were set to play Pakistan for a place in the semifinals. In the preceding days, there had been much joking between Mr. Khokhar's family and myself as to who was going to win the tie. As play was about to begin, I asked Mr. Khokhar which team he would be supporting. After a few seconds' thought, he said, "I think this time I will support England." I asked what he meant by "this time," to which he replied, "Well, last year, you know, Pakistan were champions, Pakistan won the World Cup. This time, I think it's England's turn, so I will support them." England went on to win the tie and the event's final, after which everyone around me greeted me with beaming grins and handshakes. At other times, we would walk through the bazaar (market) of a nearby town and would be frequently stopped in the street by strangers. "Where are you from?" I would be asked. When I replied "Bradford," the stranger would exclaim, "Aha! Bradford! I have many family there. Bradford is a very nice place." A conversation in Urdu would then flow about the best restaurants in Bradford, whose family owned them, and where the family lived in relation to me.

31. As the city expanded, mills and workers' houses, built with yellow Yorkshire sandstone, sprawled across the valley and up the dales in a steep rise of rapid urbanization. On the edges of the city, terrace houses gave way to fields separated by dry-stone walls, and in many places this remains the case to this day. As well as building model villages to house their workers, industrial philanthropists such as Sir Titus Salt (1803–1876) and Sir Samuel Cunliffe Lister (1815–1906) built large municipal parks on land they subsequently donated to the city.

32. Magnus Marsden (2007, 479) has made similar observations of Chitrali masculinity at musical gatherings: "Mahfils, thus, emphasize a style of Chitrali male subjectivity that focuses on the cultivation of cultural connoisseurship and taste as well as the nurturing of emotional sensitivity."

33. I heard this proverb from *Saif-ul-Malook* many times over the following years.

34. For excellent linguistic analysis of Mian Muhammad Bakhsh, see Nabil Syed Ali (2010).

35. The words *gora*, *gori*, and *gorey* translate as "white man," "white women," and "white people."

36. Mirpuri youth culture and education in Bradford will be discussed in depth in chapter 3.

37. Like *qawwali* performances, Pothwari gatherings begin and end with passages from the Qur'an, and these serve to legitimize the gatherings (Qureshi 1986, 115).

38. Mr. Khokhar's poetry is examined in more detail in chapter 5.

39. Most of the musicians were from the surrounding area, but several were from the town of Redditch, south of Birmingham. With the exception of Abid Qadri, all of the musicians relied on other forms of employment in order to earn a living. For the most part, this meant driving taxis, working in restaurants, and occasionally tailoring. Music for these musicians was a part-time endeavor rather than a professional occupation, yet it remained central to Mirpuri life. Devotion to music—and the public display of that devotion—was a marker of esteem.

40. Broadly speaking, a *ghara* serves two purposes in life. Its primary function is as a water pot, and its second is as a percussive instrument in Pothwari music; occasionally it serves a tertiary function as an ashtray or a doorstop in between performances. The *ghara* is a medium-size earthenware pot with a large belly that tapers up to a circular opening at the top. A *ghara* player will sit cross-legged on a mat on the floor, with the instrument between their legs at an angle of approximately forty-five degrees. The player will wear a series of metal rings (*challa*) on the fingers of their left hand and strike the side of the *ghara* with them to produce sharp, fast, and metallic rhythms. While the left hand strikes the body of the *ghara*, the right hand beats the cylindrical opening of the pot to produce bass notes of varying pitches. The *ghara* player will wear a band of bells (*ghungru*) on their right wrist, and in between playing bass notes, they may raise and wave their right wrist to shake the bells before striking the top of the pot. The *ghara* and its performer thus emit three main sounds: the metallic rhythm of the left hand; bass notes when the mouth of the pot is struck; and bells when the right wrist moves or is shaken. The dominant sound comes from the left hand, which creates movement and drives the rhythm along. The bass and bells of the right hand and wrist punctuate this loud, driving rhythm. In a Pothwari performance, there are often two *ghara* players who play in tight unison.

41. The *dholak*, a hand-held version of the larger *dhol* drum, is a common instrument across South Asia. It is a wooden, double-headed hand drum with a treble

skin at one end and a bass skin at the other. Each skin is stitched over an iron ring onto the body of the drum, which allows the performer to alter the two pitches of the instrument. The *dholak* is usually played in the person's lap, using fingers and palms to create high and low pitches. In sound, technique, and rhythm (*tala*), the *dholak* is comparable to the *tabla*; however, the *dholak* is primarily a folk instrument and more common in North Indian styles including *qawwali*, *bhangra*, and Punjabi folk music such as Pothwari.

42. In terms of melody and meter, Pothwari music follows similar principals to other North Indian light classical music—particularly *rāg* (melodic mode) and *tāl* (metric cycle). The sung melody in Pothwari music is used to articulate the lyrics of the given poetry and often is mimicked by the other melodic instruments, which improvise around the scale in between verses. The lines of the poetry are sung in couplets that together form a complete thought and, similar to the sung poetry of Kalam Kohistani *rō* in northwest Pakistan, can also stand alone as individual poems (see Baart [2004]).

43. This kind of circular seating arrangement follows a similar pattern to other South Asian musical practices and is usually organized according to local etiquette (*adab*). For more on *adab* in South Asian musical practices—particularly between teacher (*ustad*) and student (*shagird*)—see Silver (1984). In a practical sense, this circular seating arrangement is also arranged so as to direct the loudest percussion sounds away from the audience and allow the quieter instruments and vocals to come through. For such a large concert, however, the venue had provided a powerful amplification system. When the concert began and I felt the full force of the sound system, I understood why Mr. Khokhar's friends had been so amused by my finding the small concert in Pakistan loud. The concert in Rochdale was, by contrast, almost deafening.

44. The connections between audience and performer are, in this sense, similar to those in *qawwali* performances described by Qureshi (1986, 5): "Experiencing Qawwali means charting a process of interaction between musicians and listeners, between music and audience responses; in short, a performance." Silver (1984) has also written about the role of gesturing in relation to *adab* during musical performance: "Going beyond purely musical performance, the musician will often use gestures and histrionics, as well as dress, as part of his strategy or *adab*. Some musicians eschew any sort of showiness, and prefer to let their music make its own impact. Others employ many different head motions, facial expressions, and hard and arm gestures to add extra effect to their music" (325). See also Clayton and Leante (2011).

45. In a *qawwali* performance, the devotee hands money to the sheikh as a spiritual offering. It is then transformed from a spiritual offering to worldly pay as it passes from the sheikh to the musician. Through this process, the circulation of money becomes an incidental reward for the musician's performance rather than an integral part of the *qawwali* (Qureshi 1986, 138). As such, the audience remunerates the performer implicitly rather than explicitly.

46. Regula Qureshi also recognized the material importance of money in a *qawwali* performance, saying, "The operation of this social norm does highlight the importance of money as a material of social status" (Qureshi 1986, 129). Sam Cherribi (2010) also noted elsewhere how money, as a material rather than financial object, can carry emotional significance for people in diaspora: "Money has a far greater emotional significance than is immediately apparent. It buys flowers for lovers, shoes for babies taking their first steps, chocolate for aging parents who may have been feeling neglected. . . . All of these make up the fabric of life, and the currency that affords them

down through the centuries becomes a kind of common ground within a given culture" (24).

47. Qureshi (1986), 228.

48. In addition, the majority present at the performances I attended were elder or first-generation Mirpuris. As mentioned, the staggered arrival of people throughout a Pothwari evening made clear that these were working Mirpuris who came at the ends of their shifts. There were occasionally exceptions: besides Mr. Khokhar's grandson and me, a few boys were there with their parents, and there was a small group of men in their early thirties.

49. The remaining seats are usually unreserved, and the rows fill up on a first come, first served basis. Throughout the evening, however, people move seats, either to get a better view or to sit closer to a friend or relative.

50. This act of forming relations and networks between people around a shared musical tradition has a long history on the Indian subcontinent. As Katherine Schofield has identified, among the Mughal elite, "music was patronized through a series of friendships circles with mutual interests in music, poetry, and Sufism" (Schofield 2010, 495; see also Brown 2006). Arguably, however, less attention has been paid to the act of patronizing music among lower-class, low-caste peoples. Historiographically, this has been due to a range of factors, including a lack of available written sources resulting from low literacy levels among lower-caste people on the subcontinent and sung poetry being a largely oral tradition. This is not as true for the performance of music by lower-caste musicians, as Mahmudabad (2020), Kapuria (2023), and Khan (2013) have been at pains to correct. Baily (1990, 154), too, has observed that "the condemnation of music has important implications for the status of musicians in Muslim societies. The performance of music at public or semi-public gatherings, such as wedding parties and concerts, is very often in the hands of hereditary professional musicians. They usually occupy a low position in society, often stereotyped as social deviants. Popular imagination connects musicians with drinking alcohol and prostitution."

51. *Mirza* is the name given to describe a man of high rank or princely status.

52. Asked why there seemed to be only Mirpuris at these concerts, Mr. Khokhar replied, "This is a very traditional music. Only Pothwari people listen to this music." I followed this question up by asking why there were no women at the concert. Mr. Khokhar found this question funny and quipped, "They are at home!"

53. "Ashrafisation" is a tendency for Indian Muslims to claim descent from Arabian ancestors and their adoption of Arabic caste or family names such as Qureshi, Shaikh, or Khalifa (Baily 2006).

54. Harold Powers (1980), quoted in Katherine Schofield (2010). Other criteria for music to attain classical status are, according to Powers and quoted by Schofield: (1) That the music is "purveyed by performers who a) regard themselves and are regarded as highly skilled *specialists*, who must be b) taught and *indoctrinated* into their speciality . . . over a long period of time"; (2) That it is "said to conform to a *music-theoretical norm* which is part of a Great Tradition"; (3) That it is "both a) connected with and supportive of cultural performances to which it is ancillary, and at the same time b) conceived as an independent domain that can stand on its own as the centrepiece of a cultural performance"; (4) Finally, that it is "patronized by individuals or groups, belonging to the ruling elite, who profess *connoisseurship*."

55. There are resonances here with the work of Magnus Marsden (2007), in which gatherings such as those described here as exemplify ways of understanding

complex interactions between performer and listener that take into account both local sensibilities and broader political pressures.

56. Broadly speaking, these "political and social pressures" might perhaps be better summed *as* multiculturalism—or, as Stokes (2010) describes it, "the regulation of diversity," to which the following chapter will turn.

CHAPTER 3

1. See "Saquib—Shafaqat No Taqat Ft Liaquat (Official Music Video)," https://www.youtube.com/watch?v=kOm3iPLushg (accessed May 29, 2024).

2. See Herzfeld (2005).

3. See Zeshan Sajid YouTube channel, https://www.youtube.com/@ZeshanSajid (accessed June 12, 2023).

4. For more on the anthropology of humor, see Maurice Said (2016).

5. Interview by the author, February 17, 2010.

6. Oriental Arts was also heavily involved in the programming of the Bradford Mela during this period, which I explore in detail in chapter 4.

7. See chapter 4.

8. Interview by author, February 17, 2010.

9. This has some important side implications for how we might historically understand the origins of world music as a genre. Much has been written about it being invented by predominantly white record label executives. Yet we can actually trace this music being performed in Britain much further back. This suggests that postwar migration and the multicultural cities it created played a crucial role in fostering emergent live music markets and international tours.

10. Interview by the author, January 17, 2010.

11. Interview by the author, January 17, 2010. Elsewhere in the city is the record label Integrity Beatz. Established in 1996 as an educational project to provide studio-recording time for local communities, the label has become so successful and popular that it has now developed into a full-time record label and music promoter with a number of extremely promising and talented young Pakistani rappers and producers. And then, on a more mundane level, there is the everyday music that inflects peoples' lives. One Mirpuri taxi driver explained to me, with no small touch of irony, that he knew he was going to hell for listening to music, but he needed to have something to "bounce" to, just to get him through the day.

12. This sense of optimism seems to have been a condition of much writing on so-called postmigrant urban youth culture in the 1990s. As Swedenburg's (2001) study suggests, there was a tendency for scholars of South Asian music to focus on the more prominent, acclaimed, famous, or notorious musicians among South Asian groups in Europe. Swedenburg's study on Islamic hip-hop in Britain, for example, also focuses on Aki Nawaz, lead singer of Fun-Da-Mental (FDM), which emerged in the early 1990s at a time of heightened racial awareness in Britain. The Rushdie affair was still being hotly debated by academics (Ruthven 1991; Parekh 1990), and an argument was being put forward that politically, Pakistanis were beginning to find a voice (Lewis 1994). Amid these discussions, however, perceptions of Islam were becoming increasingly reified and characterized by the burning of books, the repression of women, and an opposition to music (for the latter, see Baily 1990). Fun-Da-Mental set out to challenge these characterizations by incorporating into their music Islamic themes, verses from the

Qur'an, and references to the Black Power movement in the United States. Swedenburg argues that "Fun-Da-Mental's uses of 'Islam' are therefore central to its multipronged intervention: Islam instills religio-ethnic pride among Asian youth, serving as an image of antiracist mobilization, and creating links between Asians and Afro-Caribbeans, shocking and educating white leftists and alternative youth" (Swedenburg 2001, 62).

13. *Nasheed*s are a form of popular Islamic worship song.

14. There is little doubt that this was indeed the intention of Aki Nawaz. Aki is a highly articulate, politically astute front man who has repeatedly asserted in interviews (academic and media-led) what he intends his music to represent. But arguably, there has been little attention paid to whether the music of FDM actually does, or did, any of the stuff the musicians and academics claimed. Part of the tendency for sociologists in the 1990s to latch onto FDM was because they were, in many respects, the first British Asian group to reflect upon the racial and religious stereotyping that were central to the multiculturalism debate. While Swedenburg's study provides an important perspective on the experience of British Asian youth in Britain, there is a danger that the perspective is actually Aki Nawaz's. Swedenburg isn't alone in identifying FDM's music as in some way speaking on behalf a generation of Asian youth who, in reality, constitute a large, heterogeneous group of people.

15. These tensions were also played out within academia. In their edited volume, Sharma, Hutnyk, and Sharma (1996) set out to create a "space in academia for Asian academics" because they believe that "white" people writing about "Asian" culture is automatically orientalist and racist. Sharma in particular accused the anthropologist Gerd Baumann of being "another one of those modern 'ethnically sensitive' white ethnographers still directing the anthro-colonial gaze on Black folks' cultures" (34). His argument suggests that Baumann, as an anthro-colonial outsider, essentializes Asian youth culture and negates other possible narratives of syncretic identity formulations. This, for Sharma, "flattens out differences and contestations across class, caste, ethnicity and gender" (36). Despite blaming Baumann for "sustaining a neo-Orientalist understanding of anterior Asian youth cultural formations," Sharma, at the same time, absolves him of this crime by saying that, after all, it's not his fault: the Otherness of *bhangra* is culturally inaccessible to white ethnographers. Their book, on the other hand, "signifies a new space and recognition being claimed for and by emergent Asian academics and cultural critics operating both inside and outside British universities" (10). Orientalism is seen, by Sharma, Hutnyk, and Sharma, as the hegemonic discourse of the Imperial West, embodied in the academic writings of scholars such as Baumann and Les Back (1996). It is a one-way discourse written in and out of the West about what is thought of the Orient. Sharma's assertion seems to stem from what Pnina Werbner (2008) has described as the "distinctly skeptical, un-cosmopolitan assumption that just because one happens to come from a certain society, one is incapable of understanding other societies, empathising with their members' predicaments and joy, learning their languages, poetry, myth making and story telling, appreciating their material culture, the challenges of their environment, their mundane everyday lives" (23).

16. For more on the topic of gender and the South Asian underground scene in Britain, see Falu Bakrania's (2013) excellent ethnography *Bhangra and Asian Underground: South Asian Music and the Politics of Belonging in Britain.*

17. These are, namely, Kala Sangam, Manasamitra, and Oriental Arts. These organizations will be explored in more detail in the following chapter.

18. See Arts Council England, https://www.artscouncil.org.uk.

19. John Baily (2006) has shown that in Bradford, where there are areas that have been identified as racially segregated, interactions among different social and ethnic groups are contested and contextually contingent, but music can play a mediating role. His study of Gujarati Khalifa Muslim barber musicians in Bradford shows that there is resistance among Khalifas to let Mirpuris become involved in their community societies. As one Khalifa put it, "People from outside, even though they are Muslim, cannot join the Khalifa community. This community is meant for the Khalifas only [so that] outsiders cannot interfere in the welfare [of the Khalifas]. I'll give you one example. We've got our own madressa, religious classes, which are run there. And the Pakistani community, which is also Muslim, they wanted to join us, they wanted to join with our community, they said, 'Oh we want to be a member, whatever the fee is, we'll pay'. But the rules and regulations and objectives is for the Khalifa community only.... The other Muslims cannot join it. Otherwise there will be too much interference culture-wise, their culture will be different" (Baily 2006, 261). With this entrenchment and fortification of "community," however, comes a reification of how "others" are assumed to behave: "The Mirpuris are regarded by other Asian communities in Bradford, and apparently elsewhere, as rather unsophisticated people.... There can be no doubt that there is strong pressure within the Mirpuri community to maintain a way of life which is in harmony with the values of Mirpur" (Baily 1990, 157). Baily goes on to show, however, that these seemingly rigid social distinctions—or areas identified as segregated—are transgressed in Khalifa musical ensembles, which include Muslim, Hindu, Sikh, and English members and whose songs include lyrics sung in Hindi, Urdu, Punjabi, and Gujarati.

20. The Associated Board of the Royal Schools of Music (ABRSM) is an educational body that provides practical and theoretical examinations in music. Practical examinations are based primarily on a recital of classical (i.e., baroque, romantic, or contemporary classical) music. In addition, candidates are tested on scales and arpeggios, sight-reading, and aural skills.

21. Studies that do exist have often focused on statistical data at the expense of more nuanced ethnographic depth. In their survey of 83 young Pakistanis, for example, Din and Cullingford identify that "girls were more likely to listen to 'pop' music (90 per cent v 78 per cent), dance (42 per cent v 33 per cent) and Bhangra (16 per cent v 15 percent). Boys were more likely than girls to listen to rock (18 per cent v 3 per cent), metal (13 per cent v 2 per cent), Quawali [sic] (6 per cent v 3 per cent) and rap (37 per cent v 25 per cent)." Having established these musical proclivities, Din and Cullingford identify one of the limitations of their statistical approach: one "reason for the 17 percent of young people who said that they enjoy listening to both English and Asian music may be the result of some Asian singers who have incorporated a combination of Western type pop/dance into traditional Asian music such as Qawali." Their variable spellings of *qawwali* aside, Din and Cullingford do not take notice of this insight and continue to make rigid distinctions between two apparently homogeneous cultures: "Asian" and "English." Part of the study sought to establish the musical tastes of young Pakistanis and the relationships and pressures exerted on them by their parents. To introduce this element of his research, Din asks, "Do they [young Pakistanis] enjoy listening to English or Asian music and what kind of films do they enjoy watching?" Citing his statistical data, Din answers his question: "these young people have a definite preference for, and enjoy listening to, English music and watching English films."

According to Din, "We need to know why they prefer one type of culture over what is considered their parents' 'native' culture." However, Din stops short of outlining precisely why we need to answer such a question and, indeed, what he means by such broad categories as "English" and "Asian" music.

22. Patricia Jones (1984), quoted in Baily (1990, 158).

23. Interview by the author, January 21, 2010.

24. Lewis (2007), 26.

25. "Tony Blair Talks about Education, Education, Education," HuntleyFilm Archives, 1997, https://www.youtube.com/watch?v=kz2ENxjJxFw.

26. See Furlong and Cartmel (2004).

27. In this sense, the chapter builds upon recent anthropological and ethnomusicological studies of young Muslims and music in Europe and beyond (Shannon 2006; Kapchan 2007; Gazzah 2008; Nieuwkerk 2011) by showing that young Mirpuris often unravel and articulate their cultural and religious identities lightly and in relation to context.

28. Carlton Bolling College is a larger than average mixed comprehensive school for 1,402 students ages 11 to 18, of whom 309 are in the sixth form. The school is located in the Undercliffe area of Bradford, approximately one mile outside the city center, and is the one of the historical homes of the Bradford Mela, which I discuss in the next chapter. The area is recognized as having significant socioeconomic deprivation, and a high proportion of students are eligible for free school meals. Nearly all of the students are from minority ethnic backgrounds, and the majority speak English as an additional language. The students' attainment on entry to the school is well below average, and higher than average numbers of students have learning difficulties and/or disabilities. For many years, Carlton Bolling struggled in its Ofsted reports and teetered on the brink of being shut down. Recently, however, it has undergone something of a renaissance and was the first school in the Bradford area to receive "outstanding" status from Ofsted.

29. According to the Ofsted (2008) report, "The school serves an area with average levels of social and economic disadvantage. The percentage of students from minority ethnic groups is above average, with students with a Pakistani heritage as the largest minority ethnic group. The number of students with learning difficulties and/or disabilities is also above average."

30. Carlton Bolling College, like Beckfoot, also sees remarkably few Mirpuri students take up music as an option at GCSE. The disparity here is more marked than at Beckfoot because the majority of students at the school are of Mirpuri heritage. Rather than offer music as an option at GCSE, then, the school has been grouping together music, drama, and dance under a Performing Arts syllabus. In this option, there is less emphasis placed on music, and there is no prerequisite to take up an instrument. One reason for this may be that the school has recently been made a "center for maths and science." As such, many more resources (time, money, and equipment) are directed to science courses rather than music. Indeed, the head teacher explained to me that the school's recent success in Ofsted reports has been partly due to a conscious effort to "concentrate on the school's strengths." At first, speaking to the students seemed to confirm this. None of them, when asked, expressed any desire to learn an instrument or, for that matter, to take music as a course at school. Some students openly laughed at the suggestion. Many others said they did not like music but rather enjoyed math and science. This emphasis on the sciences rather than the humanities shows that at an early

stage, young Mirpuris are already moving down the science route rather than toward the arts and humanities.

31. Fulat (2005), quoted in Lewis (2007, 33).

32. Several themes run through these responses to the *Telegraph & Argus* article: race, integration, religion, ethnicity, nationality, education. Indeed, in a wider sense, and in another word, these are concerns about multiculturalism. Wherever the commentators' ire is directed, however, it is clear that one set of people is to blame: Pakistani Muslim youth. There are clear, structured uses of language in these quotes to identify a distinction between "us" and "them." Ultimately, soaked in a sense of inevitability, one reader asks rhetorically, "Is it not now perfectly clear that they do not wish to integrate?" (*Telegraph & Argus*, July 10, 2001). These distinctions cut through not only oversimplified demarcations of race but also religion and ethnicity (Alexander 2003, 526; see also Alexander 2000). The Pakistan Christian association wants nothing to do with young Pakistani Muslims while one Indian commentator goes further by implying that Indians, with their higher levels of education and integration, could never be associated with such insurrections.

33. Wright, "Letters to the Editor." *Telegraph & Argus*, July 12, 2001.

34. Anon, "Letters to the Editor." *Telegraph & Argus*, July 12, 2001.

35. Dutt, "Letters to the Editor." *Telegraph & Argus*, July 12, 2001.. In academia, too, the Asian youth "problem" has been identified and critiqued. With specific reference to writings on Pakistani and Bangladeshi youth, Alexander (2000, 18) reflected that "however it is explained, excused or demonized, it seems all are agreed on one thing—Asian men are out of control and in trouble." In the aftermath of the 2001 Bradford riots, the anger directed at the "out-of-control youth" continued, reaching its zenith in the now infamous campaign run by the *Telegraph & Argus*, in partnership with West Yorkshire Police, to "name and shame" those involved in the disturbances. The newspaper ran a full front-page spread with pictures of Pakistani youth taken from closed-circuit television footage of the riots. Readers were asked to contact the paper and disclose the names of recognized faces, which would then be passed on to the police. Once the suspects had been named, the paper then fulfilled the remainder of its campaign: shaming the young men by publishing their names and photos in subsequent editions. Within the city, the campaign was praised for its tough and effective stance on bringing to justice those involved in the riots. This level of police and public attention on Mirpuri youth is not an isolated occurrence. At the 2010 Bradford Mela, groups of young Mirpuris were followed around the site by police officers armed with large video cameras, effectively placing the teenagers under a spotlight for all to see. Indeed, whatever the perceived effectiveness of these police measures and the *Telegraph & Argus* campaign had, their respective approaches have had the much broader and enduring effect of marginalizing young Mirpuris.

36. Phillips has argued that this marginalization occurs within a range of spaces including "the political arena, the media, and other institutional settings to the level of the neighborhood and the street. . . . British Muslim families [are] frequently pathologised as inward looking, reluctant to learn English, and clinging to 'unacceptable' traditions, such as forced marriages and the ritual slaughter of animals" (2006, 26). In other contexts, Michael Herzfeld has argued that "the less literally face-to-face the society we inhabit, the more obviously cultural idioms become simulacra of social relations" (2005, 6).

37. In Bradford, this point was emphasized with reference to "Muslim schools" that were underresourced and underachieving. However, it has been counterargued (Modood 2005, 202) that, rather than being Islamic schools, the schools that the reports referred to were state-run and simply had a Muslim intake of over 90 percent. The schools in question were local comprehensives that suffered from "white flight" and decades of underinvestment. For critics of multiculturalism, however, they came to symbolise the "problem" of divided cities, cultural backwardness, riots, lack of Britishness, and a breeding ground for militant Islam.

38. Never mind that the areas they lived in had long experienced white flight and decades of underinvestment. What became clear is that the language of *parallel lives* was about ethnicity and cultural difference at the expense of racialized inequalities in power, education, and status (Phillips 2006, 38). Anwar (1979, preface) traces this back to the late 1970s, suggesting that Pakistanis were "resistant to change and non-participation on an individual level in British institutions, in particular where they have a choice, [this] is a feature of the majority of Pakistanis. . . . Their participation is limited due to both the external constraints such as prejudice, discrimination and the internal cultural norms and values." At the same time, government reports into the 2001 disturbances as well as media coverage discussed inner-city clustering by ethnic minorities in terms of negative inevitability (that it fosters social depravation, drugs, crime, and poverty). Pakistani Muslim respondents described their areas positively—as vibrant social spaces, local networks of support and care, institutions and *biraderi*. Indeed, many Mirpuris' choice to live in Manningham is as much about wishing to live close to friends, family, and the *biraderi* as it is about economic disadvantage, racism, and inequalities in the housing market (Phillips 2006). As one elderly man responded regarding Manningham, "Everything is here, our culture our shops, mosque . . . and the best thing about this area: no racism."

39. Philip Charles's own heritage is not epiphenomenal to the cultural makeup of these workshops. The convergence of Pakistani Mirpuris and Afro-diasporic communities in Bradford has long produced musical collaborations that address their shared experiences of racism in postwar Britain. The most striking example, perhaps, is Fun-Da-Mental, whose members include artists from both communities and whose music explicitly addresses racism, inequality, and the double standards by which they are held. For more, see Sharma, Hutnyk, and Sharma (1996).

40. According to the school's Ofsted report at that time, Belle Vue Boys' "students are predominantly from Pakistani backgrounds and a small proportion, about 10%, [are] at an early stage of learning English when they join the school. Students from other Asian backgrounds and White British students form a small minority of the population. The proportion of students eligible for free school meals is high at around the 40% mark; that of students with special educational needs and/or disabilities is above average. Many students join or leave the school at times other than the start or end of an academic year." The report goes on to describe the school's standards as well below the national average, with exceptionally low attainment levels on entry. For the full report, see https://reports.ofsted.gov.uk/provider/27/148062 (accessed May 25, 2011).

41. For example, "Once I drove my mum's car into the wall, I know it was stupid but I am only young after all. . . . Don't mean to make you jealous, she's the best cook ever. No one can touch her now not your auntie or your mother."

42. Significantly, Ofsted's 2010 report describes the school's curriculum thus: "The school's curriculum is good. There is an appropriate curriculum policy in place which is supported by good quality schemes of work for all subjects from the National Curriculum except for music." See Ofsted (2010).

43. For more on this, see also Phillip Lewis (2007). For Tahir Abbas (2006, 2009), this meant that Mirpuris were "compounded by the traditional rural origins of first-generation migrants, who have largely organized community and political culture around clan-based kinship networks [*biraderi*], where opportunities for the subsequent generations to break out do not always exist. Local Muslim leadership is weak, and inter-generational tensions are not being resolved, particularly in relation to patriarchy. . . . [Many young Muslims] are trapped in a cycle of decline," quoted in Lewis (2007, 7). Cornel West (1993, 210) has argued that such processes of marginalization result in a "relative lack of [cultural and political] power to present themselves and others as complex human beings and thereby to contest the bombardment of negative, degrading stereotypes," quoted in Alexander (2000). In the Netherlands, the social positioning of young Muslims has been described by Cherribi (2010, 4) as "the trifecta of coercion" whereby migrants and postmigrant individuals are subjected to three types of social pressure simultaneously. I am slightly uneasy with the use of the word *trifecta*, however, given that it is most commonly used in gambling contexts.

44. Prior to the partition of India in 1947, Kashmir was a princely state under the suzerainty of the British Crown. Following Partition, it was expected that Kashmir would accede control to Pakistan, due in part to its majority Muslim population. In anticipation of this, Pakistani forces advanced into Kashmir, only for the Maharaja to accede control to India. Since then, control of Kashmir has been split and disputed among three nations: Pakistan, India, and, to the north, China.

45. Tahir Abbas (2009) has argued that Pakistanis and Azad Kashmiris, more so than other South Asian migrant groups, live "excluded lives, existing near or at the bottom of local area economic and social contexts." In particular, Abbas cites the higher number of men employed as taxi drivers as evidence of their "marginal nature."

46. See CrimeRate (2023).

47. See Ali (2017).

48. On his radio show, Changis had been trying to encourage young Kashmiris to take ownership of the pejorative term, *Paki* by reassociating it with its original meaning: the prefix *pāk* means "the pure" in Urdu. Yet the boys in the room did not appear interested in such linguistic nuance. Racist abuse should be met in kind: "It doesn't matter who they are, if they come here we'll give them a kicking."

49. According to the government Office for Standards in Education (Ofsted) in 2009.

CHAPTER 4

1. This quote is featured in Irna Qureshi's (2010, 83) coffee-table book *Coming of Age: Celebrating 21 Years of Mela in the UK,* for which I worked as a researcher. I reuse several interviews from this project in this chapter.

2. For comparison, see also Diamond and Trimillos (2008).

3. While the Bradford Mela was the first of its kind in the UK, it follows a long tradition of *mela*s held across the Indian subcontinent such as those I attended at Khari

Sharif. In some areas of India, *melas* have expanded to vast proportions. The Kumbh Mela—a Hindu pilgrimage and festival—regularly attracts over sixty million people who gather and bathe in the Ganges at Hardwar, a city in the Himalayan foothills.

4. As Steven Vertovec and Susan Wessendorf recognized, multiculturalism around this time came to mean many possibly related but nevertheless discrete things, including "a demographic condition, a set of institutional accommodations, objectives of a political movement or a broad body of state principals" (2010, 7). Ralph Grillo, on the other hand, sees multiculturalism as best understood as "a political project, involving strategies, institutions, discourses, practices, seeking to address a multicultural reality" (2010, 27). Les Back (1996) negotiates this dynamic—of the physical versus the conceptual—by talking about physical urban multiculture, as opposed to the concept of multiculturalism. This is an important distinction because it recognizes that historically, the application of multiculturalism as a concept by policymakers has had profound ontic effects on individuals and groups. This is because, Back argues, an uncritical understanding of multiculturalism risks perpetuating "simple cultural archetypes that reify 'minority' and 'host' cultures respectively" (1996, 8). Indeed, for Bhikhu Parekh (2006), multiculturalism should ultimately be about valuing cultural diversity rather than simply the rights of minority cultures. Tariq Modood, drawing on Parekh, goes further by suggesting that "the value of the presence of a variety of cultures in a society cannot be understood as increasing our options, for other cultures are rarely options for us. Rather, their sense of contrast gives us a deeper understanding of our own culture and makes us reflect and learn about the diversity of humanity" (2005, 173).

5. The Rushdie affair in particular placed Bradford and its Mirpuri population at the center of national focus. For more on these debates, see Ruthven (1991); Rushdie, (1992); Lewis (1994); and, Parekh (1990).

6. At the time of going to press, preparations for the second Jaag Festival to take place on June 22, 2024, were already well underway, with a wide range of speakers and panels. For the program, see https://www.literaturemustfall.co.uk/jaag-festival-programme-and-speakers (accessed May 15, 2024).

7. Over ten years after the "multiculturalism backlash" (Vertovec and Wessendorf 2010), migration remains one of the key policy issues in Britain, and indeed Europe, today. A series of current (refugee) and ongoing (climate) crises suggests that along with more conventional forms of economic migration, nation-states will need to continually rethink how they respond to increasing levels of diversity within their borders. Historically, this has been the work of multicultural politics. Yet narratives surrounding multiculturalism appear to have stalled. Despite playing host to increasingly diverse societies, nation-states are still often understood as more or less distinct cultural entities. Multiculturalism—as a policy and a lived practice—must, if it is to be effective, bridge this plurality of cultures on the one hand with the singularity of the nation-state on the other. Given the likelihood that globalization and climate change will produce ever-increasing levels of migration (Wallace-Wells 2019), the need for a more nuanced understanding of multiculturalism today is arguably more important than ever before.

8. The philosophical assumptions made in the conception of a liberal multiculturalism—that the power to denote which aspects of culture are valued and which are less valued—are rarely distributed equally among the populace, regardless of

how equitably the law is set out in the constitution. In this sense, "procedural" liberal multiculturalism, in Charles Taylor's term, is based on the primacy of the individual and the regulative authority of an unbiased judicial system. Unanswered in this formulation, however, is the question of how cultures, or aspects of cultures—like music—survive amid increasing levels of cultural diversity. This cuts to the core of many of the anxieties surrounding multiculturalism across Europe today.

9. For more on the Rushdie affair in Britain, see Parekh (1990, 2000) and Ruthven (1991). For discussions of the Rushdie affair in relation to music, see Sharma, Hutnyk, and Sharma (1996) and Hyder 2004.

10. See also Weldon (1989).

11. Qureshi (2010, 15).

12. During my fieldwork, I volunteered for Champak and his company, Oriental Arts. Champak started the company in 1976 while studying pharmacy at Bradford University. He held the first ever live public South Asian music show in Bradford in 1976, in the library building of Bradford College. There was a 25p admission charge to watch live Bollywood music and dance, and the event proved extremely popular. Since then, Champak has been at the center of Bradford's South Asian music scene and has been involved with the organization and programming of the *mela* since it began in 1988. Over several months, I built up a strong working and personal relationship with Champak, and his knowledge and experience of music and Bradford itself proved invaluable. On a personal level, volunteering felt particularly productive because it developed a two-way relationship, or *lena-dena* (give and take; see also Shaw 2000). My volunteering began with simple, mundane office jobs: stuffing envelopes, writing invitations, replying to queries, and so forth. Over time, however, I began to help with funding applications and proposals—two of which attracted a significant amount of funding. In return, Champak introduced me to many people in and around Bradford, including local youth workers, school workers, promoters, and Mr. Khokhar.

13. Champak Kumar quoted in Qureshi (2010, 16).

14. The *mela*s that occurred in the 1990s included performances by Nachda Punjab, Naseeb, Holle Holle, Alaap, Asian Dub Foundation, Fun-Da-Mental, and Jazzy B. In the buildup to the *mela*, the Bradford Festival also organized music and arts workshops in various local parks, schools, and community centers in and around Bradford. These events culminated in the Lord Mayor's Parade, in which a series of floats built by community groups and schools wove their way through the streets of Bradford to the city center, much akin to London's Notting Hill Carnival.

15. Qureshi (2010, 12).

16. Lister Park is one of the large Victorian municipal parks briefly touched upon at the start of this chapter. The park owes its name to Samuel Cunliffe Lister, a prominent industrialist and philanthropist who was influential in the development of Manningham. Lister was responsible for the construction of Manningham Mills— also known as Lister Mills—which dominates the local area and landscape and is where many local Mirpuris came to work in the aftermath of World War II and the construction of the Mangla Dam.

17. Qureshi (2010, 17).

18. Qureshi (2010, 82).

19. Despite being located within a mile of the city center, Peel Park is one of the largest public parks in the Bradford area, covering over twenty hectares of land. Like Lister Park, Peel Park was also built during Bradford's period of economic prosperity

by some of the city's wealthy industrialists. Land for the park was bought in 1847 using a combination of public money (1,500 pounds was given as a grant by the government) and contributions of 1,000 pounds each from Bradford's first and second lord mayors, Sir Robert Milligan and Sir Titus Salt. Completed in 1863, Peel Park was built at the height of the municipal borough's wealth during the Industrial Revolution. The park itself was named after the Conservative prime minister, Sir Robert Peel, and became the first large, publicly owned park space in Bradford. Situated high up on the east side of Bradford's valley, the park has a sweeping view across the valley of Lister's Mill, Lister Park, and Manningham.

20. The process whereby local councils and institutions absorb grassroot festivals has been noted elsewhere, particularly in relation to the Notting Hill Carnival (see Cohen 1993). With this came not only increases in budget through sponsorship levels but also an increasing awareness of the *mela*'s social and political potential. What began as a local, ground-level event organized by a small, disparate group of people quickly became absorbed by the hegemony of the local council. The *mela* soon became a means of expressing policies of multiculturalism as imagined and interpreted by the council. As Stokes has noted in a different context, "Culture assumes a particularly important role in mediating the relations between state and non-state. 'Multiculturalism,' understood as a regulation of diversity, is thoroughly implicated in this process" (2010, 5).

21. Qureshi (2010, 18).

22. For example, according to audience research data, of the two hundred thousand or so people who attended the 2009 Bradford Mela, over 50 percent were "non-Asian" (see Qureshi 2010).

23. According to the manifesto, "the purpose of 'Only Connect,' Bradford District's Cultural Strategy, is to link the work of all the individual people, organizations, agencies and services who have a bearing on the quality of life here and to focus on delivering together the shared goals." See https://publications.parliament.uk/pa/cm201012/cmselect/cmpubadm/902/902.pdf (accessed July 9, 2010).

24. In 2008, the Arts Council England, in collaboration with other funding councils, began an initiative to work with local councils with the aim of developing a framework for the improvement of community-level culture and sport. As part of this framework, a number of targets were set, which mostly comprised percentage increases in certain groups of people engaging in council-sponsored cultural activities.

25. This selective ordering of culture bears striking resemblance to the way Timothy Mitchell (1988) described the World Fairs of the nineteenth century in cities like London, Paris, and New York. Rather than deconstructing the physical power relations between the colonizer and the colonized, Mitchell seeks out the more subliminal structures behind the means of colonial domination. In a departure from previous scholarship, he asserts that ideologies of colonialism are as much "internal" as they are "external." For example, through processes of standardization, regulation of the marketplace, and careful replanning of living quarters and educational systems in nineteenth-century Egypt, Egyptians were ideologically driven into a subjugated position by British occupation.

26. Qureshi (2010, 50).

27. See Qureshi (2010, 18).

28. Steven Vertovec and Susan Wessenorf (2010) suggest that, within the last decade, multiculturalism has been subject to a vociferous "backlash" by politicians and the media, who claim that it stifles debate, fosters separateness, refuses common values, denies social problems, supports reprehensible practices, and harbors terrorists. At the risk of invoking an anachronism, the British Isles have been multicultural for millennia. In other words, these isles have always been subjected to flows of people from other lands: through migration, through invasion, and, more darkly, through trade. Asari, Halikiopoulou, and Mock (2008) suggest that the history of multiculturalism in Britain begins in 1066 at the Battle of Hastings. They argue that the positivistic way in which the Battle of Hastings is presented in schools as a defining moment in English history reveals much about the pathology of English identity versus civic nationalism. It was a moment, after all, when "a foreign force defeated and subjugated a local, indigenous one" (2008, 8). As Benedict Anderson (2006) wryly noted, this history of mongrelization is inextricably intertwined with the history of nationalism, which, by extension, is also part of the more recent history of multiculturalism. Back (1996) emphasizes this by pointing out that even such quintessentially English institutions as a cup of tea or fish and chips are, in themselves, products of intercultural influence that are bounded up with the history of empire and imperialism. In sum, national identity in the UK is, and has always been, "multicultural." Multiculturalism as a policy in the late twentieth/early twenty-first centuries, however, can only really be understood in relation to postwar migration to Britain.

29. Indeed, drawing on Krims, imagining the *mela* in this way, "affords the observer one way to observe changes in the cultural feel for the city, as cities are described and projected throughout great swathes of musical history, across numerous genres" (Krims 2007, xxxv).

30. See Bradford Mela 2010, https://web.archive.org/web/20100611093436 /http://www.bradfordmela.org.uk/bradford_mela_2010/faq (accessed September 19, 2024).

31. For more, see Cohen (1993).

32. This kind of affective power of music has been noted elsewhere (Weber 1975; Krims 2007; DeNora 2000). DeNora argues that "if music can affect the shape of social agency, then control over music in social settings is a source of social power; it is an opportunity to structure patterns of action" (2000, 20).

33. For example, avenues of retail and food outlets, through which people are channeled and encouraged to part with their money, link music stages while the stages themselves are protected behind security barriers, separating audience from performer. Musicologists have long recognized that the use of music in public spaces constitutes a form of social power. Different areas of a festival's site will often cater to specific tastes in music. The Dance area, World Music, and an Indie Stage are common features of recent large music festivals (such as the Glastonbury Festival, WOMAD, Latitude Festival etc.), and people are encouraged to flow between them via food and retail corridors.

34. This point was emphasized to me in an interview with the festival's organizer, Ben Pugh. Interview by the author, June 11, 2009.

35. While there is little existing scholarship on *mela*s in the UK, Abner Cohen's (1993) *Masquerade Politics* is of relevance here. Cohen's book provides an important structuralist analysis of the Notting Hill Carnival. His approach first sets out the

historical development of the festival, tracing its origins and development over the years. This diachronic analysis is then complemented by contextualizing the modern festival in the theoretical framework of cultural theory. The result takes time to delineate the power relations between organizers and participants, highlighting how these have changed as the hegemony of the local council and police absorb and exert their control over the carnival's running. For Cohen, Carnival represents a creative expression of dynamic power relations, embodying the tension between subculture and dominant culture.

36. It is worth noting that Rochdale, Birmingham, and Keighley are all areas with significant Mirpuri populations.

37. It should be emphasized at this point that as well as being a hairdresser, Mr. Khokhar is a musician. Indeed, on several occasions, when the last of his customers left, Muhammad would bring out his *sitar* and Mr. Khokhar and Asif would sing Punjabi poetry in the Pothwari style. Some of the time, he would sing well-known poetry, but for the most part, he would sing his own verse—eliciting cries of "*Wah ji wah!*" from Muhammad and his friends. He is an extremely competent poet and singer, and I have witnessed his performances being met with strong approval both in Bradford and in Pakistan.

38. Both the Hussain Brothers and Haji Ameer Khan are originally from Karachi in southern Pakistan but are now based in London.

39. I have put *representation* in scare quotes here because while it is impossible to completely represent an entire group of people (there will always be cases of cross-interests, tastes, identifications, and loyalties), there is, nevertheless, a clear imbalance between the amount of Indian classical music at the festival and the relative paucity of *qawwali* and Pothwari music. This goes contrary to the relative population sizes (see the introduction). For more on previous debates on representation, see also Clifford and Marcus (1986); Geertz (1988); and, Baumann (1996).

40. This overview was augmented by a tour of the site with the event's producer, Ben Pugh, who explained the rationale and thought processes behind the layout.

41. I had also arrived back in Bradford in time for the *mela*'s twenty-first year, an occasion marked by a Coming of Age celebration supported by a £50,000 grant from the Heritage Lottery Fund grant. The project aimed to collect people's memories of past *mela*s and weave them into a historical narrative that would form the basis of a coffee-table book. I became involved with the project by conducting interviews with members of the public, organizers, and artists. The data from those interviews proved to be useful to both my own research and the Coming of Age project. After the *mela*, I continued to be involved by transcribing interviews as well as providing critical feedback on the manuscript through the writing process and its final draft. Some of the data used in chapter 5 has been collected from the outcome of the Coming of Age project, titled *Coming of Age: Celebrating 21 Years of Mela in the UK*, written by Irna Qureshi. Another outcome of the project was an exhibition held between August 7 and November 7, 2010, in Cartwright Hall, Lister Park. For the exhibition, I filmed and edited a twenty-minute short film of the 2009 and 2010 Bradford Melas, which was shown on a large flat-screen television.

42. See Kala Sangam, http://www.kalasangam.org (accessed September 12, 2010).

43. Their mission is to "deliver art and cultural activities that bring communities together by promoting understanding and mutual respect." They are, in this respect,

aligned with the city council's multicultural policy, which "embraces the city's rich cultural heritage as a legacy for the future generations."

44. At the foot of this area was the *mela*'s main stage: the Mango Stage, a large, blue big top and the biggest of the stages at the *mela* with a capacity of around ten to fifteen thousand people. Despite it being the largest of the stages at the 2009 festival, at previous events it had been much larger and not contained within a big-top tent. The move to smaller stages was part of a push by the festival organizers to reduce the audience sizes that a single large stage encouraged and increase variety and diversity across the site. Consequently, the Mango Stage was popular throughout the weekend and attracted a variety of audiences. The stage promised "tasty national and international music flavours" with performances from prominent South Asian musicians including Jazzy B, Adeel, Bombay Rockers, and Channi from Alaap.

45. The Kiwi Stage was a scaled down version of the Sunset Stage from the previous year.

46. For more on *bhangra* in Britain, see Banerji and Baumann (1990); Baumann (1996); Sharma, Hutnyk and Sharma (1996); Din and Cullingford (2004).

47. This analysis of the festival layout has strong resonances with the way in which William Weber used the development of the concert hall in the nineteenth century as a way of identifying patterns of class organization (1975, 2008).

48. There are some resonances here, perhaps, with Christopher Small's assertion that "'to music' is to take part, in any capacity, in a musical performance" (1998: 1).

49. Interview by the author, July 2013.

50. Ibid.

51. In 2010, the UK government axed their entire university teaching grant for the humanities (though the sciences were protected as a government priority).

52. See also Hodgson (2014). There are also significant and relevant parallels to be drawn here with how the Notting Hill Carnival developed in London. For more on this, see Cohen (1993).

53. As Phillips suggests, the "use of the term 'self-segregation' within the context of racialized political and media discourses implies that ethnic minorities are choosing to opt out of British society; that British Muslims in places like Bradford are withdrawing from active citizenship, sustaining cultural *differences*, and choosing not to mix" (2005, 34). Phillips's empirical research, however, challenges this myth and shows that spatial segregation in Bradford is a multifaceted process that need not necessarily be thought of in negative terms.

54. Imran Khan is a Dutch Pakistani rap singer/songwriter and producer.

55. For more on these workshops and other examples of young Mirpuri music in Bradford, see chapter 3.

56. See also Hodgson (2011).

57. See UK Gov (2022).

58. See UK Gov (2022).

59. See McKenna (2023).

60. See McKenna (2023).

61. See Mark Bosworth (2018), "Does Being a UK City of Culture Create a Lasting Legacy?" BBC.com, April 22, 2018, https://www.bbc.com/news/uk-england-43485141.

CHAPTER 5

1. Kunial (2019).

2. For an ethnography of migrant labor in Qatar in the buildup to the 2022 World Cup, see John McManus's (2022) *Inside Qatar: Hidden Stories from one of the Richest Countries on Earth.*

3. In 2022, Zaffar Kunial was the recipient of Yale University Windham-Campbell Prize. His debut collection, *Us* (2018), was short-listed for a number of prizes, including the Costa Book Award for Poetry and the T. S. Eliot Prize. In 2019, he was poet in residence at the Oval cricket ground as part of the Places of Poetry project. See https://poetrysociety.org.uk/projects/the-places-of-poetry.

4. Kunial (2019, 23).

5. In a 2018 interview with Headstuff, Zaffar described how when "writing about impersonal things, the confusions and the confused energy of personal history is probably still there beneath the floorboards. Sometimes I'm looking away from my stuff, and at other kinds of history and how they intersect with my 'own'. Sometimes personal history comes through memories around individual words, often very small words—like the word *the*, or the word *yours*, and of course the word *us*." See Murphy (2018).

6. In this respect, "Hill Speak" is also clearly a deeply personal and emotional poem that explores how language and memory are intertwined in our sense of belonging. Through his vivid imagery, brought to mind with a playful use of multiple dialects, there is an undercurrent of nostalgia and longing for the cultural and linguistic landscapes of his father, driven by Zaffar's own memories of his journeys to Kashmir as a young boy. "Hill Speak," in this sense, is a kind of testament to the importance of poetry in shaping our sense of self and our relationship to the world around us, and to the potential for language to serve as a site of creative exchange, negotiation, and connection between different cultures and generations. The form and structure of "Hill Speak" also plays a role in its evocation of place and belonging. Its structure is loose and free-flowing, following the organic, spontaneous quality of the language and places he is trying to understand. There are also a number of subtle and complex literary devices—alliteration, repetition, and imagery—that generate a kind of sonic unity and coherence, linking together words and sounds from different languages and dialects to arrive at a sense of shared linguistic identity. The poem's repetition of key words and phrases, such as "hill speak" and "moss speak," emphasize the importance of these linguistic markers in shaping Zaffar's sense of self and his deeper relationship to the natural world.

7. Kunial (2019, 23).

8. To give a sense of how hard Mr. Khokhar has worked, he has been in his barbershop seven days a week for decades, breaking only to travel back to Kashmir once every year or two, usually for a period of a month.

9. In 1962, the British government attempted to stem the flow of migrants arriving in the UK by introducing the Commonwealth Immigrants Act. In the eighteen months preceding when the act was passed, a total of 50,170 Pakistanis entered Britain, compared with 17,120 between 1955 and 1960 (Lewis 1994, 18). After this point, migrants were given vouchers for entry that depended on their skills and prospects of employment. There were still loopholes in the system, however, in that young men below the age of sixteen were allowed to join their fathers as dependents. This allowed

the young men to avoid the 1962 Immigrants Act, which effectively barred unskilled male workers. When a boy migrated to Britain at the age of fourteen or fifteen, it would not be long before he could enter the workplace and contribute economically to the *biraderi* (Ballard 1990, 238). For more, see chapter 2.

10. For more on the relationship between empire and early forms of globalization, especially in a Victorian Era context, see Chris Bayly's *Imperial Meridian: The British Empire and the World*. Jurgen Osterhammel's focus on things and objects in *The Transformation of the World: A Global History of the Nineteen Century* is also relevant to the discussions in this book. And for a more local and Islamicate take on circulation around the eastern Indian Ocean in the Victorian and Edwardian period, Nile Green's *Bombay Islam* is a must. See also Eric Hobsbawm's *The Age of Empire, 1875–1914* (1987).

11. The debate over educational provisions for new migrants would crystallize some years later in the Honeyford affair. For more, see Halstead (1988).

12. Many of these strong communal and familial ties were maintained and perpetuated when the early recruits to the merchant navy, known as lascars, began to form shifting and semipermanent settlements in British ports—notably, Cardiff, Liverpool, South Shields, Hull, and London (Lewis 1994, 11). For more on Alison Shaw's (2000) brilliantly insightful and ethnographically rich overview of postwar Kashmiri chain migration to Britain, see chapter 2.

13. As I explore in more detail in chapter 4, the question of integration has long been at the heart of debates about multiculturalism in Britain. Deborah Phillips (2006) and Katharine Charsley and Marta Bolognani (2020) push back against a narrative of "self-segregation," which has typically, and negatively, framed much antimulticultural discourse.

14. For more Europe-wide engagement with the multiculturalism debate, see Vertovec and Wessendorf (2010).

15. In an Urdu translation of *Saif-ul-Malook*, for example, Sayyid Zamir Jafari (1987) described the everyday influence of Mian Muhammad Bakhsh on his own family in Dadyal: "*Bai Ji* [mother] used to wake early in the morning and after reading *nafal* prayers, she would grind some flour for four to six chappatis and separate the milk from the curd before morning prayer. After this she would remain seated on her prayer mat and read on her rosary of a thousand beads and then make supplications in Arabic and Panjabi. As children we could not understand Arabic but we could make sense of some words in Panjabi. The prayers were read in such a beautiful, melodious way that it seemed to us that it was part of her worship. She had memorised these prayers from our grandmother. As I grew up, I learned that these Panjabi prayers were from Mian Muhammad Bakhsh's long poem, *Saif al-Muluk*" (cf. McLoughlin and Khan 2006).

16. In the early twentieth century, praxis (i.e., the theory of practice) emerged as a key concept in understanding the production, dissemination, and transmission of collective memory (Ortner 2005). This turn toward praxis built upon the methods of oral history, which had long challenged the binary distinction between memory and history. Jan Vansina (1985), for example, argued that oral traditions, when documented, offer representations of the past that are embedded in present contexts, such as those described in this chapter. This broader perspective on historiography recognizes the significance of both personal memory and objective historical accounts, bringing a more comprehensive understanding to scholarly interpretations of the past and its relevance in today's world. By incorporating subjective experiences alongside traditional historical analysis, it deepens our understanding of history and its ongoing

significance in the present. In the context of migration, then, the relationship between memory and movement becomes even more intricate. By leaving one's home and adapting to new environment, poetry offers a means of navigating shifts in personal and collective memories. The experiences, stories, and identities carried by migrants shape memories and contribute to the formation of transnational collective memories. Similarly, the encounter with new cultural and historical contexts may challenge or transform established collective memories, prompting a negotiation between personal and shared histories.

17. For more on the relationship between *ṭarīqāh* (spiritual path) and the *murshid* (spiritual guide) in Mian Muhammad Bakhsh's poetry, see Nabil Syed Ali's (2010) MSci dissertation *To Be Is to Love: The Semantic Field of Love in the Works of al-Hallaj, Rumi, and Miyan Muhammad Bakhsh*. Syed writes how "the poet insists on himself standing outside his work and leaving the discovery to the capacity of the reader's eye" (2010, 124). Indeed, for Syed, the significance of the *ṭarīqāh* (spiritual path) and the crucial role of the *murshid* (spiritual guide) in traversing this path is crucial to understanding Mian Muhammad Bakhsh's poetry: "According to Bakhsh, the *ṭarīqāh* cannot be successfully undertaken without the guidance of a *murshid*. The *murshid* is portrayed as a *malāḥ* or boatman who is familiar with the river (the *ṭarīqāh*) and its dangers." Bakhsh believed that the *murshid*, having traversed the path himself, possesses the knowledge and experience required to navigate the spiritual journey. The *murshid* is aware of the obstacles, pitfalls, and challenges that the *sālik* (spiritual wayfarer) may encounter along the way. By providing guidance, the *murshid* acquaints the *sālik* with the *ṭarīqāh* and assists them in safely navigating its intricacies. Drawing on this metaphor, Bakhsh compares himself to a *malāḥ*, implying that he serves as a guide for those seeking spiritual enlightenment. Just as the *malāḥ* is intimately familiar with the river, Bakhsh claims to possess an innate understanding of the *ṭarīqāh*. His role as a *murshid* is to help individuals embark on and progress through their spiritual journey, ensuring they avoid the perils and pitfalls that may obstruct their progress. Bakhsh emphasizes that without a *murshid*, individuals may become overwhelmed by the challenges of the *ṭarīqāh*, just as someone without a *malāḥ* would drown in the river.

18. Recently, ethnographers studying people and their experiences have strived to go beyond the politics of memory and focus instead on examining the personal and family dynamics involved in shaping things like national memory. See, for example, Gable and Handler's (2000) study of Colonial Williamsburg and White's (2000) ethnography on testimonies at a Pearl Harbor museum. Both these studies show how individual and familial memories often align with larger narratives of belonging, shining a light on the emotional and relational aspects of remembering. Their studies emphasize how personal recollections and witnessing accounts at moments of memory-making contribute to a sense of belonging and personalize national memory. Janet Carsten (2007) also explored how family relations intersect with memory processes, focusing on the emotional and embodied experiences of passing down difficult historical events; similarly, Carol Kidron (2009) investigated the lived experiences of descendants of Holocaust and genocide survivors. Kidron, in particular, was able to show how the family home is situated as a place where the traumatic past is silently present, manifesting through embodied practices, interactions, and interpersonal dynamics. According to Kidron, these silent traces create an experiential framework that sustains familial "lived memory" and transmits tacit knowledge within everyday private life.

19. In this respect, I am following the calls of anthropologists such as Lambek and Antze (1996) for a shift in focus within the realm of memory studies, moving away from theoretical accounts of memory discourses and politics and instead directing attention toward grounded research on the actual practices and phenomenological lived experiences of memory.

20. These grand narratives are realized during performances of sung poetry through a process of what Berger (2009) has described elsewhere as "auditory perception . . . intimately enmeshed with bodily action" (13, quoted in Chávez). In this sense, *action* is taken to mean not only bodily movement in the present but how such corporeality embodies collective memories of migration through what Chávez terms "aesthetic labor" (2017) and what Walter Andrews and Mehmet Kalpaklı have described in other contexts as "undocumented emotional histories" (2005, 8), moments when poetic themes of love and the beloved become enacted.

21. See also Lila Abu-Lughod (1986).

CONCLUSION

1. For more, see Ralph Grillo (2010).

2. Including Trevor Phillips, who chaired the government's Commission for Racial Equality, and the scholar Bhikhu Parekh.

3. In his preface to the 2002 white paper *Secure Borders, Safe Haven: Integration and Diversity in Modern Britain*, the then home secretary David Blunkett wrote, "To enable integration to take place and to value the diversity it brings, we need to be secure within our sense of belonging and identity and therefore to be able to reach out and to embrace those who come to the UK. . . . Having a clear, workable and robust nationality and asylum system is the pre-requisite to building the security and trust that is needed. Without it, we cannot defeat those who would seek to stir up hate, intolerance and prejudice." Quoted in Back et al. (2002).

4. During this period, heads of state across Europe queued up in support of these views, proclaiming that "under the doctrine of multiculturalism," different cultures have been encouraged to live separate lives (British Prime Minister David Cameron), that it is "too concerned with the identity of person arriving and not enough about the identity of the country" (French President Nicolas Sarkozy, quoted in the *Daily Telegraph*, February 11, 2011), and, as a result, "society is too watered down" (Dutch Deputy Prime Minister Maxime Verhagen, quoted in *Crethi Plethi*, February 18, 2011). In other words, multiculturalism has "utterly failed" (German Chancellor Angela Merkel, quoted in the *Guardian*, October 17, 2010). It is pretty clear to whom these proclamations were directed: such statements are almost ubiquitously qualified by a perceived need to tackle Islamic extremism and terrorism.

5. See Cameron (2011).

6. See Wingate (2023).

7. This is a point I previously made in relation to the Conservative government's Big Society policy, in a 2011 op-ed for the *New Statesman*. See Tom Hodgson, "Multiculturalism v the 'Big Society,'" *New Statesman*, April 30, 2011, https://www.newstatesman.com/author/tom-hodgson.

8. See "Greece Migrant Boat Disaster: Pakistan to Hold Day of Mourning after Hundreds Die in Tragedy," SkyNews, June 18, 2023,

https://news.sky.com/story/greece-migrant-boat-disaster-pakistan-to-hold-day-of
-mourning-after-hundreds-die-in-tragedy-12905034.

9. Coke Studio is a popular music program in Pakistan that—broadly speaking—
reimagines the country's folk traditions within a global pop aesthetic. For more, see
Williams and Mahmood (2019).

10. See Workers' Welfare and Labour Rights,
https://www.workerswelfare.qa/en/workers-welfare (accessed June 12, 2023).

11. See "Revealed: 6,500 Migrant Workers Have Died in
Qatar since World Cup Awarded," *Guardian*, February 23, 2021,
https://www.theguardian.com/global-development/2021/feb/23/revealed-migrant
-worker-deaths-qatar-fifa-world-cup-2022.

12. See "How to Drive with Uber in Qatar," Uber.com,
https://www.uber.com/qa/en/drive/requirements (accessed September 19, 2024).

13. See Anwar (1979).

14. For more on the growing centrality of digital technologies and new media in the
circulation of music among migrant communities, see Stefan Fiol (2018).

15. For more on entrepreneurialism among South Asian diasporic communities, see
Roger Ballard (2003).

Sources

Abbas, Tahir. 2006. "British Islam Bounces Back." *Prospect*, September 24, 2006.
———. 2009 "Multiculturalism, Islamophobia and the City." In *Pakistani Diasporas: Culture, Conflict, Change*, edited by V. S. Kalra, 285–99. Karachi: Oxford University Press.
Abu-Lughod, Lila. 1986. *Veiled Sentiments: Honor and Poetry in Bedouin Society*. Berkeley: University of California Press.
Alexander, Claire. 2000. *The Asian Gang: Ethnicity, Identity, Masculinity*. Oxford: Berg.
———. 2003. "Imagining the Asian Gang: Ethnicity, Masculinity and Youth after 'the Riots.'" *Critical Social Policy* 24 (1): 526.
Ali, Hassan. 2017. "The Crofo Song." https://www.youtube.com/watch?v=aiwKVpI7qXY (accessed May 29, 2024).
Ali, Nabil Syed. 2010. "To Be Is to Love: The Semantic Field of Love in the Works of al-Hallaj, Rumi, and Miyan Muhammad Bakhsh." MSci diss., University of Georgia.
Ali, Nasreen. 2009. "The Making of Kashmiri Identity." *South Asian Diaspora* 1 (2): 181–92.
Allen, Sheila. 1971. *New Minorities, Old Conflicts: Asian and West Indian Immigrants in Britain*. New York: Random House.
Anderson, Benedict. 2006. *Imagined Communities: Reflections on the Origins of Nationalism*. London: Verso.
Andrews, Walter, and Mehmet Kalpaklı. 2005. *The Age of the Beloveds: Love and the Beloved in Early-Modern Ottoman and European Culture and Society*. Durham, NC: Duke University Press.
Anjum, Uzma, and Ahmed F. Siddiqi. 2012. "Exploring Attitudinal Shift in Pothwari: A Study of the Three Generations." *Pakistan Journal of History and Culture* 33:1–27.
Anonymous. "Letters to the Editor." *Telegraph & Argus*, July 12, 2001.
Anwar, Muhammad. 1979. *The Myth of Return: Pakistanis in Britain*. London: Heinemann Educational.
———. 1986. *Race and Politics: Ethnic Minorities and the British Political System*. London: Tavistock.
Anzaldúa, Gloria E. 1987. *Borderlands/La Frontera: The New Mestiza*. San Francisco: Aunt Lute.
Asari, Eva-Maria, Daphne Halikiopoulou, and Steven Mock. 2008. "British National Identity and the Dilemmas of Multiculturalism." *Nationalism and Ethnic Politics* 14 (1): 1–28.

Asher, Catherine B. 2009. "The Sufi Shines of Shahul Hamid in India and Southeast Asia." *Artibus Asiae* 69 (2): 247–58.

Assman, Jan, and John Czaplicka. 1995. Collective Memory and Cultural Identity. *New German Critique* 65:125–33.

Baart, Joan L. G. 2004. "Tone and Song in Kalam Kohistani (Pakistan)." In *On Speech and Language*, edited by Sieb G. Nooteboom, Hugo Quence, and Vincent van Hueven, 5–16. Utrecht: Netherlands Graduate School of Linguistics.

Back, Les. 1996. *New Ethnicities and Urban Culture: Racisms and Multiculture in Young Lives*. London: University College London Press.

Back, Les, Michael Keith, Arza Khan, Kalbir Shukra, and John Solomos. 2002. "The Return of Assimilationism: Race, Multiculturalism and New Labour." *Sociological Research Online* 7 (2): 1–10.

Bakrania, Falu Pravin. 2013. *Bhangra and Asian Underground: South Asian Music and the Politics of Belonging in Britain*. Durham: Duke University Press.

Baily, John. 1986. *Lessons from Gulam: Asian Music in Bradford* (film), London: Royal Anthropological Institute.

———. 1988. *Music of Afghanistan: Professional Musicians in the City of Herat*. Cambridge, UK: Cambridge University Press.

———. 1990. *The Making of Lessons from Gulam: Asian Music in Bradford. A Study Guide to the Film*. London: Royal Anthropological Institute.

———. 1995. "The Role of Music in Three British Muslim Communities." *Diaspora: A Journal of Transnational Studies* 4 (1): 77–87.

———. 2006. "'Music Is in Our Blood': Gujarati Muslim Musicians in the UK." *Journal of Ethnic and Migration Studies* 32 (2): 257–270.

Baily, John, and Michael Collyer. 2006. "Introduction: Music and Migration." *Journal of Ethnic and Migration Studies* 32 (2): 167–82.

Ballard, Roger. 1990. "Migration and Kinship: The Differential Effect of Marriage Rules on the Processes of Punjab Migration to Britain." In *South Asians Overseas: Migration and Ethnicity*, edited by Colin Clarke, Ceri Peach, and Steven Vertovec, 219–250. Cambridge, UK: Cambridge University Press.

———, ed. 1994. *Desh Pardesh: The South Asian Presence in Britain*. London: Hurst.

———. 2003. "A Case of Capital-Rich Under-Development: The Paradoxical Consequences of Successful Transnational Entrepreneurship from Mirpur." *Contributions to Indian Sociology* 37 (1/2): 25–57.

Banerji, Sabita. 1988. "Ghazals to Bhangra in Great Britain." *Popular Music* 7:207–213.

Banerji, Sabita, and Gerd Baumann. 1990. "Bhangra 1984–8: Fusion and Professionalisation in a Genre of South Asian Dance Music." In *Black Music in Britain*, edited by Paul Oliver, 137–151. Milton Keynes, UK: Open University Press.

Barth, Fredrick, ed. 1969. *Ethnic Groups and Boundaries: The Social Organization of Cultural Difference*. Oslo: Scandinavian University Books.

Barthes, Roland. (1980) 2000. *Camera Lucida*. London: Vintage.

Bates, Eliot. 2012. "The Social Life of Musical Instruments." *Ethnomusicology* 56 (3): 363–95.

Baumann, Gerd. 1996. *Contesting Culture: Discourses of Identity in Multi-ethnic London*. Cambridge, UK: Cambridge University Press.

———. 1999. *The Multicultural Riddle: Rethinking National, Ethnic and Religious Identities*. London: Routledge.

———. 2004. *Grammars of Identity*. New York: Berghahn.

Bayly, Christopher. 1989. *Imperial Meridian: The British Empire and the World*. London: Longman.

Beaster-Jones, Jayson. 2016. *Music Commodities, Markets, and Values: Music as Merchandise*. New York: Routledge.

Bennett, David, ed. 1998. *Multicultural States: Rethinking Difference and Identity*. London: Routledge.

Berger, Harris M. 2009. *Stance: Ideas about Emotion, Style, and Meaning for the Study of Expressive Culture*. Middletown, CT: Wesleyan University Press.

Bhabha, Homi. 1994. *The Location of Culture*. London: Routledge.

Bhatti, Rafiq Muhammad. 2013. "Language, Culture and Heritage of Mirpur." *Himalayan and Central Asian Studies* 17, no. 2 (Jan–March): 33–56.

Blunkett, David. 2002. *Secure Borders, Safe Haven: Integration and Diversity in Modern Britain*. London: Home Office.

Bolognani, Marta. 2007a. "Islam, Ethnography and Politics: Methodological Issues in Researching among West Yorkshire Pakistanis in 2005." *International Journal of Social Research Methodology* 10 (4): 279–93.

———, Marta. 2007b. "Community Perceptions of Moral Education as a Response to Crime by Young Pakistani Males in Bradford." *Journal of Moral Education* 36 (3): 357–69.

Bor, Joep, Jane Harvey, Delvoye Francois Nalini, Emmie to Nijenhuis, eds. 2010. *Hindustani Music: Thirteenth to Twentieth Centuries*. New Delhi: Manohar.

Bradford Congress. 1996. *The Bradford Commission Report*. Bradford: Stationary Office Books.

Britton, Liz, Balbir Chatrik, Bob Coles, Gary Craig, Carl Hylton, Saira Mumtaz, Paul Bivand, and Roger Burrows. 2002. *Missing ConnecXions: The Career Dynamics and Welfare Needs of Black and Minority Ethnic Young People at the Margins*. London: Joseph Rowntree Foundation.

Brown, Katherine. 2006. "If Music Be the Food of Love: Masculinity and Eroticism in the Mughal Mehfil." In *Love in South Asia: A Cultural History*, edited by Francesca Orsini, 61–86. Cambridge, UK: Cambridge University Press.

Butt, G. 2001. "Letters to the Editor." *Telegraph & Argus*, July 12, 2001.

Cameron, David. 2011. "Prime Minister's Speech at Munich Security Conference." In *Speeches and Transcripts*. London: British Prime Minister's Office. https://www.gov.uk/government/speeches/pms-speech-at-munich-security-conference (accessed September 17, 2024).

Canetti, Elias. 1973. *Crowds and Power*. Harmondsworth, UK: Penguin.

Cantle, Ted. 2001. *Community Cohesion: A Report of the Independent Review Team*. Great Britain: Home Office Community Cohesion Review Team.

Cantwell, Robert. 1993. *Ethnomimesis: Folklife and the Representation of Culture*. Chapel Hill: University of North Carolina Press.

Carsten, Janet, ed. 2007. *Ghosts of Memory: Essays on Relatedness and Remembering*. Oxford, UK: Blackwell.

Caton, Steven Charles. 1990. *"Peaks of Yemen I Summon": Poetry as Cultural Practice in a North Yemeni Tribe*. Berkeley: University of California Press.

Charsley, Katharine, Marta Bolognani, Evelyn Ersanilli, and Sarah Spencer. 2020. *Marriage Migration and Integration*. Cham, UK: Springer International.

Chauhan, Abha. 2021. *Understanding Culture and Society in India: A Study of Sufis, Saints and Deities in Jammu Region*. Singapore: Springer.

Chávez, Alex E. 2017. *Sounds of Crossing: Music, Migration, and the Aural Poetics of Huapango Arribeño*. Durham, NC: Duke University Press.

Cherribi, Sam. 2010. *In the House of War: Dutch Islam Observed*. Oxford, UK: Oxford University Press.

Chowdhary, Rekha. 2021. *Shared Sacred Spaces: The Sufi Shrines of Jammu Region*. Singapore: Springer.

Ciucci, Alessandra. 2012. "The Text Must Remain the Same": History, Collective Memory, and Sung Poetry in Morocco. *Ethnomusicology* 56 (3): 476–504.

———. 2022. *The Voice of the Rural: Music, Poetry, and Masculinity among Migrant Moroccan Men in Umbria*. Chicago: Chicago University Press.

Clayton, Martin, and Laura Leante. 2011. "Imagery, Melody and Gesture in Cross-Cultural Perspective." In *New Perspectives on Music and Gesture*, edited by Anthony Gritten and Elaine King. Surrey, UK: Ashgate.

———. 2015. "Role, Status and Hierarchy in the Performance of North Indian Classical Music." *Ethnomusicology Forum* 24 (3): 414–442.

Clifford, James. 1986. "Part Truths." In *Writing Culture: The Poetics and Politics of Ethnography*, edited by James Clifford and George Marcus. London: University of California Press.

———. 1988. *The Predicament of Culture: Twentieth-Century Ethnography, Literature, and Art*. Cambridge, MA.: Harvard University Press.

———. 1994. "Diasporas." *Cultural Anthropology* 9 (3): 302–38.

Clifford, James, and George Marcus, eds. 1986. *Writing Culture: The Poetics and Politics of Ethnography*. London: University of California Press.

Cohen, Abner. 1993. *Masquerade Politics: Explorations in the Structure of Urban Cultural Movements*. Oxford, UK: Berg.

Cohen, Robin. 1997. *Global Diasporas*. London: University College London Press.

Cohen, Sara. 2007. *Decline, Renewal and the City in Popular Music Culture: Beyond the Beatles*. Aldershot, UK: Ashgate.

Cole, Ross. 2019. *The Folk: Music, Modernity, and the Political Imagination*. Oakland: University of California Press.

Cooley, Timothy. 1999. "Folk Festival as Modern Ritual in the Polish Tatra Mountains." *World of Music* 41 (3): 31–55.

Cressey, Gill. 2006. *Diaspora Youth and Ancestral Homeland: British Pakistani/Kashmiri Youth Visiting Kin in Pakistan and Kashmir*. Leiden, Netherlands: Brill.

CrimeRate. 2023. "Walsall." https://crimerate.co.uk/west-midlands/walsall (accessed June 12, 2023).

Daily Mail. 2012. "Farewell to a Martyr to Political Correctness: Bradford Headmaster–Hounded for Warning of the Perils of Multiculturalism–Dies Saddened but Vindicated." February 10, 2012.

Daily Telegraph. 2012. "Obituary: Ray Honeyford." February 20, 2012.

Dave, Nomi. 2019. *The Revolution's Echoes: Music, Politics, and Pleasure in Guinea*. Chicago: University of Chicago Press.

DeNora, Tia. 2000. *Music in Everyday Life*. Cambridge, UK: Cambridge University Press.

Dermaine, Jack. 1993. "Racism, Ideology and Education: The Last Word on the Honeyford Affair?" *British Journal of Sociology of Education* 14 (4): 409–14.

Deva, B. C. 1975. "The Double-Reed Aerophone in India." *Yearbook of the International Folk Music Council* 7:77–84.

Diamond, Heather A., and Ricardo D. Trimillos. 2008. "Introduction: Interdisciplinary Perspectives on the Smithsonian Folklife Festival." *Journal of American Folklore* 121 (479): 3–9.

Din, Ikhlaq. 2006. *The New British: The Impact of Culture and Community on Young Pakistanis*. Aldershot, UK: Ashgate.

Din, Ikhlaq, and Cedric Cullingford. 2004. "Boyzone and Bhangra: The Place of Popular and Minority Cultures." *Race Ethnicity and Education* 7 (3): 307–320.

Dundes, Alan, and Alessandro Falassi. 1975. *La Terra in Piazza: An Interpretation of the Palio of Siena*. Berkley: University of California Press.

Dutt, G. "Letters to the Editor." *Telegraph & Argus*, July 12, 2001.

Dworkin, Ronald. 1978. *Taking Rights Seriously*. London: Duckworth.

Ernst, Carl W., and Bruce B. Lawrence. 2002. *Sufi Martyrs of Love: The Chishti Order in South Asia and Beyond*. New York: Palgrave.

Feld, Steven, and Keith Basso, eds. 1996. *Senses of Place*. New Mexico: School of American Research Press.

Finnegan, Ruth. 1989. *The Hidden Musicians: Music Making in an English Town*. Cambridge, UK: Cambridge University Press.

Fiol, Stefan. 2017. *Recasting Folk in the Himalayas: Indian Music, Media, and Social Mobility*. Urbana: University of Illinois Press.

———. 2018. "Listening to Garhwali Popular Music in and out of Place." *Himalaya* 38 (1): 113–26.

Foster-Carter, Olivia. 1987. "The Honeyford Affair: Political and Policy Implications." In *Racial Inequality in Education*, edited by Barry Troyna, 44–59. London: Routledge.

Fox, Aaron. 2004. *Real Country: Music and Language in Working-Class Culture*. Durham, NC: Duke University Press.

Frembgen, Jürgen Wasim. 2012. *Nocturnal Music in the Land of the Sufis: The Unheard Pakistan*. Karachi: Oxford University Press.

Frishkopf, Michael. 2008. "Globalizing the Soundworld: Islam and Sufi Music in the West." In *Sufis in Western Society: Global Networking and Locality*, edited by Ron Greaves and Markus, 46–76. London: Routledge.

Fulat, S. 2005. "Caught between Two Worlds: How Can the State Help Young Muslims?" In *Islam, Race and Being British*, edited by Madeleine Bunting, 23–30. London: *Guardian* in association with Barrow Cadbury Trust.

Furlong, Andy, and Fred Cartmel. 2004. *Vulnerable Young Men in Fragile Labour Markets: Employment, Unemployment and the Search for Long-Term Security*. York, UK: York Publishing.

Gable, Eric, and Richard Handler. 2000. "Public History, Private Memory: Notes from the Ethnography of Colonial Williamsburg". *Ethos: Journal of Anthropology* 65 (2): 237–52.

Gardner, Katy. 1993. "Desh-Bidesh: Sylheti Images of Home and Away." *Journal of the Royal Anthropological Institute* 28 (1): 1–15.

Gazzah, Miriam. 2008. *Rhythms and Rhymes of Life: Music and Identification Processes of Dutch-Morrocan Youth*. Amsterdam: Amsterdam University Press.

Geertz, Clifford. 1973. *The Interpretation of Cultures: Selected Essays*. New York: Basic.

———. 1988. *Works and lives: the anthropologist as author*. Stanford: Stanford University Press.

Giddens, Anthony. 1990. *The Consequences of Modernity*. Cambridge, UK: Polity.

Gidley, Ben. 2007. "Youth Culture and Ethnicity: Emerging Youth Multiculture in South London." In *Youth Cultures: Scenes, Subcultures and Tribes*, edited by Paul Hodgkinson and Wolfgang Deicke, 145–60. London: Routledge.

Gill, Denise. 2018. "Listening, Muhabbet, and the Practice of Masculinity." *Ethnomusicology*. 61 (2): 171–205.

Gilmartin, David. 2012. "Environmental History, the Biraderi, and the Making of Pakistani Punjab." In *Punjab Reconsidered: History, Culture, and Practice*, edited by Anshu Malhorta and Farina Mir, 289–319. Oxford, UK: Oxford University Press.

Goldberg, David, ed. 1994. *Multiculturalism: A Critical Reader*. Oxford, UK: Blackwell.

Graeber, David. 2001. *Toward an Anthropology of Value: the False Coin of Our Own Dreams*. New York: Palgrave.

Green, Nile. 2011. *Bombay Islam: The Religious Economy of the West Indian Ocean, 1840–1915*. Cambridge, UK: Cambridge University Press.

Grillo, Ralph. 2010. "An Excess of Alterity? Debating Difference in a Multicultural Society." In *Anthropology of Migration and Multiculturalism*, edited by Steven Vertovec, 19–38. London: Routledge.

Gross, Joan, David McMurray, and Ted Swedenburg. 1996. "Arab Noise and Ramadan Nights: Rai, Rap, and Franco-Maghrebi Identities." In *Displacement, Diaspora, and Geographies of Identities*, edited by Smadar Lavie and Ted Swedenburg, 119–55. Durham, NC: Duke University Press.

Halbwachs, Maurice. 1992. *On Collective Memory*. Chicago: University of Chicago Press.

Hall, Stuart. 1988. "New Ethnicities." Institute of Contemporary Art, *Black Film/British Cinema*, Documents 7, London: ICA/BFI.

———. 1996. *Critical Dialogues in Cultural Studies*. London: Routledge.

Halstead, Mark. 1988. *Education, Justice and Cultural Diversity: An Examination of the Honeyford Affair, 1984–85*. London: Falmer.

Hegland, Mary Elaine. 1998. "Flagellation and Fundamentalism: (Trans)forming Meaning, Identity, and Gender Through Pakistani Women's Rituals of Mourning." *American Ethnologist* 25 (2): 240–66.

Herzfeld, Michael. 2004. *The Body Impolitic: Artisans and Artifice in the Global Hierarchy of Value*. Chicago: University of Chicago Press.

———. 2005. *Cultural Intimacy: Social Poetics in the Nation-State*. Abingdon, UK: Routledge.

Higgins, Duncan. 2001. "Letters to the Editor." *Telegraph & Argus*, July 10, 2001.

Hobsbawm, Eric. 1987. *The Age of Empire, 1875–1914*. London: Weidenfeld and Nicholson.

Hodgson, Thomas. 2011. "Multiculturalism v the 'Big Society'." *The New Statesman*. April 30, 2011. https://www.newstatesman.com/politics/2011/04/society -multiculturalism.

———. 2014. "Le Mela de Bradford." *Les Cahiers d'Ethnomusicologie* 27:243–60.

Holbrook, Victoria Rowe. 1994. *The Unreadable Shores of Love: Turkish Modernity and Mystic Romance*. Austin: University of Texas Press.

Hyder, Rehan. 2004. *Brimful of Asia*. Burlington, VT: Ashgate.

Imran, Irna, and Tim Smith. 1997. *Home from Home: British Pakistanis in Mirpur*. Bradford, UK: City of Bradford Metropolitan District Council, Arts, Museums and Libraries.

Imran, Irna, Tim Smith, and Donald Hyslop. 1994. *Here to Stay: Bradford's South Asian Communities*. Bradford, UK: Bradford Metropolitan District Council.

Jafari, S.Z. 1987. *Man Mela*. Islamabad: Lok Virsa.

Jairazbhoy, Nazir. 1970. "A Preliminary Survey of the Oboe in India." *Ethnomusicology* 14 (3): 375–88.

———. 1980. "Colloquy: The South Asian Double-Reed Aerophone Reconsidered." *Ethnomusicology* 24 (1): 147.

Jankowsky, Richard C. 2021. *Ambient Sufism: Ritual Niches and the Social Work of Musical Form*. Chicago: University of Chicago Press.

Jones, Patricia. 1984. *An Investigation into Curriculum Music in Middle Schools and the Role of Music in the Lives of Muslim Children, as a Basis for Development of a Music Education More Relevant to a Multi-cultural Society*. BEd diss., Bradford College.

Kapchan, Deborah. 2007. *Traveling Spirit Masters: Moroccan Gnawa Trance and Music in the Global Marketplace*. Middletown, CT: Wesleyan University Press.

Kapuria, Radha. 2023. *Music in Colonial Punjab: Courtesans, Bards and Connoisseurs*. Oxford, UK: Oxford University Press.

Khan, Pasha M. 2013. *The Broken Spell: The Romance Genre in Late Mughal India*. PhD thesis, Colombia University.

———. 2019. *The Broken Spell: Indian Storytelling and the Romance Genre in Persian and Urdu*. Detroit: Wayne State University Press.

Khan, V. S. 1977. "The Pakistanis: Mirpuri Villagers at Home and in Bradford." In *Between Two Cultures: Migrants and Minorities in Britain*, edited by James Watson, 54–77. Oxford, UK: Blackwell.

Kidron, Carol. 2009. "Toward an Ethnography of Silence: The Lived Presence of the Past among Holocaust Trauma Descendants in Israel." *Current Anthropology* 50 (1): 5–27.

Knott, Kim, and Sean McLoughlin, eds. 2010. *Diasporas: Concepts, Identities, Intersections*. London: Zed.

Kosnick, Kira. 2007. *Migrant Media: Turkish Broadcasting and Multicultural Politics in Berlin*. Bloomington: Indiana University Press.

Krims, Adam. 2000. *Rap Music and the Poetics of Identity*. Cambridge, UK: Cambridge University Press.

———. 2007. *Music and Urban Geography*. London: Routledge.

Kunial, Zaffar. 2018. *Us*. London: Faber & Faber.

———. 2019. *Six*. London: Faber & Faber.

———. 2022. *England's Green*. London: Faber & Faber

Lambek, Michael, and Paul Antze. 1996. "Introduction: Forecasting Memory." In *Tense Past: Cultural Essays in Trauma and Memory*, edited by Paul Antze and Michael Lambek, xi–xxxvi. New York: Routledge.

Lewis, Philip. 1994. *Islamic Britain: Religion, Politics, and Identity among British Muslims*. London: I. B. Tauris and Co.

———. 2007. *Young, British and Muslim*. London: Continuum.

Lomax, A. 1959. "Folk Song Style." *American Anthropologist* 61 (6): 927–54.

Lorea, Carola E. 2018. "Migrating Songs Connecting the Ocean: Displacement, Bengali Identity, and the Performance of Homeland." *Rivista degli studi orientali*, XCI Supplemento 2:51–65.

Lornell, Kip, and Anne Rasmussen. 1997. *Musics of Multicultural America: A Study of Twelve Musical Communities*. New York: Schirmer.

Lortat-Jacob, Bernard. 1995. *Sardinian Chronicles*. Chicago: University of Chicago Press.

Lothers, Michael, and Laura Lothers. 2010. *Pahari and Pothwari: A Sociolinguistic Survey*. Dallas: SIL International.

Magee, Gary Bryan. 2010. *Empire and Globalisation: Networks of People, Goods and Capital in the British World, c. 1850–1914*. Cambridge, UK: Cambridge University Press.

Mahmudabad, Ali Khan. 2020. *Poetry of Belonging: Muslim Imaginings of India 1850–1950*. Oxford, UK: Oxford University Press.

Marsden, Magnus. 2005. *Living Islam: Muslim Religious in Pakistan's North West Frontier*. London: Hurst.

———. 2007. "All-Male Sonic Gatherings, Islamic Reform, and Masculinity in Northern Pakistan." *American Ethnologist* 34 (3): 473–90.

Mauss, Marcel. 1925. *The Gift: The Form and Reason for Exchange in Archaic Societies*. London: Routledge.

McKenna, David. 2023. "Bradford 2025: UK City of Culture to Receive £10m from Government." https://www.bbc.com/news/uk-england-leeds-66121711.

McLoughlin, Sean. 2006. "Writing a British-Asian City: Race, Culture and Religion in Accounts of Postcolonial Bradford." In *A Postcolonial People: South Asians in Britain*, edited by Salman Sayyid, Virinder Kalra, and Nasreen Ali, 110–49. London: Hurst.

McLoughlin, Sean, and Muzamil Khan. 2006. "Ambiguous Traditions and Modern Transformations of Islam: The Waxing and Waning of an 'Intoxicated' Sufi Cult in Mirpur." *Contemporary South Asia* 15 (3): 289–307.

McManus, John. 2022. *Inside Qatar: Hidden Stories from One of the Richest Countries on Earth*. London: Icon.

Meeker, Michael. 1979. *Literature and Violence in North Arabia*. Cambridge, UK: Cambridge University Press.

Métraux, G. S. 1976 "Editorial: Of Feasts and Carnivals." *Festivals and Carnivals: The Major Traditions*. Boudry, France: UNESCO.

Mitchell, Timothy. 1988. *Colonising Egypt*. London: Cambridge University Press.

Modood, Tariq. 1997. *Ethnic Minorities in Britain: diversity and disadvantage*, London: Policy Studies Institute.

———. 2000. *Multiculturalism*. Cambridge, UK: Polity.

———. 2005. *Multicultural Politics: Racism, Ethnicity and Muslims in Britain*. Edinburgh, Scotland: Edinburgh University Press.

Murphy, Sam. 2018. "Through Small Mysteries That Add Up / Interview with Zaffar Kunial." *Headstuff*. https://headstuff.org/culture/literature/poetry/interview-with-zaffar-kunial (accessed June 12, 2023).

Nazir, Farah. 2014. *Light Verb Constructions in Potwari*. PhD thesis, University of Manchester.

———. 2020. "We Code-Switch Like Riz Ahmed." *Creative Multilingualism* (Blog). Last modified May 1, 2020. https://creativeml.ox.ac.uk/blog/exploring-multilingualism/we-code-switch-riz-ahmed.

Nettl, Bruno. 1998. *In the Course of Performance*. Chicago: University of Chicago Press.

Neuman, Daniel M. 1990. *The Life of Music in North India: The Organization of an Artistic Tradition*. Chicago: University of Chicago Press.

Nieuwkerk, Karin van. 2011. *Muslim Rap, Halal Soaps, and Revolutionary Theater: Artistic Developments in the Muslim World*. Austin: University of Texas Press.

Niranjana, Tejaswini. 2006. *Mobilizing India: Women, Music, and Migration between India and Trinidad*. Durham, NC: Duke University Press.

Ofsted. 2008. "Beckfoot School." https://reports.ofsted.gov.uk/provider/23/107386 (accessed September 17, 2024).

———. 2010. "M A Institute." https://files.ofsted.gov.uk/v1/file/1440673 (accessed September 17, 2024).

Oliver, Paul. 1990. *Black Music in Britain*. Milton Keynes, UK: Open University Press.

Olszewska, Zuzanna. 2015. *The Pearl of Dari: Poetry and Personhood among Young Afghans in Iran*. Bloomington: Indiana University Press.

Ortner, Sherry. 2005. "Subjectivity and Cultural Critique." *Anthropological Theory* 5 (1): 31–52.

Osterhammel, Jürgen. 2014. *The Transformation of the World: A Global History of the Nineteenth Century*. Princeton, NJ: Princeton University Press.

Pannke, Peter. 2014. *Singers and Saints: Sufi Music in the Indus Valley*. Karachi: Oxford University Press.

Parekh, Bhikhu. 1990. *The Rushdie Affair and the British Press: Some Salutary Lessons*. London: Commission for Racial Equality.

———. 2000. *The Future of Multi-Ethnic Britain*. London: Profile.

———. 2006 *Rethinking Multiculturalism: Cultural Diversity and Political Theory*. London: Palgrave Macmillan.

Patel, Ameen. 2001. "Letters to the Editor." *Telegraph & Argus*, July 12, 2001.

Phillips, Deborah. 2006. "Parallel Lives? Challenging Discourses of British Muslim Self-Segregation." *Environment and Planning. D, Society & Space* 24 (1): 25–40.

Phillips, Trevor. 2005. *After 7/7: Sleepwalking to Segregation*. Manchester: Manchester University Press.

Powers, Harold. 1980. "Classical Music, Cultural Roots, and Colonial Rule: An Indic Musicologist Looks at the Muslim World." *Asian Music* 12 (1): 5–39.

Puri, Rakshat. 1997a. "Bulleh Shah in Punjabi Poetic Tradition." In *Crossing Boundaries*, edited by Geeti Sen. New Delhi: Orient Longman.

———. 1997b. "Bulleh Shah in Punjabi Poetic Tradition." *India International Centre Quarterly* 24 (2/3): 125–38.

Qureshi, Irna. 2010. *Coming of Age: Celebrating 21 Years of Mela in the UK*. Bradford, UK: City of Bradford.

Qureshi, Kaveri. 2012. "Pakistani Labour Migration and Masculinity: Industrial Work, the Body and Transnationalism." *Global Networks* 12 (4): 485–504.

Qureshi, Regula. 1986. *Sufi Music of India and Pakistan: Sound, Context, and Meaning in Qawwali*. Cambridge, UK: Cambridge University Press.

Ramnarine, Tina K. 2007. "Musical Performance in the Diaspora: Introduction." *Ethnomusicology Forum* 16 (1): 1–17.

Ronström, Owe. 1991. "Concerts and Festivals: Public Performances of Folk Music in Sweden." *World of Music* 43 (2/3): 49–64.

Rose, Tricia. 1989. "Orality and Technology: Rap Music and Afro-American Cultural Resistance." *Popular Music and Society* 13 (4): 35–44.

———. 1991. "'Fear of a Black Planet': Rap Music and Cultural Politics in the 1990s." *Journal of Negro Education* 60 (3): 276–90.

Runnymede Trust. 1980. *Britain's Black Population*. London: Heinemann Educational.

———. 2000. *The Future of Multi-Ethnic Britain*. London: Profile.

Rushdie, Salman. 1992. *Imaginary Homelands: Essays and Criticism 1981–1991*. London: Granta.

Ruthven, Malise. 1991. *A Satanic Affair: Salman Rushdie and the Wrath of Islam*. London: Chatto and Windus.

Said, Maurice. 2016. "Humour and Lying: Male Sociality among Coastal Sinhalese." *Etnofoor* 28 (1): 97–109.

Schimmel, Annemarie. 1975. *Mystical Dimensions of Islam*. Chapel Hill: University of North Carolina Press.

Schofield, Katherine. 2010. "Reviving the Golden Age Again: 'Classicization,' Hindustani Music, and the Mughals." *Ethnomusicology* 54 (3): 484–517.

Schreffler, Gibb. 2010. *Signs of Separation: Ḍhol in Punjabi Culture*. PhD diss., University of California, Santa Barbara.

———. 2021. *Dhol: Drummers, Identities, and Modern Punjab*. Urbana: University of Illinois Press.

Schwartz, Barry. 1996. "Introduction: The Expanding Past." *Qualitative Sociology* 19 (3): 275–82.

Shackle, Christopher. 1990. "Sacred Love, Lyrical Death." *Critical Muslim* 5 (1).

———. 2007. "The Story of the Sayf al-Maluk in South Asia." *Journal of the Royal Asiatic Society* 17 (2): 115–29.

———. 2012. "Punjabi Sufi Poetry from Farid to Farid." In *Punjab Reconsidered: History, Culture, and Practice*, edited by Anshu Malhorta and Farina Mir, 3–34. Oxford, UK: Oxford University Press.

Shannon, Jonathan. 2006. *Among the Jasmine Trees: Music and Modernity in Contemporary Syria*. Middletown, CT: Wesleyan University Press.

Sharma, Sanjay, John Hutnyk, and Ashwani Sharma, eds. 1996. *Dis-Orienting Rhythms: The Politics of the New Asian Dance Music*. London: Zed.

Shaw, Alison. 1988. *A Pakistani Family in Britain*. Oxford, UK: Basil.

———. 2000. *Kinship and Continuity: Pakistani Families in Britain*. Amsterdam: Harwood Academic.

Silver, Brian. 1984. "The *Adab* of Musicians." In *Moral Conduct and Authority: The Place of Adab in South Asian Islam*, edited by Barbara Daly Metcalf, 315–32. Berkeley: University of California Press.

Slobin, Mark. 1993. *Subcultural Sounds: Micromusics of the West*. Hanover, NH: University Press of New England.

Small, Christopher. 1998. *Musicking: The Meanings of Performance and Listening*. Hanover, NH: Wesleyan University Press.

Somayaji, Sakarama, and Smrithi Talwar. 2011. *Development-Induced Displacement, Rehabilitation and Resettlement in India: Current Issues and Challenges*. Abingdon, UK: Routledge.

Stokes, Martin. 1994. *Ethnicity, Identity and Music*. Oxford, UK: Berg.

———. 2004. "Music and the Global Order." *Annual Review of Anthropology* 33 (1): 47–72.

———. 2007. "On Musical Cosmopolitanism." Institute for Global Citizenship: The Macalester International Roundtable.

———. 2010. *The Republic of Love: Cultural Intimacy in Turkish Popular Music*. Chicago: University of Chicago Press.

———. 2017. "Musical Ethnicity: Affective, Material, and Vocal Turns." *World of Music* 6 (2): 19–34.

———. 2021a. "Migration and Music." *Music Research Annual* 1 (1): 1–24.

———. 2021b. "On the Beach: Musicology's Migrant Crisis." *Representations* 154 (1): 34–46.

Stuart, Forrest. 2020. *Ballad of the Bullet: Gangs, Drill Music, and the Poer of Online Infamy*. Princeton, NJ: Princeton University Press.

Sugarman, Jane C. 1997. *Engendering Song: Singing and Subjectivity at Prespa Albanian Weddings*. Chicago: University of Chicago Press.

Swedenburg, Ted. 2001. "Islamic Hip-Hop vs. Islamophobia: Aki Nawaz, Natacha Atlas, Akhenaton." In *Global Noise: Rap and Hip-Hop outside the USA*, edited by Timothy Mitchell, 57–85. Middletown, CT: Wesleyan University Press.

Taylor, Charles. 1994. *Multiculturalism: Examining the Politics of Recognition*. Princeton, NJ: Princeton University Press.

Tölölyan, Khachig. 1996. "Rethinking Diaspora(s): Stateless Power in the Transnational Moment." *Diaspora* 5 (1): 3–36.

Toynbee, Jason, and Byron Dueck, eds. 2011. *Migrating Music*. London: Routledge.

Turino, Thomas. 2000. *Nationalists, Cosmopolitans, and Popular Music in Zimbabwe*. Chicago: University of Chicago Press.

Turino, Thomas, and James Lea., eds. 2004. *Identity and the Arts in Diaspora Communities*. Warren, MI: Harmonie Park Press.

UK Census Data. 2001. http://www.ons.gov.uk/ons/guide-method/census/census -2001/index.html (accessed June 12, 2023).

UK Gov. 2022. "UK City of Culture 2025: Full Application Guidance." https://www .gov.uk/government/publications/uk-city-of-culture-2025-full-guidance-for-long -listed-bidders/uk-city-of-culture-2025-full-application-guidance (accessed June 12, 2023).

Vansina, Jan. 1985. *Oral Tradition as History*. Madison: University of Wisconsin Press.

Vertovec, Steven. 1997. "Three Meanings of 'Diaspora,' Exemplified among South Asian Religions." *Diaspora*. 6 (3): 277–99.

———. 2007. "Super-Diversity and Its Implications." *Ethnic and Racial Studies* 30 (6): 1024–55.

———. 2009. *Cosmopolitanism in Practice*. London: Routledge.

Vertovec, Steven, and Robin Cohen, eds. 1999. *Migration, Diasporas, and Transnationalism*. Cheltenham, UK: Elgar.

Vertovec, Steven, and Susanne Wessendorf, eds. 2010. *The Multiculturalism Backlash: European Discourses, Policies and Practices*. Abingdon, UK: Routledge.

Wallace-Wells, David. 2019. *The Uninhabitable Earth: A Story of the Future*. London: Allen Lane.

Waterman, Christopher. 1990. *Jùjú: A Social History and Ethnography of an African Popular Music*. Chicago: University of Chicago Press.

Watson, James, ed. 1977. *Between Two Cultures: Migrants and Minorities in Britain*. London: Billing and Sons.

Weber, William. 1975. *Music and the Middle Class: The Social Structure of Concert Life in London, Paris and Vienna*. London: Croom Helm.

———. 2008. *The Great Transformation of Musical Taste: Concert Programming from Haydn to Brahms*, Cambridge: Cambridge University Press.

Weldon, Fay. 1989. *Sacred Cows: A Portrait of Britain Post-Rushdie, Pre-Utopia*. London: Chatto & Windus.

Werbner, Pnina. 1990. *The Migration Process: Capital, Gifts and Offerings among British Pakistanis*. Oxford, UK: Berg.

———. 2002. *Imagined Diasporas among Manchester Muslims: The Public Performance of Pakistani Transnational Identity Politics*. Oxford, UK: James Currey.

———. 2008. *Anthropology and the New Cosmopolitanism*. Oxford, UK: Berg.

Werbner, Pnina, and Helene Basu, eds. 1998. *Embodying Charisma: Modernity, Locality, and Performance of Emotion in Sufi Cults*. London; New York: Routledge.

West, Cornel. 1993. *Race Matters*. Boston: Beacon.

West, Patrick. 2005. *The Poverty of Multiculturalism*. London: Civitas.

White, Geoffrey. 2000. "Emotional Remembering: The Pragmatics of National Memory." *Ethos: Journal of Anthropology* 27 (4): 505–29.

Williams, Richard. D., and Rafay Mahmood. 2019. "A Soundtrack for Reimagining Pakistan? Coke Studio, Memory and the Music Video." *South Asian Screen Studies* 10 (2): 111–28.

Wingate, Sophie. 2023. "Braverman: Multiculturalism Has 'Failed' and Threatens Society." *Independent*. September 26, 2023. https://www.independent.co.uk/news/uk/europe-home-secretary-united-states-multiculturalism-prime-minister-b2418911.html.

Wolf, Richard. 2000. "Embodiment and Ambivalence: Emotion in South Asian Muharram Drumming." *Yearbook for Traditional Music* 32 (1): 81–116.

———. 2006. "The Poetics of 'Sufi' Practice: Drumming, Dancing, and Complex Agency at Madho Lal Hussain (and Beyond)." *American Ethnology* 33 (3): 246–68.

———. 2009. *Theorizing the Local: Music, Practice and Experience in South Asia and Beyond*. New York: Oxford University Press.

———. 2013. "The Manifest and the Hidden: Agency and Loss in Muslim Performance Traditions of South and West Asia." In *Music, Culture and Identity in the Muslim World: Performance, Politics and Piety*, edited by Kamal Salhi, 122–59. London: Routledge.

———. 2014. *The Voice in the Drum: Music, Language and Emotion in Islamicate South Asia*. Urbana: University of Illinois Press.

———. 2021. "The Musical Poetry of Endangered Languages: Kota and Wakhi Poem-Songs in South and Central Asia." *Oral Tradition* 35:103–66.

Wright, David. "Letters to the Editor." *Telegraph & Argus*, July 12, 2001.

Zerubavel, Eviatar. 1996. "Social Memories: Steps to an Ecology of the Past." *Qualitative Sociology* 19 (3): 283–308.

Zuberi, Nabeel. 2001. *Sounds English: Transnational Popular Music*. Chicago: University of Illinois.

Index

Page numbers in italics refer to figures.

Printed and bound by CPI Group (UK) Ltd, Croydon, CR0 4YY

24/07/2025

14708434-0004